Saving Community Journalism

A good newspaper is an anchor in a community. A newspaper reminds a community every day of its collective identity, the stake we have in one another, and the lessons of its history.

—Ron Heifetz, John F. Kennedy School of Government, Harvard University

SAVING COMMUNITY JOURNALISM

The Path to Profitability

PENELOPE MUSE ABERNATHY

THE UNIVERSITY OF NORTH CAROLINA PRESS | CHAPEL HILL

All rights reserved. Designed by Sally Scruggs. Set in Calluna types by codeMantra.
Manufactured in the United States of America. The paper in this book meets
the guidelines for permanence and durability of the Committee on Production
Guidelines for Book Longevity of the Council on Library Resources. The University
of North Carolina Press has been a member of the Green Press Initiative since 2003.

Library of Congress Cataloging-in-Publication Data
Abernathy, Penelope Muse.
Saving community journalism : the path to profitability / Penelope Muse Abernathy.
    pages cm
Includes bibliographical references and index.
ISBN 978-1-4696-1542-4 (hardback) — ISBN 978-1-4696-1543-1 (ebook)
1. Community newspapers—United States 2. Newspaper publishing—United States.
I. Title.
PN4888.C594A24 2014
070.4'33—dc23
2013041253

18-17-16-15-14—5-4-3-2-1

Dedicated to those who have both inspired and helped create this book, most especially the next generation of journalists and media executives whom I have taught, and the owners, publishers, and editors of newspapers who fight the good fight every day for the residents of the communities they serve.

Contents

Figures

Introduction

It has been a little less than two decades since the Internet revolution began, and yet the change to the news landscape—and the business model that supported it—has been seismic. In the 1930s, economist Joseph Schumpeter coined the term "creative destruction" to describe how a new technology makes one industry obsolete while creating the opportunity for another to subsume or replace it—which is exactly what is occurring in the news business today. In purely economic terms, resources flow away from the aging industry (in this case, newspapers) to a vibrant successor or successors (search engines, social networks, blogs, or portals). Something of an optimist, Schumpeter believed that creative destruction was capitalism's way of "reshuffling the deck" and renewing itself.

The recent experience of other industries that have faced creative destruction—from software companies to financial service providers—leads to this unmistakable conclusion: newspapers, both large and small, need to re-create themselves for the twenty-first century. If they do not develop a plan for confronting and accommodating today's very intrusive and disruptive technological innovations, they risk being lost in the "reshuffling of the deck" and going the way of black-and-white motion pictures and other outdated media forms, consigned to the periphery with severely diminished prestige, influence, and profitability.

Newspapers, of course, differ from other industries in two ways: their traditional business model and their historic mission. In contrast to other manufacturing or retail industries, which make a profit by selling directly to customers, newspapers have traditionally acquired readers at "below the cost" of producing a paper and then made a profit by selling access to these readers to local advertisers.

Because the creative destruction wrought by the Internet has undermined the traditional business model of news organizations by siphoning off both readers and advertisers, the critical and unique historic mission of newspapers—informing and educating the public instead of just maximizing profit—is now in jeopardy. This situation has been observed and documented by a number of governmental and nonprofit organizations. One 2010 report, *Informing Communities: Sustaining Democracy in the Digital Age*, commissioned by the Knight Foundation, warned that the financial pressures that this disruption has inflicted on newspapers "could pose a crisis for democracy" in the near future.

That report also noted that the "watchdog" role of the nation's smaller "community newspapers" becomes even more important as larger regional and metro news organizations pull back circulation and coverage from outlying communities. According to the most recent census, there are more than 55,000 legally or politically recognized entities in this country, ranging from urbanized counties to vast rural townships. Since there are only 1,500 or so daily newspapers, the Knight report reasoned, "[i]t follows that hundreds, if not thousands, of American communities receive only scant journalistic attention on a daily basis." Therefore, it is vital for the health of our grassroots democracy that the country's community newspapers find a path to renewal.

Traditionally, papers with less than 15,000 circulation have been categorized as community newspapers. Using this definition, there are 8,000 community newspapers in the United States today, the vast majority of which are published on a weekly or semiweekly schedule. But in a digital age, when print circulation for almost all newspapers is dropping yearly—and an increasing number of readers are accessing a paper's digital edition only—that definition seems limiting and out-of-date. Many daily newspapers in small and midsized markets, for example—especially those with a circulation of less than 100,000—also position themselves as "community newspapers." The same is true of papers serving ethnic populations in cities around the country.

Therefore, this book has used a much more expansive and modern definition of community newspapers, one based not on a publication's circulation but rather on its mission and the characteristics of the markets it depends on for revenue. This definition encompasses newspapers that serve geographic communities as well as those bound together through a shared affiliation or ethnic identity. It includes nondailies ranging in size from a 7,000-circulation weekly in West Virginia to a 150,000-circulation Spanish-language weekly for Chicago's Hispanic residents. It also includes daily newspapers serving small and midsized markets, ranging from an 8,000-circulation daily in a coastal North Carolina community to a 90,000-circulation publication in Salt Lake City, Utah, that serves a community of readers and advertisers who value "faith and family."

This new definition, based on mission and market characteristics, encompasses almost all of the country's more than 11,000 regularly published newspapers, excluding only the largest ninety or so regional and national dailies (papers with print circulations well above 100,000). Like those with smaller circulations, these large papers also face a crisis of identity and market erosion. If they are to survive and thrive in the twenty-first century, all newspapers—including national dailies such as the *New York Times* and metro and regional papers such as the *Boston Globe* and the *New Orleans Times-Picayune*—must pursue a three-pronged strategy (outlined in this book) that addresses cost reduction as well as readership and revenue growth across multiple platforms. But even though some investors who have recently purchased large metropolitan newspapers have talked about them as "community treasures," these businesses face implementation issues and market challenges that are very different from those faced by other newspapers. This book focuses primarily on the choices that community-based newspapers must confront, circling back in the closing pages to discuss the implications of the new world order for the entire newspaper ecosystem, including the regional and metropolitan papers.

During times of immense disruption such as is now occurring in traditional news organizations, the data gleaned from various "experiments" and case studies often appear to be ambiguous, and as a result, it is often not clear how the lessons learned in one circumstance can be applied in another. Such ambiguity can lead to paralysis and the temptation to move slowly and cautiously, or even do nothing. There is a window of opportunity for community newspapers, but they need to have a well-conceived and flexible game plan to address the issues head-on.

Therefore, *Saving Community Journalism* methodically explores both the risks and opportunities that publishers and editors face as they attempt to reimagine and re-create their newspapers while facing ferocious headwinds. All authors call on their own personal experiences. Mine include more than three decades working as both a journalist and a business executive, developing and implementing strategies on newspapers ranging from 7,000-circulation weeklies to national newspapers with more than 1 million readers. But this book is also based on extensive research, including almost five years of in-field strategy work conducted by the School of Journalism and Mass Communication of the University of North Carolina at Chapel Hill (UNC) and funded initially by a grant from the McCormick

Foundation, which was an early advocate of developing business models to sustain quality community journalism in both rural and urban areas of the country, such as the Appalachian region and Chicago. The pilot project involved three small prize-winning newspapers in rural North Carolina serving economically depressed communities. Two of those papers had won Pulitzer recognition for their investigative journalism. Over the intervening years, the research study has grown to incorporate the efforts of more than two dozen community newspapers in ten states from California to Vermont and Florida.

In addition, this book synthesizes and marries two avenues of relevant research, identifying and applying insights from recent industry studies as well as academic inquiries conducted by the faculty at some of the nation's leading business and communication schools during the last fifty years. Among the new and useful information presented here:

- An analysis of specific ways in which the Internet has attacked both the business model and the competitive landscape of community newspapers, and the strategies that these papers must pursue if they are to survive and thrive.
- An explanation of why time is of the essence and how newspapers must immediately change and continue to evolve over the next five years to avoid being overwhelmed by "the gales of creative destruction."
- The critical moves that newspapers, during this time of disruption and transition, must make to take advantage of cross-platform delivery (print and digital) and become competitive again, engaging readers and offering advertisers unique value.
- A definition of "community" in a digital age and the ways that newspapers can profitably create and nurture it in their print and digital editions among both readers and advertisers.

This book is divided into three parts. The first part, "Creating a New Strategy," consisting of three chapters, focuses on helping all newspaper publishers and editors—regardless of a paper's size or location—understand why they must create a new strategy to deal with creative destruction. Chapter 1, "Why It Is Critical That Newspapers Survive," reviews the vitally important mission of newspapers—that of informing, nurturing, and advancing the communities they serve. Chapter 2, "Why Newspapers Must Change," examines how the traditional business model of community newspapers has been undermined from both a cost and revenue standpoint. It relates these new economic realities to both reader and advertiser changes in media consumption. Chapter 3, "How Newspapers Must Change," articulates a three-pronged strategy requiring newspapers to simultaneously (1) shed the "inefficient" costs associated with the pre-digital era; (2) build "community" online; and (3) pursue a host of new, profitable revenue opportunities. This chapter also prescribes a timeline and a goal for implementing change.

The second part, "Implementing a New Strategy," consisting of four chapters, focuses on the organizational and operational challenges facing community newspapers, particularly as they attempt to implement this new three-pronged strategy. Chapter 4, "How to Lead Change," explores what other organizations have learned about adjusting to massive change and what role publishers, editors, and advertising directors can play in bringing about successful change. Chapter 5, "How to Shed Legacy Costs," helps publishers come up with a game plan for intentionally phasing out costs associated with the print editions. It ends by asking the basic question: if you were building your business today, how would you do it? Chapter 6, "How to Build Vibrant Community on Many Platforms," examines why readers remain loyal to community newspapers and proposes ways that editors can build on that loyalty—especially in the digital realm—to engage both readers and advertisers. Chapter 7, "How to Pursue New Revenue Opportunities," explores how and why community newspapers must retool their advertising sales efforts so they can profitably pursue new sources of revenue and be competitive with traditional rivals (such as local radio and billboards) as well as with new digital entrants.

The third and final part, "The New World Order," consisting of two chapters, zooms back out and explores the implications of the recent technological transformation for the entire newspaper ecosystem. Chapter 8, "The Far-Reaching Implications," examines the ripple effects of the changed economics in community journalism on metro and regional newspapers, nonprofit news organizations, state press associations, and journalism schools as each of these organizations and institutions attempts to reinvent itself. Chapter 9, "Crafting a New Beginning," sets the stage for community newspapers to step forward with a new strategy and reaffirm their vital mission and role in the digital age.

As any businessperson who has ever led a strategy process knows, creating a vision and a strategy is only the first step. The more demanding journey is actually implementing the new strategy. It requires an organization and its leaders to make constant judgments about what is succeeding and then either make course corrections or hold steady.

The endeavors of publishers and editors at eleven innovative community newspapers are presented through in-depth profiles, and at the end of each chapter in the second part of the book, we focus on the struggles and successes of the Pulitzer Prize–winning, twice-weekly *Whiteville News Reporter* (print circulation 10,000) in eastern North Carolina as it has attempted over the last five years to implement a new strategy. Of all the newspapers the UNC team worked with, the experiences of the staff at the *News Reporter* are especially relevant for several reasons:

- The *News Reporter* was the first out of the gate. As one of the three North Carolina community papers involved in the initial phase of our research, it has made substantial progress in implementing the strategic initiatives and therefore has practical, feet-on-the-ground information to share.
- It is still independently owned. Decisions are made by the family owners and not imposed by company headquarters. This makes it much easier to set market-specific goals and measure the success or failure of a strategy. It is also easier to understand the logic behind choices a publisher or editor makes in response to the unique challenges he or she faces.
- Finally, it is one of the smallest newspapers involved in the study. Those who work at the *News Reporter* must juggle on a daily basis the demands of "getting out the paper" while also "reinventing" themselves "for the future." The publisher and editor must constantly weigh where to deploy scarce resources. Therefore, if the *News Reporter* can successfully implement the three-pronged strategy, other larger papers—which have more resources—can as well.

While many of the country's community newspapers share similar characteristics—such as a small staff and limited resources—each of the thousands of "markets" they serve is unique. By following the strategic process laid out in this book and on the website, some news organizations may conclude, for example, that it is in their long-term interest to eliminate the print edition altogether, move to digital-only delivery of news and information, and charge readers more. Others may decide that during a time of immense confusion in the marketplace, offering cross-platform delivery of advertising messages is actually a competitive advantage. So they may decide instead to totally revamp and retool the way advertising is sold and priced in both the print and online editions.

This book envisions a five-year process that involves creating a new strategy and implementing and revising it as needed. At the end of five years, publishers and owners who follow the path laid out in these chapters should have made substantial progress in turning around their newspaper and adapting to the digital era. As General Dwight D. Eisenhower once famously said: "In preparing for battle, I've always found that plans are useless, but planning is indispensable." Our goal is to lay out a detailed process for creating, and then adjusting, strategy in the course of battle.

Accompanying this book is an instructional website (http://businessofnews.unc.edu), which has an abbreviated summary of the main points covered here along with accompanying video interviews with many of the featured publishers and editors and numerous examples of how their newspapers executed successful strategies. It also gives publishers and editors opportunities both to interact with the faculty and students at UNC who have assisted community papers in implementing new strategies and to share their own stories. Information on how to use the website and share your experiences is provided in the back of the book.

Over the last four years, through a seminar class titled "Leadership in a Time of Change," approximately 200 graduate and upper-level undergraduate students at UNC's School of Journalism and Mass Communication have worked with five professors to conduct market and reader research, analyze the results, and then assist editors and advertising directors at community newspapers throughout the country in implementing changes. This digitally savvy generation has approached the project unencumbered by the past and its outmoded ways. When they speak about "creative destruction," they are much more likely to focus on the creative *possibilities* brought about by the digital age than on the *destruction* of the "old-school" newspaper business. Several of them have contributed articles and examples of proposed Web designs that are incorporated into this book or are available on the website.

"Not only would a project of this magnitude have been cost-prohibitive for us to employ a private consultant," says Les High, managing editor of the *Whiteville News Reporter*, "[but] I doubt we'd have gotten the level of emotional investment and intellectual commitment our student team has had in this project. I see great potential for what the project can continue doing for us—and how our experiences can benefit other community newspapers."

As publishers and editors of community newspapers use the strategic framework laid out in this book, they will want to view "creative destruction" as the UNC students have—acknowledging it but quickly turning their gaze toward the future, focusing on the creative potential unleashed by the Internet and how that can be used to chart a path for renewal.

PART I Creating a New Strategy

For a lot of reasons, many people are still embracing the twentieth-century growth model. Sometimes complacency is the problem. . . . Sometimes they have no clear vision for the twenty-first century so they don't know how they should change. But often, fear is a key issue. . . . [So] they cling defensively to what they currently have. In effect, they embrace the past, not the future.

—John P. Kotter, *Leading Change* (Harvard Business School Press, 1996)

CHAPTER ONE

Why It Is Critical That Newspapers Survive

The early 1950s were tense and dangerous times for the publisher and editor of the *Whiteville News Reporter*. Publisher Leslie Thompson, who had just secured a loan to buy out his long-standing business partner, watched as both circulation and advertising for the small twice-weekly newspaper in rural southeastern North Carolina spiraled downward in reaction to an editorial stance against the violence spawned by the Ku Klux Klan in nearby communities.

But Thompson had more than his business to worry about. Both he and editor Willard Cole had received numerous threats—anonymous notes and pamphlets placed on their car windshields or slid under the door of the newspaper office warning that the Klan was watching. In response, Cole began carrying a loaded pistol everywhere, and Thompson, breaking with tradition in the small town of Whiteville, began locking the front door of his house and established a family curfew and protocol for entering the home.

In many ways, Whiteville, population 5,000, was a sleepy southern postcard town in 1951. It was the seat of Columbus County, one of the state's largest in area—954 square miles of farms and swampland interspersed with villages and crossroad communities. Social life and the economy revolved around the tobacco season. In late summer and early fall, local farmers sold their cured crop at one of the fifteen auction houses in Whiteville (or the smaller markets of nearby Tabor City and Chadbourn in the southern part of the county) and then settled up their accounts with the downtown merchants. In the postwar era, life was relatively simple— mules pulling farm wagons were still a common sight on Saturdays around the courthouse square. Life was also segregated for the county's 50,000 residents, of whom 65 percent were white, 30 percent were African American, and 5 percent were Native American.

Roughly twenty miles south of Whiteville, Tabor City (population 2,000) adjoined Horry County in neighboring South Carolina, which had become a hotbed of Klan activity in the late 1940s. On July 22, 1950—a sultry Saturday night—a twenty-nine-car motorcade, with a spotlighted cross attached to the lead car, appeared on the streets of Tabor City. A week later, in an editorial, the *News Reporter* took note of the motorcade of 100 armed and masked men, stating: "Columbus County. . . . has no need for the Klan."

Over the next three years, along with Horace Carter, the editor of the weekly *Tabor City Tribune*, Whiteville's Thompson and Cole would print dozens of editorials and front-page articles documenting, exposing, and excoriating Klan beatings, floggings, and drive-by shootings in the southern portion of the county. Several of the editorials, issuing a clarion call to action among community citizens, ran on the front page of the *News Reporter*.

"Front-page editorials are unheard of today, but Cole and Thompson knew this was necessary to keep the public focused on the seriousness of the issue," says Jim High, Leslie Thompson's son-in-law and the current publisher of the *News Reporter*. The activist editor, he points out, even traveled to Charlotte 150 miles away to meet with the FBI and ask them to intervene. In 1953 more than 300 reputed Klansmen were arrested, and sixty-two—including the police chief of Fair Bluff—were convicted and served time.

The Klan activity in Columbus County ultimately attracted the attention of media outside the area, including *Life* magazine photographers who covered a Klan rally of 5,000 just south of Whiteville in August 1951. Still, the perseverance, tenacity, and courage of these two small community newspapers—one a weekly of 2,000 circulation and the other a semiweekly with only 4,500 subscribers—so impressed Jonathan Daniels, the editor of the *News and Observer* of Raleigh, one of the state's largest newspapers, that he nominated them both for journalism's highest honor, the Pulitzer Prize for Public Service, which they were awarded in 1953—becoming the smallest papers ever to be awarded the Gold Medal.

Cole, who later used the Pulitzer medal as a paperweight on his desk, acknowledged the recognition, but he added in an editorial that the greatest reward of the three-year investigative endeavor was not the award itself. "We believe the richest harvest from this experience," he wrote, "is a renewal of our faith in the soundness of awakened citizenry and a restoration of full confidence that right and justice can triumph in any community."

In 1958, after the death of his father-in-law, High, newly graduated from college with a degree in business administration, became Whiteville's publisher. He came home to Columbus County to find a paper on the financial brink, with half the circulation and advertising that it had prior to the Pulitzer Prize–winning journalism it had produced in the early part of the decade. After consulting with several journalists and businesspeople, High decided to "take a gamble" that investing was the best way to revive the fortunes of the *News Reporter* "so that we could continue to be the 'paper of record' for Columbus County."

High built a new plant and purchased one of the first offset presses in the state, which allowed the *News Reporter* to begin attracting a new and steady source of income from printing other newspapers in the area. To reverse the slide in circulation and advertising, High also committed to making the *News Reporter* "the source of news for the county by providing better coverage than a community of this size might expect." Luck and the economy were with him. By the late 1960s, "the circulation and advertisers were back and we were back on our feet."

Today, Jim High, in his eighties, is still publisher. His son Les—named for his grandfather Leslie Thompson—is the managing editor, responsible for making most of the day-to-day and strategic decisions for the *News Reporter*, which was founded in 1896 and is one of a rapidly shrinking number of family-owned publishing enterprises in the state. The paper, with a circulation today of 10,000, is still published two days a week (Mondays and Thursdays). On those days, Les can look out his office window and observe a time-honored ritual in Whiteville: a carrier standing on the street selling roughly 400 copies to cars queued up in front of the newspaper building.

But Les also realizes that those days may be numbered. Like his father a half century before, he faces a dual dilemma. He knows he must "modernize" and keep pace with the digital revolution if the paper is to attract a new generation of readers and advertisers. But a dramatic decline in print advertising revenue in recent years has limited the funds he has to invest in the newspaper's digital efforts, which include the website (established in 1998), Twitter, and Facebook. Not only have many of the local advertisers that traditionally supported the *News Reporter* begun to defect to other traditional and digital media, but Columbus County also remains mired in an unprecedented economic slump, limiting the ability of the *News Reporter* to "grow" with the market.

Publisher Jim High reflects on rejecting "a nice offer we got to sell out to a chain in the 1980s. I think we made the right decision. I sure hope we did." In the office next door, Les High reflects on the economic challenges facing Columbus County and the imperative he feels to find a "path" for the *News Reporter* to remain a vital source of information for the residents of that community in the coming years. He ticks off the problems facing Columbus County sixty years after the newspaper's journalistic crusade to oust the Klan. Per capita household income in the large county is the lowest in the state, and—since Georgia-Pacific shuttered its operation—Columbus has one of the highest rates of unemployment (double the state average). In addition, it has the highest rate of obesity and diabetes of any county in the state. "The economy, health, education—we know there are a lot of quality-of-life issues here in Columbus that will affect our future," says Les. "And if we don't cover them, no one else will."

Almost 600 miles northwest of Whiteville—and halfway across the country—in the heart of Chicago's bustling downtown, thirty-six-year-old Fabiola Pomareda, managing editor of *La Raza*, is also on a journalistic mission. Her forty-year-old newspaper (circulation 153,000) serves a very different "community": Chicago's Latino population, which, according to the 2010 census, numbers roughly 800,000, or a third of the city's 2.6 million residents.

Born in the United States and raised in Peru, Guatemala, and Costa Rica, Pomareda says her inspiration and "role model" was the mother of a teen-aged friend, a Costa Rican journalist who covered "human rights issues" during Nicaragua's civil war. Pomareda began her career as a journalist with a weekly newspaper in Costa Rica. After receiving a master's degree in journalism at the University of Barcelona, she moved to Chicago and became a freelance writer and then a reporter for the Spanish-language weekly. Her audience, she says, are first- and second-generation Latinos—mostly from Mexico, Guatemala, and Colombia—ages eighteen to sixty, who communicate primarily in Spanish. "I keep very much in mind who I was when I came here. I try not to forget," she says. "Immigrants who come here need to understand this city and how it works—everything from how to use city transportation to how to buy clothes for the winter."

Over the last seven years, Pomareda has written extensively about immigration ("I've dedicated myself to it because I've seen a lot of sad stories"), as well as to politics and the economy. "My job is different from what someone at the *Chicago Tribune* might write about," she says. "Their stories are much broader in scope. I always have to explain to my audience what everything—every issue—means to them." Believing "this job—'being a reporter'—is a mission," she is also constantly monitoring traditional media to see what is not being covered. "In recent years, I started writing a lot about organized crime and drug trafficking because no one else was. As the drug wars have heated up in Mexico, it's spilled over here and people want to know what it means to them in Chicago."

Appointed managing editor of *La Raza* in 2012, Pomareda and her staff of four reporters try to cover "everything local," keeping a balance between "hard news" and what she refers to as "news you can use and positive news." She says she is constantly impressed by the readership of *La Raza*, which includes "congressmen and -women, members of the Chicago City Council, even the DEA [the Drug Enforcement Agency]."

Fabiola Pomareda is one of a long line of passionate and tenacious Chicago journalists reporting on the issues and events that affect the city's diverse population and communities. A half century ago, for example, at the same time that a crusading editor at a small semiweekly newspaper in Whiteville, North Carolina, was exposing the Klan, African American reporters for the *Chicago Defender* and the *Chicago Crusader* were journeying south to cover the Civil Rights struggle, sending their stories back home to inform their city's black communities about what they saw and witnessed. Today, both publications—like many of Chicago's other 300 ethnic news outlets—are struggling to adapt to a changing media landscape and to a readership that has largely moved on and "assimilated" into the Chicago landscape. "Race-based publications and foreign-language publications[,] . . . essentially their existence depends on being able to resist assimilation," says veteran media analyst John Morton. "Unfortunately, assimilation in this country is pretty much an inexorable force and most of them are going to lose out."

Stephen Franklin, former award-winning foreign correspondent and workplace reporter for the *Chicago Tribune*, is working hard to make sure these diverse viewpoints and voices are still heard in the digital age. He is the ethnic-news director of the Community Media Workshop, which aims to provide editorial and business guidance to the city's print, broadcast, and digital ethnic news outlets. "The greatest problem for much of the ethnic media is time. Many were founded by immigrants long ago and failed to catch up," says Franklin. "This problem translates into a failure to stay modern and learn all of the tools of reaching their audiences. But the ethnic media is also horribly discriminated against by advertisers who harbor stereotypes that counter the reality of the black and immigrant communities. And so, the ethnic news media is largely understaffed."

Most of the ethnic publications are very small "mom and pop" operations that live month to month with few resources, if any, to invest in converting to digital. Even those that are part of a larger media company or owned by an investment firm with headquarters elsewhere often face the same financial struggles as their small, independent counterparts.

Since it was founded in 1970, *La Raza* has been owned by two different individuals—including a restaurateur and a marketer—and, recently, by a private equity firm and two publishing companies. The newspaper's renovated three-story loft on West Ohio Street is in stark contrast to its humble beginnings—a second-floor walk-up office over a Mexican restaurant. Its weekly circulation in the 1970s was 5,000. Its second owner, Luis Rossi—a marketing executive as well as an event and music promoter—purchased *La Raza* in 1983 and invested heavily in the publication, often promoting it at the various entertainment events he sponsored. After ImpreMedia purchased the paper in 2004, company founder and then-CEO John Paton—a long-standing evangelist for "digital first"—implemented a strict protocol for distributing news, which is still in effect today at *La Raza* and its sister Spanish-language publications in six other U.S. cities. Every story is sent out first as a mobile alert; then it is posted on the website, and that posting is announced on Facebook and Twitter. Next, an enhanced audio and video version is posted on the site. Finally, it is published in the print edition. Recent research estimates that more than 65 percent of Latino readers of *La Raza* have mobile phones with texting capabilities. "Much of our Web traffic comes from mobile, people reading us on phones," says Pomareda.

Beginning in 2008, ImpreMedia also moved to aggressively "modernize" and shed "inefficient" costs—centralizing administration, print production, Web production, and technology and cutting back on print circulation in certain areas of the city. With most of the "inefficient" costs shed a half decade ago, the future success of *La Raza*—now owned by the Argentinian company S. A. La Nacion—depends both on its ability to attract new readers (at a time when Latino immigration is slowing) and grow revenue across its various digital platforms. Its publisher, Jimena Catarivas, points to the many efforts the paper makes to connect with and interact with its readers and its advertisers—from face-to-face meetings at numerous cultural events that the newspaper sponsors to exchanges across multiple digital platforms from Facebook to mobile.

As veteran journalist Franklin points out, all residents of Chicago should care whether *La Raza* and the city's ethnic community news outlets survive. "They are vitamin supplements for their communities and more," he says, citing "the mainstream media's failure to write about immigrants. This involves stories ranging from merely acknowledging the way that they have changed Chicago's cultural DNA to examining the terrible problems faced by immigrants and especially those without papers. The great gift of newspapers like *La Raza* is that week after week they do not have to apologize to their readers for their social conscience when they write about crime or discrimination or the problems encountered by immigrants."

How the Mission Has Changed

The founders of our country envisioned newspapers as "watchdogs" of our democracy and sanctioned that mission with a First Amendment guarantee that set the press apart from other for-profit businesses. Over the last two centuries, many newspapers, such as the small semiweekly *News Reporter* in rural North Carolina, have performed that mission by serving as a steadfast conscience for the communities they covered—issuing courageous clarion calls for justice and fairness despite great personal and professional risk. Or, like the journalists at *La Raza,* they have sought out and covered the burning issues of the day, bubbling just below the surface in the vast and diverse neighborhoods and communities of the sprawling Chicago metropolis. Without their vigilance, such concerns might well be overlooked and ignored, and these stories would never be told.

While most recent media attention has focused on the financial travails of the large regional and "metro" newspapers like the *Chicago Tribune*, community newspapers are facing an equally dangerous transitional period as their revenues decline so rapidly that publishers do not have the funds necessary to invest in their digital future. Like that of their big-city cousins, their survival is equally important to ensuring that democracy remains vibrant in the twenty-first century—especially at the grassroots level.

In *Losing the News: The Future of the News That Feeds Democracy* (2009), the Pulitzer Prize–winning journalist Alex Jones estimates that 85 percent of the enterprising journalism that ultimately affects major public-policy change has traditionally originated with newspaper reporters—on both small and large papers. "When we look back on the civil rights era, there's a tendency to give credit to the national networks and newspapers, like the *New York Times*, for exposing racial injustice in the South," says Hodding Carter III, journalist and former public official in the Carter administration. "But more than a decade before the national reporters headed South, courageous newspaper editors on small papers were already covering the story, at *great* risk to themselves and their families. They didn't cover it because it was good for business, because it wasn't. They did it because they cared about the community they served, and knew the story had to be told, despite the personal and professional sacrifices." Carter's father, Hodding Carter II, editor of the *Delta Democrat-Times* in Greenville, Mississippi, won the Pulitzer Prize in 1946 for a series of editorials decrying intolerance in the South (especially the mistreatment of Japanese-American soldiers returning from World War II) and often spoke out in editorials and articles, both in his own paper and national publications, against racial injustice throughout the 1950s and 1960s.

In the beginning of the Internet age, most assumed the digital revolution would provide professional journalists and citizens alike with technological tools that would make government and democracy even more transparent and allow injustices to be quickly corrected. But as the past decade has shown, most "citizen journalists" rarely have the know-how, tenacity, and resources to pursue and write about the public-policy issues simmering below the surface. And they lack the bully pulpit—a credible editorial page—that newspaper editors have used historically to rally citizens in this democracy.

Further complicating matters, the digital revolution has upended the business models of all print publications, resulting in a dramatic decline in profitability and a significant cutback in the number of "professional journalists." As a result, "in many communities we now face a shortage of local, professional accountability reporting," according to *The Information Needs of Communities: The Changing Media Landscape in a Broadband Age*, a 2011 report by the Federal Communications Commission (FCC).

The FCC report describes two types of "accountability journalism" at which newspapers have historically excelled: beat reporting, in which a journalist covers the public meetings of local, regional, or state officials; and investigative and interpretative reporting on "quality of life" issues that affect a community, ranging from government corruption to environmental and health issues. In the twentieth century, newspapers typically employed many more reporters than the local broadcast outlets. With this staffing advantage, newspapers—especially the dailies—could cover more "beats" and afford to let reporters spend weeks, sometimes even months, ferreting out wrongdoing or uncovering inequality. Therefore, newspapers—through the breadth and depth of their coverage—did most of the original reporting on public-policy issues and then became a sort of tip sheet for broadcast media who followed up with "second day" stories.

But the most recent Pew Research Center report, titled *State of the News Media* (2013), estimates that newsroom staffing levels have decreased by one-third since peaking in 2000, bringing the total below 1978 levels, when the annual survey was first done. And not surprisingly, as the amount of "accountability journalism" fed into the information ecosystem by newspapers has declined, coverage of government news has shriveled on broadcast outlets—falling by half. Sports, weather, and traffic now account for 40 percent of total air time on local television newscasts, according the Pew report. The FCC report notes that 20 percent of the country's licensed television stations and more than half of the radio stations have no local news programs.

Simultaneously, there has been a marked trend in recent years toward consolidation of ownership of papers in small and midsized markets (those with less than 100,000 population), further diminishing the diversity of voices and public-policy stories in the news "food chain." Many papers—especially those in smaller markets—are being purchased by investment firms and private equity groups that are employing what Harvard Business School professor Michael Porter calls a "harvesting strategy"—cutting costs and withholding reinvestment of the savings into the newspaper.

The most civic-minded of these firms focus on coverage of hyperlocal news ("a story about the reader himself or his neighbor will be read to the end") or extensive coverage of local governmental meetings, but often not on the more expensive and time-consuming investigative or interpretive journalism that, ultimately, improves the quality of life in a community but can alienate advertisers. In the end, both types of investors are focused on managing profit margins in a declining industry.

Without strong community newspapers performing their customary watchdog function, the FCC report predicts an increase in "the kinds of problems that are, not surprisingly, associated with a lack of accountability—more government waste, more local corruption, less effective schools, and other serious community problems." As referenced in the introduction, the Knight Foundation report *Informing Communities: Sustaining Democracy in the Digital Age*, issued in 2010, puts it even more succinctly: "The current financial challenges facing news media could pose a crisis for democracy."

Publishers and editors often assume that everyone in a community—readers, public officials, advertisers, employees, and shareholders—intuitively know the mission of the newspaper and its value to the community. Yet "the public, for its part, is not very aware of the financial struggles that have led to the news industry's cutbacks in reporting," according to the

Pew 2013 media report. "Fully 60 percent of Americans say they have heard little or nothing at all about the financial problems besetting news organizations. Even so, 31 percent have stopped turning to a news outlet because it no longer provided them with the news they were accustomed to getting." Therefore, reaffirming a newspaper's mission—and its importance to the entire community—is a critical first step in charting a path to survival and renewal for the nation's community newspapers.

What exactly is a "community newspaper"? According to the traditional definition, it is a newspaper—usually a nondaily publication—with less than 15,000 circulation. But in the digital age, that definition is rapidly becoming antiquated and useless, as more and more readers get their news from digital sources.

In the predigital twentieth century, the newspaper ecosystem consisted of five different types of publications. At the very top were the national newspapers—the *New York Times*, the *Wall Street Journal*, and *USA Today*—with an extensive network of national and foreign correspondents and an editorial focus on covering national trends. Next were the large metropolitan and regional papers, such as the *Boston Globe*, the *Los Angeles Times*, the *Philadelphia Inquirer*, and the *Charlotte Observer*, with a newsroom staff that numbered in the hundreds. This gave them the ability to tackle long-term journalistic investigations that won Pulitzer recognition. Many of these papers, especially the largest metro papers, had an extensive network of bureaus in other cities (including Washington, D.C.) and maybe even several foreign reporters. But the primary editorial focus of the metro papers centered on stories of consequence in the expansive region they covered.

The third tier consisted of daily newspapers in small and midsized markets, such the *Rutland Herald* in Vermont and the *Winston-Salem Journal* in North Carolina, which have both won Pulitzer recognition—the *Herald* for its editorials and the *Journal* for its investigative reporting of environmental issues. Their newsrooms were much smaller, but they saw their editorial mission as giving statewide context to important public-policy issues that affected the quality of life of their readers. The fourth tier consisted of traditional "community newspapers" (a group composed primarily of weeklies with circulation under 15,000) that covered issues of local concern. Occasionally, those issues would rise to the level of regional and national significance, and they would be nominated for Pulitzer Prizes—as was the case with the Whiteville and Tabor City papers for their aggressive coverage of the Klan.

The final tier was composed of hundreds of ethnic newspapers, most located around major metropolitan areas. These papers, like *La Raza* or the *Polish Daily News*, focused on the concerns of recently arrived immigrant groups or, like the *Chicago Defender*, on those of African American communities throughout the North and South. The journalists on these ethnic papers wrote about the American experience from a very different perspective than the mainstream newspapers.

As the swift adoption of the Internet over the last decade has eroded the profit margins of most papers, many mainstream dailies have pulled back on news coverage of outlying areas. A recent study notes that in response to the increased availability of national newspapers in even the most remote areas of the country, many dailies—both large and small—have focused increasingly on covering the local scene in an attempt to find a niche that differentiates them from the competition. Also, many ethnic papers have focused increasingly on connecting their readers to the community in which they live and helping them assimilate quickly into American society. As a result, the five tiers have collapsed into three tiers composed of the national newspapers, the metro and regional papers, and community-based publications.

Therefore, the term "community newspaper" (as used in this book) encompasses almost all of the country's 11,000 newspapers. In addition to the 8,000 or so weeklies and semiweeklies traditionally considered "community newspapers," it includes more than a thousand dailies in small and midsized markets (such as the *Rutland Herald* and the *Winston-Salem Journal*) and hundreds of ethnic publications (such as *La Raza*). It excludes only ninety of the nation's dailies—the three national newspapers as well as the metro and regional papers that circulate more than 100,000 copies of their print edition. (These larger papers have somewhat different market and editorial issues, which will be addressed in chapter 8 as we consider the implications of this "new world order" on the entire newspaper ecosystem.)

Using this new definition of community newspapers, what is important is not the size of a paper's print circulation but, rather, the mission of the paper. Therefore, articulating and emphasizing that vital mission helps everyone, from readers and advertisers to employees and shareholders, understand what is at stake if a community newspaper ceases to exist. It then sets up a productive discussion about how a newspaper needs to change if it is to survive the threats posed by the digital revolution.

Publishers and editors can begin by asking this simple question: if your newspaper ceased publishing tomorrow, who has the most to lose? The answer in most communities—rural and urban, large and small—is that there would be a tremendous vacuum for many, including readers and public officials, who depend on the newspaper to be a credible and comprehensive source of news and information that affects the community; advertisers, who depend on the newspaper to connect them with local consumers of their goods and services; and shareholders, employees, and vendors, who rely on the newspaper for income.

Extensive research at the University of North Carolina at Chapel Hill, as well as dozens of interviews with stakeholders in communities large and small, has revealed an expansive mission and role that goes significantly beyond the original "watchdog" function envisioned by our nation's founders. As numerous stakeholders—from advertisers and readers to government officials—have pointed out, even in the digital age, newspapers are quite simply "the glue that binds" a community together politically, socially, and financially, as well as journalistically.

Three Critical Roles of Community Newspapers

SETTING THE AGENDA FOR PUBLIC-POLICY DEBATE

Seminal research at UNC in the 1970s established that newspapers—more than any other traditional medium—essentially determine the "hot-button" issues that are debated and voted on in communities large and small. As result, they have historically wielded disproportionate influence on policy making at all levels of government.

How did newspapers set the agenda for public debate of issues? First, by singling out certain issues that editors perceive are important and then devoting the necessary resources to documenting and reporting on those issues. Second, by placing certain stories on the front page, or in a prominent "can't-miss" position, with headlines that attract attention. As one reader summed it up: "I always scan the headlines on the front page to see what the editors consider are the most important stories." And third, by following up these stories with editorials that argue for a specific course of action.

This "agenda-setting" role is especially important in the digital age, when readers often suffer from information overload. Ironically, as the FCC report points out, "in many ways, today's media landscape is more vibrant than ever, with fewer barriers to entry and more ways to consume information." What is often missing, though, is the context and analysis that professional reporters and editors have historically provided.

And with a range of new reporting tools that allow professional journalists to both access and drill down into all sorts of publicly available data and then zoom back out to provide a big-picture perspective on the numbers, community newspapers in the digital age are even better equipped to ferret out and spotlight important issues. In addition, in an age when anyone can create and post opinions in the "blogosphere," the measured and rational voice of a community newspaper's editorial page can lift an important issue above the din of a thousand voices.

The *Rutland Herald*, circulation 12,000, won a Pulitzer Prize in 2000 for its series of editorials encouraging the state legislature to recognize same-sex civil unions. At that time, it was an emotionally fraught issue that surfaced deep cultural divisions among the state's populace and resulted in death threats for the paper's editorial page editor, David Moats, and publisher and owner, John Mitchell. Yet the paper persisted in its measured stance (with the legislature ultimately passing a law that the *Herald* endorsed) because, says Rob Mitchell, who is the third generation in his family to be editor of the independent paper: "We believe the role of a community newspaper is to commit journalism and take stands that matter."

Similarly, the *Santa Rosa (Calif.) Press Democrat* (circulation 55,000) announced soon after it was purchased by a group of local investors in early 2013 that it would resume making endorsements of candidates for local office—something that had been prohibited by the previous owners, the Halifax Group, a private-equity firm that purchased the paper from the New York Times Company in 2012. As longtime publisher Bruce Kyse wrote in a letter to readers: "It seems incongruous to us that the one time a newspaper would not offer its opinion is when it comes to making the most important decision a community makes—choosing elected leaders."

Whiteville's Les High considers editorials "an integral part of the paper. They help set the agenda for what we believe is important and will help move the county in a positive direction, whether it be supporting a good cause or criticizing government officials on the issue of transparency, to cite a recent example. Sometimes we take what many would consider a liberal view of issues, which isn't looked upon favorably by a majority of our readers, but bottom line, we call 'em like we see 'em, even if it's not popular." Remembering the crusading front-page editorials on the Klan that resulted in a Pulitzer Prize for the *News Reporter* in 1953, he asks philosophically: "Would we ever run a front-page editorial today? You bet we would—if the issue rose to that level of importance."

As director of the Institute for Rural Journalism and Community Issues, Al Cross, a longtime political reporter for the *Louisville (Ky.) Courier-Journal*, helps rural newspapers "grasp the ideas and issues that will affect a community and then define the public agenda for their communities through strong reporting and commentary." The idea for the institute originated with a former White House correspondent for the *Los Angeles Times* who was touring the Appalachian region to research the area's social and economic progress over the last several decades. "He was distressed at the devolution of newspapers in Appalachia since the last time he'd been here," says Cross, "because he believed strong newspapers build strong communities."

Since 2005, the Institute for Rural Journalism and Community Issues, headquartered at the University of Kentucky in Lexington, has presented the Gish Award to rural newspaper publishers and editors throughout the country—from Oregon and Texas to Kentucky—who, through sheer perseverance, have overcome community indifference and outright opposition to bring quality-of-life issues into the public arena. The Gish Award is named for Tom and Susan Gish, a married couple who purchased the *Mountain Eagle*, a weekly newspaper (circulation 6,000) in Whitesburg, Kentucky, in the late 1950s and immediately showed "courage, integrity, and tenacity" by reporting and editorializing on everything from the closed meetings of the local school board to mining-company abuses. Like the *News Reporter*, the *Mountain Eagle* has endured advertising boycotts and personal attacks, and its office was even firebombed. And like the *News Reporter*, it perseveres today, with the couple's son now the editor.

As a state legislator in North Carolina puts it: "I trust the editors at the paper—more than any other source—to tell me what is just below the surface that I might have missed. They tie it together and tell me whether it is really an issue or a personal beef of some blogger." When a strong newspaper identifies a public-policy issue, reports on it, and then persuades others to take a stand, then everyone in the community benefits—even the nonreaders of the paper, according to Stanford University media economist James T. Hamilton. In *All the News That's Fit to Sell: How the Market Transforms Information into News* (2004), Hamilton notes that many people approach learning about a public-policy issue as "an investment decision." Since they perceive they have little say in the decision, they opt for "rational ignorance." But if a newspaper explains the significance or consequence of a certain policy—and the impact it will have on a community—the readers of the news stories and editorials in the paper become better-informed voters. "The improved precision of their (voting) decisions may benefit others (including nonvoters in the community) . . . leading to what economists term positive externalities," he writes, "with broader benefits to society."

ENCOURAGING ECONOMIC GROWTH AND COMMERCE

Community newspapers also encourage regional economic growth and commerce. They do so directly by providing a marketplace for readers and advertisers to connect. But equally important, through their "agenda-setting" function, editors and reporters encourage discussion around issues that can either impede or accelerate economic growth.

Even in this digital age, most people buy the majority of their goods and services close to home. So there is a still a need for a central marketplace—which the newspaper has historically provided—that allows local merchants to inform current and potential customers through advertisements about the multiple products and services that are available in the area. While much has been made about the death of print advertising in community newspapers, most community newspapers still deliver a more effective and efficient audience for local advertisers than competing mediums, including new digital interlopers.

Dozens of advertisers interviewed over the last four years expressed a desire to support the local newspaper. As one advertiser put it, "I realize that it is important for this community—and for my business and other small businesses—for the newspaper to survive. I just need the newspaper to understand that my business is changing, too. They [advertising sales representatives] need to help me reach new customers and not just show up and take my order and move on."

The *Hampshire Review*, a 7,000-circulation weekly in the town of Romney (population 2,000) in the eastern panhandle of West Virginia, has done just that by helping local merchants build and design Web pages and use social media more effectively. And it has been good for business, both for the paper's bottom line and for the success of area merchants. Currently, the paper hosts the websites of more than thirty small local businesses on its own server, including a carpet distributor located in a crossroads community twenty miles from Romney on the border with Maryland. "I went to the owner and said, 'You've got to have a website so people will know about you,'" says the *Hampshire Review* editor, Sallie See. "We built him a gorgeous site showing all his carpets and then sold him an ad on [the paper's] website with a link to his site that has gotten 23,000 hits over the last eighteen months. He says I turned his business around."

In later chapters, we'll discuss the various and important services that newspaper advertisements continue to provide, even in the digital era—from creating awareness of a need for a product to reinforcing the loyalty of current customers. Suffice it to say, retooled and retrained, newspaper advertising departments at dailies such as the *Santa Rosa Press Democrat* or the *Naples (Fla.) Daily News*—or weeklies such as the *Hampshire Review*—can play a very important and critical role in educating local businesses in how to best use the digital marketing tools that are now available. In doing so, newspapers can continue to nurture a vibrant local retail marketplace.

Likewise, journalists on community papers have an important role in encouraging long-term economic growth and overall prosperity in the community. Through news stories—or local summits that editors convene, host, and then report on—newspapers can highlight underlying trends that help public officials and local businesspeople focus on ways to prioritize investments that spur economic growth.

Unfortunately, "there is a sense in a lot of small towns that the local newspaper exists to promote business development," says Al Cross at the Institute for Rural Journalism and Community Issues. "So there is a lot of pressure not to print anything that is negative about a community because it might discourage a company from moving into town and providing jobs. These companies have already done their own research and will decide to come—or not—based on that research, and not on some bad publicity." But that doesn't stop local boosters from attempting to discourage aggressive reporting on key issues—such as health, education, and safety—that can cause a prolonged economic blight to settle on a community. Tom and Susan Gish met with a ferocious advertiser boycott in the 1960s and 1970s when the stories in their weekly *Mountain Eagle* spotlighted the many economic issues facing the eastern Kentucky county of Letcher—from local government corruption to inadequate public education and strip mining practices that damaged the environment.

By acknowledging a deep-seated economic problem, says Cross, a community is better off in the long term since it can begin to develop a strategy for addressing it. A report by the Manpower Development Corporation, a nonprofit organization that focuses on encouraging economic development in communities throughout the southern part of the United States, underscores that point. "Historically . . . too many communities have a culture of low expectations. Good schools, skilled people, and visionary leadership have been viewed as unnecessary, expensive, even destabilizing conceits," notes the report, entitled *Building Communities of Conscience*

Why the Public Should Care Whether Community Newspapers Survive

Why is it important for community newspapers to survive? Steven Waldman, the senior advisor to the chairman of the FCC and a visiting senior media policy scholar at Columbia University's Graduate School of Journalism, was the lead author for the commission's 2011 report, "The Information Needs of Communities" (www.FCC.gov/info-needs-communities), which analyzed the changing media landscape in the broadband age and how it affects the ability of communities to get the news they need.

Q. In the FCC report, you conclude that the digital revolution has created the best of times and the worst of times for today's media landscape. Can you explain what that means?

We're seeing tremendous innovation. Americans have access to a much wider range of information and news sources, including blogs, data straight from the government, and journalism from around the world. And they can get it in a variety of media platforms—on their phones, on desktop computers, in print magazines and newspapers—and they can get that news and information almost instantly. They can contribute to the news flow through their own photos and observations. On the other hand, the business models for sustaining full-time professional accountability reporting have collapsed.

Q. What specific areas of newspaper coverage are disappearing?

It tends to be types of coverage that are costly and have a high public benefit but not necessarily huge numbers of readers—coverage of state legislatures; investigative reporting; coverage of courts, planning boards, city hall, crime, health, the environment, etc. Newspaper employment fell dramatically in the last decade, and it takes a lot of reporters to adequately cover those public-interest beats. The pressure on newsroom staff means reporters have less time for daily beat reporting and fewer resources to produce labor-intensive stories.

Q. How can community papers step up to fill in that information gap? What challenges will they face?

Community newspapers are important because they have traditionally promoted local accountability. But while the need for community papers (or online-only versions) is greater than ever, the business model is harder than ever. The way forward will probably have to involve finding new and innovative models for making money on public-interest journalism. There's also an important opportunity to rebuild loyal community readership and engagement online.

Q. Will this require a new mindset for community paper editors and publishers as they think about fulfilling their traditional watchdog role?

I do think there's more of an opportunity for community newspapers because of the gaps left by the big-city dailies. If they could serve more of a watchdog role that would really distinguish them from their competitors. That means finding ways to overcome the ongoing business challenges facing print newspapers and committing staff resources to original reporting for those public-interest beats that have really suffered from lack of coverage. (Interview by Stephen Boss)

and Conviction. "Today, however, survival in the competitive world of global economics and political decentralization demands that these places set and reach higher standards or wither and perish."

Currently, Cross is attempting to get "small newspapers [in Kentucky] to run more stories about health-related matters because many of the counties in this [eastern] region are in the bottom of the rankings on health in the entire country." Both for the long term and the short term, he points out, this health issue is a serious impediment to the economic vitality of a community. Journalist Stephen Franklin notes: "Last year the city of Chicago shut down a number of mental health facilities in a cost-saving move. Not one mainstream paper devoted any serious coverage to the fact that Latinos were losing the only place they could find Spanish-speaking therapists at a public facility. But the Latino media covered this—just as it has written about the suicides that have afflicted immigrant teens without papers and the abuses suffered by immigrants unfamiliar with unscrupulous businesses." For low-income communities bypassed by the digital revolution, newspaper reporters and editors may be the only people who can access, analyze, and report on data and trends that point the way to civic health and economic viability.

Many economically depressed rural counties have what Cross calls "a Friday-night-lights mentality" in which community leaders believe they are always competing with the neighboring county in recruiting employers to the area. Community newspapers, especially in rural areas, can be important catalysts in reframing the discussion and helping county officials think about collaboration with adjoining counties instead of competition. "Most of these impoverished rural counties do not have the civic capital to go it alone," he says. "They need to work in combination with other counties to lift the entire region. The local newspaper can play an important role in encouraging this."

FOSTERING A SENSE OF GEOGRAPHIC COMMUNITY

In addition to setting the agenda for debate on public issues, community newspapers can play a critical role in fostering and nurturing a cohesive sense of geographic community. Even in a digital age, we still navigate multiple political, economic, and social geographic boundaries on a daily basis. A community newspaper helps us pass through these border crossings knowingly, intentionally, and—in most cases—seamlessly. It also helps us understand how those of us who live in geographic proximity are all connected and how our actions affect our neighbors.

"Effective communities appear to have more than just facts," notes a report by the Kettering Foundation titled *Community Effectiveness: What Makes the Difference?* (1987). "They know what the facts mean in the lives of diverse people who make up the community. . . . [It] is about interrelationships and consequences. It implies knowing the consequences of our own actions on people who might seem unrelated to us—but really aren't." Politically, we reside in numerous political and governmental entities—the precinct where we vote, the town or municipality in which we live, the zip code in which we receive our mail. Newspapers unite these various divisions and help us understand what our vote means to the larger community, or why we should be concerned about a certain issue that especially affects our town or zip code.

In Columbus County (population 55,000) in rural eastern North Carolina, the *News Reporter*'s Les High counts three state legislative districts, twenty-six precincts, ten incorporated municipalities, six school-board districts, seven county-commissioner districts, and nine zip codes. "I tell editors constantly that the readers of your county are not just residents of a county but of a region, a state, and a nation," says Al Cross. "So coverage of political issues should not stop at the county line." We also identify economically with the place where we work and spend money. The newspaper informs us of employment opportunities in the region and directs our shopping activities to nearby towns.

The *Fayetteville Observer* (circulation 55,000), the state's oldest newspaper (established in 1816), covers a ten-county region with a population of 750,000 in eastern North Carolina, anchored by the town of Fayetteville and the military bases of Fort Bragg and Pope Air Force Base (employing almost 100,000 military and civilian workers). Despite the geographic reach of the newspaper, its publisher, Charles Broadwell, calls the *Observer* "a community newspaper." "Cumberland County is a major retail center and Fort Bragg is a growing driver of our regional economy—affecting everything from transportation to education—and is a major employer," says Broadwell. "Where they [the soldiers] go, we go—from Kabul to Baghdad." As a result, Fayetteville has historically carried an unusually high percentage of national and international news, some of it written by reporters traveling with military units. "When most consultants come in here, they talk about how different we are from other communities of this size that just want local, local, local," he says. "Here, for us, there are two goal posts, so to speak—one for local news and one for national and international [news]—and we have to kick field goals through both every day." Not only does the *Observer* attempt to connect the political and economic dots for its readers; it also attempts to help them connect socially, "even though many are passing through and may only call this 'home' for a few months," says Broadwell.

When he was appointed publisher of the *Daily News* in 2006 in the upscale retirement and resort community of Naples, Florida, Dave Neill says one of his first priorities was to "identity and reach out to the many communities within our greater community—the Hispanic community, the Haitian community, the religious community. Forging relationships with these underserved communities gives you editorial access—and an understanding of how they experience the greater community."

In Chicago, "ethnic news outlets keep the language and culture alive," says Franklin. "They link people overwhelmed by feelings of otherness and isolation. And they are the soul that people turn to in order to find out the truth." He points to *Draugas*, a Lithuanian newspaper, "printed five days a week on an old machine that has been churning out news in the native language since its readers worked in the stockyards and became the symbols for *The Jungle*. When the Soviets banned the language in their native land, this tiny newspaper became the sole place in the world where you could read in Lithuanian."

Each week, the Chicago Spanish-language weekly *La Raza* carries at least three pages of "hometown news" in all of its editions—news from the

Latin American countries where most of the first- and second-generation immigrants still have family ties. "There are two things that our readers really care about," says *La Raza* publisher Jimena Catarivas. "Family life and what's happening in the Latino community—not just in Chicago, but in the country where they came from."

A similar identification with one's birthplace or ancestral home showed up in the UNC research, which focused on readers of rural community newspapers. A regular reader of a weekly's digital edition who lives and works in a metro area seventy-five miles from the small community in West Virginia where he spent his early years observed: "You always call the place where you grew up and graduated from high school 'home'—especially if you still have family and friends there. Reading the newspaper is the best way to keep up with people back home." Or, as another reader—a lifelong resident of a small community in the mountains of North Carolina—pointed out: "Even though I'm on Facebook a lot, I still depend on the newspaper to tell me about people in this community I don't know, or know only in passing. It's like my ticket to community membership."

After surveying the issues confronting communities throughout the South in the late 1990s, the Manpower Development Corporation published a report titled *The Building Blocks of Community Development* (2002), which concluded: "For a community to reach and maintain its full potential economically, it must be civically healthy and inclusive, or its own pathologies will prevent its sustained viability." Whether setting the agenda for debate on public-policy issues, fostering economic growth, or nurturing a sense of geographic community, newspapers—unique among other businesses and enterprises—have historically been "the glue that binds" a community together. In the digital age, the mission (or reason for being) is just as important as ever. The *Whiteville News Reporter*, *La Raza*, the *Rutland Herald*, the *Santa Rosa Press Democrat*, the *Fayetteville Observer*, and the *Whitesburg Mountain Eagle*—all of these newspapers cover often-overlooked issues or neglected communities. Their existence makes for a much richer and diverse media landscape and more inclusive democracy. Everyone in the communities they serve—whether large or small—has a tremendous stake in their survival. This includes the reader who no longer pays to receive the print edition because he can get the news "for free" on the Internet. Or the local merchant who believes the local newspaper has "not kept up with the times" and has shifted his marketing dollars online.

In the following chapters, we'll discuss how newspapers can begin to reestablish the value proposition for both readers and advertisers. But before a publisher can do that, he or she must first reconfirm that the role of a newspaper—informing, nurturing, and improving a community—is as vital in the twenty-first century as it was in previous predigital eras.

"A good newspaper is an anchor in a community," says Ron Heifetz, professor in Harvard University's John F. Kennedy School of Government and a longtime advisor to political and governmental leaders ranging from presidents and prime ministers to mayors. "A newspaper reminds a community every day of its collective identity, the stake we have in one another, and the lessons of its history."

This, then, is the vital mission of community newspapers in the digital age. A mission is born of passion, and passion allows an organization to summon both the energy to persevere and the courage to adjust to new realities. "It is hard to overstate the vitally important role that a strong newspaper can play in improving the quality of life for residents of the communities they serve," says Ferrel Guillory, former editorial page editor of the *Raleigh News and Observer* and director of UNC's Program on Public Life. "A good editor can see the big picture better than just about anyone else in the community—tying together the reality of the present with the possibility of the future."

CHAPTER TWO
Why Newspapers Must Change

Looking out on the media landscape at the turn of the millennium, most publishers of community newspapers could be forgiven for dismissing the pundits and prognosticators who viewed them as technological "dinosaurs." Despite rapid adoption of the Internet in the previous decade, the business model seemed to be holding strong. Newspaper advertising was at an all-time high, and profits were healthy. It was hard to imagine, much less believe, that the immediacy, interactivity, and interconnectedness of the Internet would wreak such havoc over the next decade on a 200-year-old industry.

Indeed, the extent and pace of change in the media landscape since 2000 has been so extensive that it is mind-boggling to contemplate. Far from being islands safe from the destruction that engulfed large city papers in mid-decade, publications in even the most remote and rural areas of the country have been affected. So while the mission of newspapers is as vital as ever in the digital age, the business model that has supported and funded good journalism in communities large and small is frayed and, in many cases, in tatters.

Les High of Whiteville's *News Reporter* remembers those "good old days" as "a time—not too long ago—when it seemed we could just sit back and count the money." Today, with profits squeezed, High worries about how he will fund the sort of watchdog, or "accountability," journalism that has long been the hallmark of the independently owned, Pulitzer Prize–winning publication. That sort of journalism, he points out, is time- and labor-intensive and requires a willingness by the newspaper to allow reporters to pursue tips that may not pan out. It also requires an ability to pay the legal fees that often result when a newspaper needs to defend itself against threatened libel suits or go to court to get government officials to release certain public documents.

What happened? How did the world change overnight for newspapers everywhere in the first half decade of the twenty-first century? Were the seeds of destruction for the old world order already planted?

Before they can begin to chart a course to survival and renewal, community newspaper publishers and editors need to understand why exactly the Internet—unlike radio and television in the twentieth century—has been such an intrusive medium, invading even the smallest and most remote communities, and why it is both a near-term and long-term threat to all newspapers, regardless of size and location.

In this chapter, we will first survey the seismic shifts that have occurred in a relatively brief period of time, comparing the stable world of the latter half of the twentieth century to the current news ecosystem, which is in transition and, at times, appears to be in convulsive flux. And then, because every community and market is unique, we will analyze how these changes in the macroenvironment play out on a local level, eroding everything from yearly profit to customer loyalty and engagement with the newspaper. The Internet has attacked both the cost and revenue structure of the traditional newspaper business model. That is why newspapers who wish to survive must change the way they do business in the twenty-first century.

How the Media Landscape Has Changed

In retrospect, the "good old days" of the 1980s and 1990s—when profit margins at small community newspapers routinely exceeded 20 percent—seem an economic aberration. Writing in 1991 in the pre-Internet era, media historian Donald Shaw noticed that the decline of a mass medium, such as newspapers, is always anticipated by the rise of a "new" medium that displaces it. And indeed, the heyday of newspapers—the era when the number of papers in this country peaked—was the early 1920s, before the emergence of radio as a mass medium.

Newspapers weathered the assault—first by radio in the 1920s and 1930s and then by television in the 1950s and 1960s—by retreating into their local communities. What followed was a fifty-year war of attrition between dueling, competing newspapers in individual cities and towns around the country. By the 1980s, most communities, large and small, were served by only one newspaper. Looking back on the latter decades of the twentieth century, Columbia University economist Eli Noam noted: "TV and radio took away some news audience and advertising, but they were not a substitute for longer news stories or many types of advertising, such as classified. The surviving papers were therefore profitable and could afford the production of the news content."

With little local competition for advertising dollars—except, perhaps, from radio, the Yellow Pages directory, or direct-mail houses—the surviving community newspaper became what economists call a "de facto geographic monopoly." Typically, de facto monopolies, especially those largely unencumbered by government regulations, have tremendous latitude in setting prices and controlling costs, which leads to higher than normal profits and operating margins.

As a result, such industries usually attract the attention of Wall Street analysts and investors. That business is viewed as a "cash cow," a term coined by the Boston Consulting Group to describe a mature industry requiring minimal investment to produce a reliable, above-average cash flow. Such was the case with the newspaper industry over the last quarter of the twentieth century, when profit margins were increasing even as readership decreased. In the 1980s and 1990s, Wall Street analysts began to recommend newspaper stocks as safe and reliable investment options ("buy and hold"), and chains bid up the price of the few independently owned newspapers in markets ranging in size from Santa Rosa, California, to Raleigh and Minneapolis.

With the focus of public companies—such as Knight Ridder Newspapers and the Times Mirror Company—on delivering profit margins that consistently met or exceeded analysts' expectations, many journalists began to worry the news operation had taken a backseat to the business side. In his 2004 book, *The Vanishing Newspaper: Saving Journalism in the Information Age*, Philip Meyer documented the steady downward trend in household penetration of U.S. daily newspapers in the twentieth century and worried how, with declining readership, newspapers could continue to fulfill their historic role of informing democracy in the twenty-first century.

But few journalists or publishers in the 1990s worried about what the Internet could do to siphon off revenue and profit. The declining household penetration, documented by Meyer, also spelled trouble for newspapers' attractiveness to advertisers, who wanted to reach as large an audience as possible. But on the back of the longest economic expansion since World War II, advertising money during the 1990s poured into all traditional media outlets, including local newspapers, masking the underlying problem. Classified advertising, which had the highest profit margins, flourished in categories ranging from help wanted to real estate.

While other media companies—such as Time Warner and the Tribune Company—were making "big bet" acquisitions and mergers at the close of the century, newspaper companies merely hedged their bets by taking out equity or partnership stakes in Internet companies. And when the big bets—such as Time Warner's "merger" with AOL—failed, newspaper owners no doubt felt vindicated by their hedging strategies.

By the middle of the first decade of the twenty-first century, however, the potential of the Internet to supplant newspapers was becoming abundantly clear. In 2005, speaking to a group of newspaper editors, News Corporation chairman and CEO Rupert Murdoch took note of the Internet's expanding global audience. Extrapolating from the downward readership trends documented by Meyer in *The Vanishing Newspaper*, Murdoch somewhat tongue-in-cheek predicted that "the last reader recycles the last printed paper in 2040."

But the demise of an industry does not often occur in a straight downward trend line. Rather, industries in the throes of creative destruction experience a tipping point or "a waterfall moment"—the point in time when an industry's revenues and profits suddenly plummet and the "old" industry's existence is put in jeopardy. Ironically, in many cases just before the waterfall, an industry's revenues may actually spike, giving its managers a false sense of permanence and encouraging complacency.

And that is exactly what happened in the years leading up to 2000 and the sudden dot-com bust. Advertising revenues for the newspaper industry, adjusted for inflation, peaked in 2000 at $64 billion. It had taken roughly fifty years for advertising revenues to climb from $20 billion in 1950 to its peak. Yet by 2010—only a decade later—ad revenues had plummeted back down to 1950 levels. A waterfall moment!

Until recently, many publishers and owners of community newspapers were still reassuring themselves and their investors that an uptick in advertising was just around the corner—"as soon as the recession lifted." Yet as Figure 1, put together by a University of Michigan economist, graphically shows, the advertising decline does not correlate with the economic cycles we have experienced since 2000. Nor does it correlate with advertising trend lines in the broadcast industry. Rather, the chart suggests there has been a significant shift in advertising, which has traditionally comprised 80 percent of the revenues at most newspapers, to other mediums. As advertising revenues declined, so have the news operations of many papers through staff layoffs and curtailment of coverage in outlying areas of the community.

To complicate matters, a second tipping point for the industry occurred in 2006, when Wall Street types—the analysts, investment bankers, and investors—began abandoning newspaper companies. As advertising revenues in the 1990s soared, so did the stock of most newspaper companies.

FIGURE 1. Newspaper Advertising Revenue,
Adjusted for Inflation, 1950 to 2012

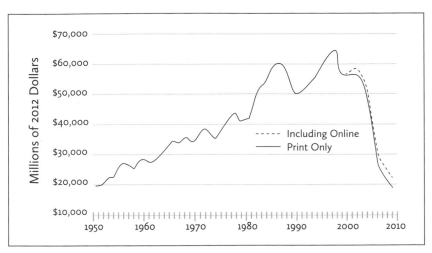

Source: Mark Perry, "Free-Fall: Adjusted for Inflation, Print Newspaper Advertising Will Be Lower This Year Than in 1950," Carpe Diem Blog posting Thursday, September 6, 2012, http://mjperry.blogspot.com/2012/09/freefall-adjusted-for-inflation-print.html.

Despite declining household penetration, Wall Street continued to view newspapers in small and midsized markets as de facto monopolies that were relatively immune from the vicissitudes of the Internet revolution sweeping the rest of the country. From 1996 to 2006, shareholders in the nation's six largest publicly held newspaper companies—most of which owned newspapers in markets with only minimal competition from broadcast outlets—reaped a return that exceeded the stock market as a whole.

But as Figure 2 shows, this above-average return to shareholders ceased in 2006, suddenly falling "off a cliff." Today, the market value (the price of the stock multiplied by the outstanding shares) of most publicly traded newspaper companies is only one-fifth of what it was in 2006. And the book value of many media companies (that is, the dollar amount listed as "assets" on a balance sheet) often exceeds its market value—indicating that Wall Street investors are very pessimistic about the prospects for a recovery.

What happened to cause the 2006 sell-off? Most likely it was the convergence of a number of technological and economic trends that had been building over the first half of the decade, including the increasing penetration of broadband and wireless in all but the most remote areas of the country and a dramatic surge in search-related advertising. Both caused Wall Street to realize that the local newspaper was no longer a de facto

FIGURE 2. Media Returns in Relation to the S&P 500

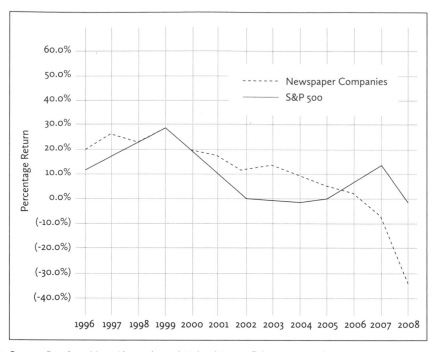

Source: Penelope Muse Abernathy and Richard Foster, "The News Landscape in 2014: Transformed or Diminished? (Formulating a Game Plan for Survival in the Digital Era)." Paper presented at the Yale University Conference on Information, the Law and Society, November 12, 2009.

geographic monopoly. It had viable *competition* for both its readers and its advertisers.

This realization and pessimism seeps through the capital markets and ultimately limits the availability of funds that newspapers can access. Complicating matters, many of the investors who bought individual newspaper properties in 2006 and 2007 assumed the past financial performance of these papers was an indication of future profitability. And it most certainly was not. So chains—such as McClatchy, which purchased Knight Ridder Newspapers Inc. in 2007—have had to funnel most of the declining profits from their newspapers into repaying the loans instead of investing heavily in a digital future. In an attempt to keep profit margins and cash flow as high as possible, many of these acquiring companies have pursued significant cost reductions, including laying off up to 50 percent of newsroom reporters and editors.

With the long-term financial viability of metro and regional newspapers in doubt, many investors have now turned their gaze toward community newspapers in small markets, where they assume—because of the lack of connectivity—that newspapers still face relatively little competition for either readers or advertisers. But as we will discuss later in this chapter, this is rapidly changing.

What is notable about this latest influx of investors into community newspapers is that they are not the "newspaper chains" of yesterday but instead predominantly private equity and investment firms. Private equity firms typically have very short time horizons for "flipping" properties—they do not "buy and hold," as the newspaper shareholders did in the 1980s and 1990s. Therefore, their emphasis is on increasing the profit margins as quickly as possible through "cost efficiencies." Consequently, they often cut as much as 50 percent of costs in the first year and consolidate most journalistic and business functions in a central location that serves many papers and many markets.

Even the investment firms considered to be "white knights" (such as Berkshire Hathaway, headed by Warren Buffett, a longtime shareholder in and board member of the Washington Post Company) must focus first on return to their shareholders—which means that expensive investigative journalism, which has historically served small and remote communities well, often takes a backseat to the easier and less-expensive "hyperlocal" content focusing on people and events and not underlying trends. In his 2013 annual letter to Berkshire Hathaway shareholders justifying the purchase of twenty-eight newspapers in small and midsized markets for $344 million, Buffett stated: "A reader's eyes may glaze over after they take in a couple of paragraphs about Canadian tariffs or political developments in Pakistan; a story about the reader himself or his neighbors will be read to the end.

"Berkshire's cash earnings from its papers will almost certainly trend downward over time," Buffett continued. "Even a sensible Internet strategy will not be able to prevent modest erosion. At our cost, however, I believe these papers will meet or exceed our economic test for acquisitions." (It is worth noting that what Buffett paid in 2012 for twenty-eight community newspapers, including the third- and fourth-largest newspapers in North Carolina, was roughly equivalent to what the McClatchy Company paid in 1996 for a single paper—the *News and Observer* of Raleigh, the state's second-largest paper.)

Surveying the changed news landscape in his 2009 book *Media Ownership and Concentration in America*, Columbia University economist Eli Noam offered his best guess as to the future for ten different mediums, from books to telecommunications. "Newspapers have been a stodgy industry for over 70 years," he wrote. "But now . . . the newspaper sector has become turbulent again." Previously, he noted, the lone surviving paper in a market could "charge fairly high prices for advertising and subscriptions. . . . But now, another generation of technology creates another wave of alternatives and undercuts the ability to charge the previous price for news and ads." Given all the disruption newspapers were dealing with, Noam concluded that the "likelihood . . . of this medium remaining the same are nil."

No longer de facto monopolies, community newspapers everywhere have emerged from a "stodgy" period to find themselves facing new and relentless interlopers. In other words, the industry is not in a cycle from which it will emerge relatively unchanged. Rather, it is in a cyclone. There is a new reality—a "new normal"—for the newspaper industry.

Zooming In: How the Internet Attacked the Business Model

These seismic changes in the macroenvironment have trickled down to the micro-level very quickly, threatening the long-term economic vitality of newspapers serving even the most remote communities. How exactly has the Internet destroyed the business model that has traditionally underpinned U.S. community newspapers? It has done so by attacking newspapers on both the cost side—making the aging printing press, once an expensive necessity, potentially a huge financial albatross—and the revenue side, first siphoning off the high-margin classified advertising and now threatening the remaining retail advertising and preprinted inserts.

In addition, the Internet has trained readers to expect to pay nothing for news and information they can access digitally. "The problem with newspapers is not, as has often been claimed, generational and sociological but technological and economical," says Columbia economist Noam. "Newspapers are under pressure, and will be still more, not because young (and older) people do not want to pay for news but because they do not have to."

In order to understand why they must change, publishers and editors first need to calculate and analyze the impact that the digital revolution has already had on the economics of their individual newspapers, as well as the likely outcome if the trend lines are not reversed. As we discussed in the previous section, on the revenue side, even in the smallest, most remote markets, print advertising revenue is unlikely to return to previous levels, even with an uptick in the economy. The business model that sustained newspapers during the twentieth century is like the battered and beaten barrel that is rapidly descending down a gigantic "waterfall." The most recent industry surveys on ad spending show continued double-digit declines in print marketing. In many communities, classified advertising—including the help-wanted, real estate, and automotive categories—has fallen by as much as 80 percent since 2000. This is especially painful for small community papers since classified advertising traditionally yielded much higher profit margins than display advertising.

To make matters worse, even as advertising revenue has fallen "off a cliff," newspapers are saddled with high fixed costs of printing and distributing the paper. In the predigital age, the cost of purchasing and operating a printing press and delivering the paper served as "a barrier to entry" that discouraged all competitors except those with deep pockets and allowed the surviving newspapers to become local de facto geographic monopolies. Now these high fixed costs are more likely to be a serious financial burden. In his study of other industries in the throes of creative destruction, Richard Foster (longtime McKinsey consultant and author of *Creative Destruction: Why Companies That Are Built to Last Underperform the Market—And How to Successfully Transform Them* [2001]) observed that mature companies carry "inefficient" legacy costs from a previous era into the current one. Not having to bear these "legacy costs," he said, is the single biggest advantage a digital start-up competitor has over a mature competitor.

Therefore, in the digital era, community newspapers are disadvantaged in three ways. First, their "geographic" market dominance and pricing power has been undermined by the Internet. Second, a good portion of the highest-margin advertising has been diverted to online sites or search engines. And finally, they carry into the digital age huge costs associated with supporting a system of printing and distribution that essentially dates to the nineteenth century. In other words, the Internet has delivered three simultaneous blows to the business model of newspapers:

- It has destroyed barriers to entry.
- It has diminished pricing leverage with readers and advertisers.
- It has decimated whole categories of advertising.

Seeing the production of a newspaper as a series of processes—some of which are more threatened by the digital age than others—helps publishers and editors begin to prioritize the changes they need to make if their papers are to survive creative destruction. Historically, the act of producing a newspaper consisted of three separate processes: creation, aggregation, and distribution. First, reporters created content—news and information. This content was then bundled together (aggregated) by editors and placed onto a geometric grid (broadsheet or tabloid, for example). Advertisers who wanted to reach the newspaper's readers purchased space in this aggregated package of news and information—generally, without regard to whether their advertisement was placed near a certain story or news item. Finally, this aggregated package of content (of both news and advertising) was printed and distributed on a routine basis—daily, weekly, or on some other schedule—to homes and businesses.

The Internet has actually enhanced the ability of community newspapers to create content. It has provided reporters and editors with new digital tools that help them more effectively analyze data and give substantive context to complex trends and stories, deliver more timely news, and communicate directly with readers. By using these new tools effectively to create unique content that no one else provides, forward-thinking publishers and editors can get a leg up on their competitors—both digital and traditional ones. Creation of content becomes an important building block in making a successful transition to a new business model since it allows newspapers to retain and attract new readers. So the value proposition for the first of the three processes—creation of content—is stronger than ever, and publishers and editors will want to invest in strengthening it.

But in order to invest, publishers need money—and that is the problem with the other two processes. The disaggregation (or unbundling) of news content siphons off readers and, most significantly, advertisers, which have historically provided the revenues and profits that support the three processes in the production of a newspaper. Simultaneously, distributing a print edition puts a newspaper at a distinct disadvantage in relation to competitors who can distribute digitally for a fraction of the cost.

So while the Internet has enhanced a newspaper's ability to create content using new digital tools, it has seriously disrupted the processes of aggregation of content as well as the distribution and delivery of the content. This double whammy to both the revenue and cost sides of the equation poses serious threats to the long-term viability of all newspapers' business models.

In order to craft a strategy for responding, publishers and editors need to quantify the dual threats to the bottom line if the trends continue. Let's look at the disaggregation threat to revenue first. Historically, newspapers have sold content to readers for a small fraction of what it costs to create it, aggregate it, and distribute it. Advertisers, who provided the majority of revenues, typically have not supported specific content generated by the newsroom. Rather, advertisers paid for "space" in an edition of a newspaper—an aggregated "package" called an "edition."

When search engines unbundle (or disaggregate) the content that newspaper editors have so thoughtfully aggregated for their readers, they undermine the newspaper's traditional revenue base with both readers and advertisers. Readers—already conditioned to pay less for a print newspaper than they did for a cup of coffee—have now learned that information (which newspapers paid reporters and editors to create and aggregate) is "free" and customizable in the digital realm.

Even more alarming is the fact that certain types of advertisers now have a much more efficient way to target their current and potential customers on these online sites, where the search engines essentially "reaggregate" the content around various special interests. Since digital advertising rates for these large online competitors are based on scale and traffic, the community newspaper is at a further disadvantage since it cannot deliver a mass audience. Nevertheless, advertisers expect the community newspaper to offer rates for their digital edition that are roughly equivalent to those they can get with the large aggregators.

As they search for options to reverse these long-term, devastating revenue trends, publishers have essentially two options: they can attempt to get the reader to pay more, or they can attempt to get more revenue from the advertiser. Let's look at the issue with reader revenue first. Here are the trends:

- Readers have historically furnished roughly 10 to 15 percent of a newspaper's total revenue. At many of the papers today, they are contributing as much as 25 percent of total revenue. This is because the revenue from advertising has declined so dramatically.
- Over the last few years, many newspapers have been forced to discount subscription prices heavily in order to attract new readers and retain current readers of the print edition, further depressing the total dollar amount received from circulation.
- As a result, only a very small portion of the costs of printing and distribution are now being covered by the revenues generated by readers.

Over the last two years, several hundred papers have opted to erect some version of an online "pay wall" (in which some material is still provided for free but the majority of the content is behind a "wall," and only subscribers to either the print or online editions are allowed unlimited access). But "publishers should not expect pay walls to be the salvation for newspapers," warns the digital editor of the *Wall Street Journal*—which in 1996 became the country's first major newspaper to charge for access to its website, wsj.com. Research with more than a dozen community newspapers (ranging in size from 8,000 to 75,000 circulation) confirms that assessment. In online reader surveys, researchers found that only one-third to one-half of frequent visitors to a typical community paper's website did not already subscribe to the print edition.

This leaves publishers with a conundrum. Offering Web content for free undermines a community newspaper's ability to charge readers for the print edition (which currently is providing the preponderance of advertising revenue). Yet charging for online access to content potentially diminishes a newspaper's ability to attract readers—and the advertisers who want to reach those readers—to the digital edition, which *must* play a significant role in the paper's future.

With the upside potential for circulation revenue somewhat limited, this forces publishers to take a harder look at what's happened on the advertising side of the equation, where newspapers have been hit by a steep decline in *both* volume—with some categories practically decimated—and rate. Here are the advertising-revenue trends:

- For many newspapers, the decline in volume from 2000 to 2007 was caused by the loss of classified advertising, especially the help-wanted and real estate categories. But the continued decline in more recent years comes from the loss of display advertising, including many "big-box" retailers who have shifted either to digital competitors or to preprinted slick inserts and coupons.
- Because of significant volume decreases in high-margin categories— such as real estate and help-wanted—low-margin slick, preprinted inserts now account for more than 25 percent of total advertising revenue in many newspapers, up from 10 percent just five years ago. These inserts bring down the overall advertising rate for the print edition, which is based solely on the paper's distribution footprint. Ironically, the way the insert rate is determined forces publishers into a vicious cycle of discounting reader subscriptions to prop up the circulation of the printed paper so they can deliver these low-margin inserts.
- Increasingly, a small number of advertisers provide a large majority of total advertising revenue. At many community newspapers,

anywhere from 50 to 80 percent of total ad revenue comes from 20 percent of the advertisers.

- Digital revenue is a small fraction (less than 10 percent) of print revenue. This is because the preponderance of the digital advertising is priced at a very low CPM (cost per thousand)—a small fraction (one-tenth to one-twentieth) of the rate for the print edition.

Interviews with more than sixty retailers in a half dozen markets provided some insights into how newspapers could address the advertising-revenue issues. For example, most of the community newspapers that the UNC team researched had experienced volume decreases of 50 to 75 percent in the real estate and automotive-display categories. Disaffected advertisers in those categories indicated that they switched to other mediums because they did not feel newspapers had "kept up with the times" in offering them viable marketing solutions.

This suggests that newspapers should focus on improving digital and print content offerings to attract more readers that the advertisers want to reach. This can be done either by creating new content or by aggregating content around specific interests that appeal to readers and providing advertisers with an efficient way to reach a desired, targeted audience. Additionally, newspapers need to rethink and retool how they price and sell advertisers on both the print and digital editions.

In the next chapter, we will discuss the specific strategies that newspapers can employ to both increase volume and rate. Our complementary website, businessofnews.unc.edu, provides publishers with a step-by-step template for analyzing the revenue trends at their paper and calculating exactly how much of a threat disaggregation poses to their business model.

This sort of quick, "back-of-the-envelope" calculation of revenue illustrates the perils of continuing to pursue business as usual—a course that will, almost certainly, lead to a decline in profitability marked by a number of "waterfall moments." Those tipping points could occur, for example, when a newspaper loses one of its major advertisers to a competitor or its preprint business because of declining print circulation.

But more important, at all the community newspapers in the UNC study, this sort of analysis also uncovered several potential short-term and long-term revenue strategies that publishers could pursue to address the disaggregation threat head-on. The key to reversing the trend was to come up with a comprehensive strategy for enticing readers and advertisers to engage with *both* the print and digital editions.

Although the Internet may have assaulted a community newspaper's business model on the revenue side—disaggregating content and siphoning off advertising dollars—forward-thinking publishers and editors still have the ability to reestablish a value proposition in the digital age for both readers and advertisers around the unique content they create and aggregate. The disruptive blow to a community newspaper's cost structure is potentially lethal. Therefore, instead of pursuing an aggressive "turn-around" strategy, newspapers need to seek to minimize the damage as quickly as possible.

When a barrier to entering a business has been destroyed (in this case, the need for expensive printing facilities), mature industries need to shed those costs as expeditiously as possible in order to be competitive, warns business consultant Richard Foster. That means that during this period of transition, publishers need to be tracking very closely how efficiently the newspaper is being produced. Put another way, they need to make sure that the value equation stays in balance—that is, the revenue generated by the three processes required to produce a paper (that of creating content, aggregating it, and distributing it) approximates the cost that each process entails.

At papers in the UNC study, costs were segregated in this way:

- Since the news is created by reporters, the salary, benefits, and expenses of the reporting staff were attributed to the process of "creating content."
- That content is then aggregated by editors. So in a similar fashion, the salary, benefits, and expenses of editors and others who package information were attributed to the aggregation process.
- Finally, the cost of printing and distributing the paper—including not only the personnel costs but also any other operating expenses, such as rent and maintenance of equipment, transportation costs, and fees to independent contractors—was tallied.

The direct cost of selling advertisements—as calculated by salaries and commissions paid to staff—was set aside in this calculation since it has a much-less-significant impact on the bottom line than the other three processes and is a secondary function. Content is created, aggregated, and distributed with the primary goal of attracting a desirable audience that a newspaper can then sell to advertisers. Advertising revenue not only covers the direct costs of selling, but, more important, it also pays for the content creation, aggregation, and distribution that attracts readers.

In the digital age, both the processes of creating and aggregating unique content—and then selling it to readers—continue to have tremendous value. However, the process of producing and distributing the physical paper is a significant drag on the bottom line. In most community newspapers in the study, the costs of printing and distributing the paper—a legacy of the predigital era—comprised more than half the total costs, placing these newspapers at a tremendous disadvantage versus other competitors (both digital and traditional broadcast outlets).

Therefore, publishers need to take an unemotional, critical look at the number of legacy traditions that add costs—but not value—to the content they create, aggregate, and sell to advertisers. The following are some of the key questions publishers should be asking.

- Staffing is the second-biggest cost at most newspapers, and all staffers should be adding to the value equation. Are all the positions in production and distribution fully utilized? Can current staff members—especially in news and advertising—be retrained? Can work among journalists be reallocated to increase the amount of content that is available for the digital edition?
- How many days a week is the newspaper actually profitable? Most daily newspapers are only profitable two or three days a week, with the Sunday edition built around retail advertising and inserts, plus two other days built around grocery ads and weekend entertainment. Whether a daily, weekly, or semiweekly, the decision to cease publishing on unprofitable days is a complicated one that risks alienating loyal readers. But publishers need to be able to weigh the costs of continuing to distribute the print edition on unprofitable days versus the value they could create by adding additional content that would attract readers and advertisers to the digital site.
- Should printing and distribution of the newspaper be outsourced? This is an especially valid question if a printing press is fully depreciated and a paper is facing a major capital expenditure. But it is also a question that every publisher should be considering on an annual basis as he or she weighs the routine costs of maintaining the current system versus outsourcing it.

Because so much advertising revenue is still tied to the print edition, most community newspapers will not be able to eliminate these "legacy" costs overnight by switching to an all-digital platform. Nor will they want to, as we will discuss in the next chapter. But during this time of transition and disruption—with the value equation in flux—publishers need to be willing to question all assumptions about costs.

As this analytical exercise shows, the value equation at most community newspapers is out of sync. The legacy costs of the predigital era (distribution of the print edition) outweigh the value drivers in the digital era (those of content creation and aggregation). If community newspapers are to survive and thrive in the digital era, then they need to funnel investment into content creation and aggregation, where they have the ability to carve out a competitive advantage based on the reputation they have earned over the years for providing unique local content that readers want. Attracting readers, in turn, attracts advertising revenue. On the other hand, funneling investment into propping up the distribution of the print edition leads to inevitable decline, as digital delivery replaces the printing press.

The current business model for community newspapers, which relies almost entirely on the print edition for revenue, is broken and needs to be significantly changed if the paper is to survive the assault leveled against it—on both the cost and revenue sides—by the Internet. How much time community newspapers have to change out that predigital model depends on how rapidly their customers' habits and expectations are changing.

How the Internet Changed the Competitive Environment

Since 1975 and the advent of the microprocessor, the pace of technological change has been dizzying. Every eighteen months to two years, we, as media consumers, are faced with adapting to a disruptive innovation. As a result, the rate at which we adopt a new technology—such as the DVD player, for example—can be much quicker than the rate at which we adopted its predecessor (the VCR).

Two national surveys—Deloitte's *State of the Media Democracy Survey* and the Pew Research Center's Project for Excellence in Journalism's *State of News Media*—have been tracking the changing media habits of consumers over the last decade. Both paint a dramatic picture, and both speak volumes about the simultaneous decline of the print newspaper and the rise of digital readership. Circulation of print newspapers continued its steady decline in the most recent Pew report, down 4 percent over the previous year. It has declined 30 percent since 2000. However, visits to the top twenty-five news sites—seventeen of which are operated by legacy media—was up 17 percent during the same period. By 2011, according to

Pew, more people received their news from online sources and sites than from printed newspapers. Three-fourths of all American homes now have computers. Almost half of the population has smartphones, and almost a third has tablets.

The Deloitte report, which annually surveys 2,000 consumers between the ages of fourteen and seventy-five on their consumption habits, found similar statistics and an emerging preference from owners of smartphones and tablets for receiving news through those devices. In the 2012 Deloitte study, 20 percent of respondents between the ages of twenty-three and twenty-eight reported reading their favorite newspaper over a smartphone in the last six months, up from 3 percent two years prior. Similarly, more than a third of the owners of tablets or e-readers expressed a preference for reading a digital newspaper versus a print one.

Citing the exploding number of households that now own smartphones (which has doubled in the last two years) and the potential for exponential growth in tablets, the Deloitte survey opens with this summary of the changing media landscape in the United States: "With new devices and media platforms being introduced at a faster clip than at any time in memory, media consumption habits are changing just as quickly."

Lest publishers and editors think that this trend is only true in the more-populated areas of the country, UNC surveys conducted in half a dozen communities beginning in the fall of 2009 reflect similar shifts in reader use of "new" media. Even in rural markets, where broadband availability still hovers at around 50 percent, a majority of newspaper readers report that their use of new media has changed significantly in recent years. This is especially true of adults under forty, but it is also true of print subscribers to community newspapers, who tend to be over fifty.

Like their city kinfolk, rural residents are addicted to texting, Facebook, and smartphones. Asked to estimate whether the time they spent with digital media had increased or decreased over the last two years, the vast majority of readers (approximately 90 percent) reported that it had increased. They estimated that they were spending two hours or more daily with new media, with cell phones and smartphones coming in first followed closely by social networking, searches, and e-commerce done on desktop computers. Some use of Twitter in rural markets among young adults and teenagers even emerged in the surveys as early as 2010.

"We like to think of some of these mountain communities in Kentucky and West Virginia as isolated—and bypassed by the digital age—since they only have broadband penetration of less than 30 percent," says Al Cross, director of Kentucky's Institute for Rural Journalism and Community Issues. "But increasingly, these rural communities are becoming 'bedroom communities.' People who live there have to commute to other communities to find employment. This means they either have access to broadband and wireless where they work or through their phones on the way to and from work."

A majority of the people who read the website of Chicago-based, Spanish-language weekly *La Raza* access it from their phones, according to managing editor Fabiola Pomareda. "From the mobile readers I've talked with online, they tend to be younger than our print readers. And they usually only read the online edition." Indeed, online editions of community newspapers everywhere appear to be connecting with new customers—readers not reached by the print editions. Almost half of the readers of online editions told researchers that they "never" or "infrequently" read the print edition. ("Infrequently" was defined as less than once a week for a daily and less than once a month for a weekly or semiweekly.) This finding is quite different from what was perceived to be the case with newspaper websites five years ago, when almost all visitors to the online site also read the print edition.

The average age of residents who read *only* the print edition of most community newspapers is sixty—approximately the same age as viewers of the major networks' evening news shows. In contrast, the readers of digital editions are much younger, better educated, and much more tech savvy than print-only readers. Online readers were an average of fifteen years younger than subscribers who read only the print edition and were twice as likely to have either an associate or bachelor's degree. They also reported being much more fluent with, and heavy users of, new media technologies such as search, social networks, and e-commerce.

The engagement of these online consumers with all types of digital media—and their fluency in navigating multiple media platforms—speaks to the potential for community newspapers to engage a new generation of readers in the twenty-first century if they invest in their digital editions. Plus, these readers, with their demographics and media consumption habits, are potentially a very attractive audience to local advertisers.

But while readers seem to be increasingly comfortable navigating across multiple media platforms, many local merchants surveyed in these same communities expressed confusion at the choices they faced in deciding where and when to advertise. Noting that their own media consumption habits have changed, a majority of advertisers said they had been considering "experimenting" with digital by allocating a portion of their marketing budget to online outlets. So while a majority of the local merchants in the small and midsized markets surveyed still expressed support for the local newspaper and its print edition, it is clear that the landscape is shifting quickly.

Even in the predigital age, when many community newspapers were de facto monopolies, there were still local competitors for the newspaper's readers and advertisers. But those competitors were always in plain sight and easy to identify—the billboard company, the Yellow Pages directory, the local shopper, the direct-mail company, or the local radio station. In the digital age, however, while a publisher's attention is focused on traditional rivals, other potent rivals can fly under the radar for months, maybe even several years, all the while amassing a sizeable or desirable audience that intrigues advertisers. As Harvard University professor Michael Porter pointed out in his business classic *Competitive Strategy: Techniques for Analyzing Industries and Competitors* (1998), the most potent competitor often comes from the periphery. This is especially true during times of upheaval and disruption such as the one newspapers are currently experiencing.

It pays to be paranoid and take an expansive view of the competitive landscape. Publishers need to be asking these three questions: Who can potentially create, aggregate, and deliver content that people care about more creatively, credibly, and comprehensively than the newspaper? What sort of audience could they attract with this content? Would it be attractive to the newspaper's advertisers?

There are three types of competitors that can challenge a newspaper's relationship with either its readers or its advertisers. First, there are the traditional rivals, such as the local radio and cable operators or regional television stations. In a digital era, local radio and television stations can offer news on their websites that was traditionally only available in the printed newspaper. This can include everything from breaking news stories to posting and acknowledging births and deaths in a community. But traditional rivals are even more potent on the advertising front. The sales representatives for these local media often come armed with "stats and facts" that can lure away longtime newspaper advertisers with claims of greater efficiency and reach.

In one market, the sole remaining car dealer had shifted all of his advertising to two regional television stations forty miles away, and the local sporting-goods retailer had shifted a substantial portion of his advertising budget to billboard advertising. In both cases, the sales representatives of these rival businesses had shared data on the reach and efficiency of their mediums while simply dismissing the local newspaper reader as "old and dying—not the audience you want."

Community newspapers also face a threat from new digital entrants into the market—the local mom-and-pop start-ups as well as regional and national firms such as cars.com or Google. The mom-and-pop digital start-ups can target an especially passionate portion of a newspaper's audience—for example, prep sports fans—and then sell access to these fans to local advertisers. Regional and national digital firms target specific audiences (such as home buyers), and, like the local broadcast outlets, their sales representatives come armed with "analytics" that convince advertisers that they deliver more customers than the local newspaper.

But while both traditional rivals (such as radio stations) and new digital entrants can siphon off readers and advertisers from newspapers, their competitive moves are relatively easy to track. A third challenger for a newspaper's readers and advertisers is a stealth competitor—a company that starts off as something else and evolves into offering advertisers and readers many of the same benefits as the newspaper. Michael Porter refers to these competitors as "substitutes," and they are the hardest to anticipate.

For example, in one rural North Carolina mountain community, a local Web design company established in 2007 decided to demonstrate its professional services by posting on its site an interactive calendar of upcoming events in the community and inviting readers to post announcements. Within two years, the Web design company's calendar had become the most credible and comprehensive source of up-to-date information on upcoming events in the community, supplanting the local newspaper's weekly printed calendar of events. Not surprisingly, the Web design company was able to sell "sponsorship" of the community calendar to several longtime newspaper advertisers.

Publishers and editors who stay on top of changing reader and advertiser habits are best positioned to take offensive action. The popularity of mobile phones, even in rural areas, suggests that editors should devise a mobile strategy for delivering content and that publishers and advertising-sales representatives should help local merchants use this third platform. By identifying the range of current and potential competitors, publishers can begin to craft a response that counters the threats. But just as important, it allows publishers to prioritize investment based on whether the threat is imminent or can easily be deflected by simply shoring up key franchises.

In his 1996 business classic *Leading Change*, Harvard University professor John Kotter says that creating "a sense of urgency" is the very first—and most essential—step to establishing a mandate for change. Without a sense of urgency, he argues, employees revert to business as usual, even if the business is about to fall off the proverbial cliff.

The realities of the newspaper industry, of the business model for individual papers, and of the competitive landscape in the digital era offer at least four compelling arguments for immediate change:

- Print advertising is unlikely to return to previous levels, even with an uptick in the economy.
- Newspapers are saddled with the high fixed costs of printing and distribution, which puts them at a competitive disadvantage as print advertising revenue declines.
- The demographics, habits, and expectations of current and future readers of community news have shifted dramatically in recent years.
- The competition is tough and getting tougher, with the swift adoption of the Internet encouraging both traditional competitors, new entrants, and "substitutes" to move into the "news space" and siphon off both readers and advertisers.

In sum, both the macro- and microeconomic trends in the twenty-first century world of community newspapering are clear and point to the need for aggressive corrective action.

CHAPTER THREE
How Newspapers Must Change

The three newspaper editors who gathered in the spring of 2009 in a conference room at the University of North Carolina at Chapel Hill shared a number of concerns. Their Internet strategies had stalled, despite their efforts to embrace a digital future. All three were facing significant succession issues over the next several years as the owners neared retirement age. Would the paper stay "in the family"? Or might it be sold?

Their most immediate concern, however, was the significant drop in advertising revenue and profit, which had occurred over the prior two years and threatened their ability to continue producing the caliber of journalism for which these three award-winning Carolina papers were known. Two of the three had won journalism's most coveted honor, the Pulitzer Prize for Public Service: the twice-weekly *Whiteville News Reporter* in 1953 for its coverage of Ku Klux Klan activity in the rural southeastern part of the state, and the 8,000-circulation *Washington Daily News* in 1990 for exposing pollution of the water system in the coastal community of "little Washington" (as it is known among residents of the state), located on the Pamlico Sound. The third paper in the group—the twice-weekly *Wilkes Journal-Patriot* (with a circulation of 12,000)—was well known among members of the state's press association for taking its role as a government watchdog seriously, aggressively pursuing local officials in the North Carolina mountain community who wanted to hide behind closed doors or withhold public documents.

All three had volunteered their papers as "working laboratories" to test out new strategies and tactics that might help other community newspapers throughout the country make a successful transition to the digital age. As they pondered what they hoped to learn from participating in the multiyear research project, Ray McKeithan, the general manager and editor of the *Daily News*, spoke first. "I need to know what I can do to get the paper back on track," he said. "Is it a small change? Or a big change?"

Both he and the owner, Ashley "Brownie" Futrell, were already considering or implementing a number of major changes that would significantly reduce the costs of producing the century-old daily newspaper. In the previous year, they had outsourced the printing and distribution of the *Daily News* to a newspaper in the nearby college town of Greenville forty miles away. In 2009 they would cease publishing on Mondays—"a really hard decision," says McKeithan, "that went to the heart of our identity and forced us to consider whether we could still call ourselves a 'daily newspaper' if we only published six days a week." But the biggest change came in 2010, when the Futrell family sold the *Daily News* to the Boone Newspapers, Inc., a chain of thirty newspapers headquartered in Alabama and Mississippi. The sale ended sixty years of family ownership.

McKeithan, who now works for a local potash mining company, looks back on that first meeting in Chapel Hill in 2009 with the UNC group and recalls: "I knew we had to change our cost structure. But I didn't realize we had to change our revenue model, too—that the market fundamentals had changed, and that there wasn't going to be a revenue rebound, like there always had been before. I simply didn't realize that any revenue the newspaper got going forward would come from what you did with your own sweat and initiative."

How much change is enough? The question that McKeithan posed in 2009 summarizes the dilemma that publishers and editors of community newspapers face constantly during this time of immense disruption—and the choices they make determine whether they survive and thrive anew.

In *The Rise and Fall of American Mass Media: Roles of Technology and Leadership* (1991), historian Donald Shaw noted three stages in the life of a mass medium: emergence of a new technology (such as the printing press), rapid growth and dominance of the "new" medium, and eventual decline. Whenever a declining medium is displaced by a new one (such as the Internet), leaders in the once-dominant industry initially "assume that only an 'adjustment' is needed," says Shaw. But that "always fails" because the fundamentals of the macroenvironment in which the medium exists have irrevocably changed.

Longtime consultant Richard Foster has noted that new technologies (such as the Internet) attack the business models of existing companies by leveling three disruptive and potentially lethal blows to cost structure, customer base, and revenue. In the digital era, print newspapers are disadvantaged in three ways. First, they carry into the twenty-first century huge costs associated with supporting a system of production and distribution that essentially dates to the nineteenth century. Second, their customers' habits are changing quickly. And third, a good portion of advertising—the primary source of revenue and profit—has been "lost" to competitors.

For many industries facing creative destruction of their business models, the advice is to embrace the new technology, even at the risk of "cannibalizing" the old one—the "cash cow." But for newspapers, that answer is too simplistic. The digital edition (not the print edition) is indeed the key to future profitability for almost all community newspapers. That is where the explosive growth in advertising revenue is occurring, and it is where readers are migrating.

But community newspapers simply cannot cannibalize the print edition (which at most papers currently furnishes more than 90 percent of revenue) without also having in place a well-thought-out strategy for significantly boosting the audience, revenue, and profitability associated with their digital editions. Therefore, they need to be simultaneously pursuing a three-pronged strategy of aggressively shedding outdated and inefficient costs associated with the print edition and then investing the savings in building a vibrant community of readers on multiple platforms, which then allows the advertising department to begin pursuing new revenue opportunities. In this chapter, we'll explore the rationale for each of those strategies and establish a timeline for change.

Simply stated, newspapers are in a period of transition. Over the next decade, the print edition may disappear entirely in some communities. In many others, it will coexist with its digital cousin—and in the process, the local newspaper will become a true cross-platform medium for both readers and advertisers. But regardless of which of these two paths a newspaper ultimately travels—digital-only or cross-platform (print and digital) delivery of news and advertising—every publisher and editor must contemplate how he or she will react to and accommodate the massive changes that are occurring.

From the experience of other industries tossed "by the gales of creative destruction," we know that it is possible to chart a course that leads to rebirth and renewal. But doing so involves more than a mere "adjustment" to the current strategy; it involves a whole new way of thinking and acting.

Building on Strengths, Addressing Weaknesses

In 2009, as McKeithan debated how much change would be enough for the *Washington Daily News*, Jule Hubbard, managing editor of the *Wilkes*

Journal-Patriot, wondered silently if his family-owned newspaper even needed to change. The community that the *Journal-Patriot* served—Wilkes County—was nestled in the foothills of the Appalachian Mountains and best known in popular culture as the home of good moonshine, bluegrass music, and famous NASCAR drivers. Hubbard's father and uncle had purchased the paper in the 1930s and followed a simple formula for success: they aggressively covered everything in the community—both the good and the bad. State press association awards for the *Journal-Patriot*'s vigilant coverage of local government hung on the newsroom walls alongside plaques given by civic clubs and organizations lauding the paper's unwavering support.

Both Julius and John Hubbard were in their early eighties and still active as publisher and editor. And both were very skeptical that any major change in strategy was needed. They especially questioned whether any investment in improving the *Journal-Patriot*'s website—a very simple PDF reproduction of the print edition—would pay off. In order to "go digital," as Hubbard put it, he would need to convince the other four members of his family who worked at the paper that "I'm not jeopardizing the paper's future and moving too fast."

Author and consultant Foster, currently a senior fellow at Yale University's School of Management, notes how very difficult it can be to gain consensus about the need for change during times of massive disruption. As a result, we engage in what is known as "confirmatory bias"—looking for signs that the world as we knew it has not changed. Because of this, we fail to grasp both what has changed and what remains unchanged.

As they survey the environment around them, newspaper publishers and editors often lose sight of the strengths they still possess and the potential opportunities to build on these strengths. But they can also fail to notice new threats that have materialized, threats that must be addressed head-on or they will destroy a franchise that has been in existence for decades. So as a first step—before beginning to craft a strategy that addresses the disruption in their markets—publishers and editors should take an inventory of their paper's current strengths and weaknesses, as well as the potential opportunities and threats that are present in the digital age.

Using simple surveys and research techniques (which will be discussed in chapter 4), publishers and editors can assess aspects of their newspapers from five different vantage points, focusing first on the strengths and weaknesses of the community they serve. They then can analyze the editorial content of their print and online editions, the audience they were delivering to the advertisers, and their advertising sales effort. And finally, with the data in hand, they can consider how well their current business model might weather the storm.

Using these techniques, publishers and editors in the UNC study uncovered enduring strengths on which their papers could rebuild, as well as weaknesses and threats that needed addressing fairly quickly. But perhaps more important, the process helped them understand what they could—and could not—control and how this affected potential strategic choices they must make.

For example, many of the newspapers served either low-income or low-growth communities. Newspapers in communities with a sluggish economy often have a tougher battle turning around advertising-revenue declines than those with growing economies and populations. However, slow growth can also discourage potential competitors from entering the market. Therefore, many of the publishers came to see this "weakness" (low economic growth in a community) as a potential opportunity since it allows them to prioritize investments based on the threats posed by a smaller number of competitors. And it also forces the newspaper's advertising department to think broadly about its market.

"We have a very small retail base here in Romney," says Sallie See of West Virginia's *Hampshire Review*. "So I look at where our readers are shopping and working in adjacent counties and I explain to those businesses why they have to be advertising with us—why we are the best way to reach their customers in Hampshire County." Mark Palmer, publisher of the 12,000-circulation *Columbia Daily Herald* in central Tennessee, relates: "For us, it was a matter of survival. When the General Motors plant closed four years ago, fully half of the businesses in the area went under. At times we felt like we were just throwing things up against the wall. But my philosophy was: don't be afraid to try something new. Fail for the right reasons."

In economically depressed communities, newspaper editors and publishers also have an opportunity to take a leading role in educating and informing the public on topics such as education and health care. "The idea for a monthly section on health and healthy living came from the editorial department," says Palmer. "I want both my editors and advertisers to look for holes in the community and come up with ways to address those shortcomings.'

Analyzing the strengths and weakness of the rural community in southeastern North Carolina that his paper serves helped Les High in Whiteville "understand where we [the newspaper and Columbus County] had come from and where we might go," he says. "Fifty years ago, we all believed Columbus County—just fifty miles from the beaches—was about to take off." But that still hasn't occurred. Doing the analysis got me to be a lot clearer in thinking about our connection to Wilmington and the beaches and to the surrounding counties. Will we ever be anything but an exit sign on the way to the beach? And is there anything the paper can do to change that?"

As High points out, all newspapers have to "live with and in" the community they serve and "build on whatever assets" they have. But when it comes to changing the direction of their newspaper—its editorial content or its advertising sales effort, for example—he and the other publishers and editors involved in the community newspaper study realized they had much more latitude to affect change.

Below are the major strategic insights gained by publishers and editors who cast a critical look at their papers, searching for both problems and possibilities.

ON EDITORIAL CONTENT:

Reader loyalty to community newspapers—both the print and digital editions—was exceptionally strong in almost all markets that UNC surveyed. An overwhelming majority of readers (80 percent or more in many markets) perceive that their local paper is the "most credible and comprehensive source of news and information" they care about. And they have an insatiable appetite for even more "hometown" news—delivered via mobile, Facebook, or the print and online editions.

But even though a significant number of readers say they are comfortable navigating between multiple platforms, many community newspapers still treat their digital edition as a stepchild to the print publication. Editors say they are reluctant to put original content on the websites for fear of cannibalizing print readership. Reader research, however, indicates this fear may be misplaced. As was reported in chapter 2, about half of the frequent visitors to online sites surveyed were also loyal subscribers to the print edition. They say they visited the digital site to get updates on breaking news or read material that wasn't in the paper. The other half of the visitors to online sites say they "rarely" or "never" read the print edition and prefer to get their news online. This tendency to see the two editions as "competing" instead of as "complementary" or "coexisting" appears to have held down the growth in readership of the digital editions, which still lag behind the print editions in many markets, and it prevents the news departments from thinking differently about how best to present news and information on the various platforms available.

ON THE AUDIENCE DELIVERED TO ADVERTISERS:

Despite recent declines in print circulation, a newspaper, in most instances, is still an efficient way to get a message across to the widest possible, most engaged audience in a community—especially if both editions are purchased. The online edition not only reaches a new audience but also draws loyal readers of the print edition for a second look. By purchasing "space" in both editions, advertisers can significantly increase the effectiveness of their ads, extending their reach (capturing a new audience that did not see the ad in the print edition) and efficiency (multiple exposures to a message by loyal, engaged readers of both print and online editions).

In addition, the demographics of the readers are attractive to advertisers. Readers of the print edition have a higher household income than online readers. But online readers are better educated and more tech savvy. And although they earn less, in many markets they often spend more on advertised products—ranging from cars and houses to groceries and staples—than the more-affluent print readers.

But even though newspapers continue to deliver a desirable audience to local advertisers, the digital rate in most markets today has been set and artificially driven down by online aggregators and search engines. Until newspapers can solve "the rate problem," digital advertising revenue will not be sufficient to support the level of journalism most papers currently provide. Solving the rate problem involves the reeducation of the sales force *and* the advertisers so that both understand the true value that a cross-platform medium—such as a community newspaper with both a print and online edition—can deliver.

ON THE ADVERTISING SALES EFFORT:

Most local businesses surveyed said that they still allocate the majority of their marketing dollars to the community newspaper. Most merchants also rated the local newspaper sales representative as more "trustworthy" than agents with the television station, the billboard company, or online sites.

However, in many markets, newspaper sales representatives are viewed by advertisers as little more than print-edition "order takers" with scarce knowledge of how to sell across multiple platforms. Local advertisers also pointed out that local newspaper representatives rarely suggested purchasing the online edition but instead continued to "push space" in the print edition. "Their idea of 'marketing' is to sell you space in a special print section, or a directory ad on the Web page," said a local sporting-goods retailer in rural eastern North Carolina. "I'd really like their help in thinking how to use digital media—like social networking or mobile—better."

The *Santa Rosa (Calif.) Press Democrat* (circulation 55,000) set up an in-house digital-ad agency that helps local advertisers with everything from search-engine optimization to website development and the use of social media. "We're just following the money," says publisher Bruce Kyse. "There's a real need in the market for that expertise, and if we don't provide it, someone else will." Similarly, the Chicago-based weekly *La Raza* offers a "360 solution" that includes mobile and event sponsorship. "Our national advertisers demand it," says publisher Jimena Catarivas. "Many of our local advertisers don't take advantage of it yet—but that is the way the market is going."

As the Chicago and Santa Rosa experiences suggest, by training sales representatives to be multiplatform marketing consultants (instead of print "order takers"), newspapers could gain a competitive edge versus other media outlets. An entire revamping of the sales process—one that includes revising the bonus and commission structure to encourage cross-platform sales and prioritizing efforts focused on high-potential advertisers—could also result in significant revenue upside (especially for the digital edition).

ON THE SOUNDNESS OF THEIR BUSINESS MODEL:
Most of the newspapers have begun cutting back on costs, focusing primarily on production and distribution. For the most part, newspapers that are part of a larger corporation have been the most aggressive, with some cutting as much as 50 percent by centralizing production, finance, and administrative functions. But few have attempted to "zero-base" the newspaper budget and focus on all costs (including those in the news and advertising areas), asking: "If we were building this newspaper today, what would it cost to create, aggregate, and distribute content so we created the most value for our readers and advertisers?" Also, much of the savings in these newspapers had been pocketed instead of invested in building up the digital edition, which has to play an important role in a community paper's future.

Taken altogether, the findings in this broad-based analysis showed that, despite the upheaval in the marketplace and the industry, most community newspapers actually have some very significant strengths on which to build a new strategy. These include strong reader loyalty, an engaged and loyal audience that is still attractive to local advertisers, and a reservoir of goodwill among many local advertisers. As Whiteville's High observed: "We don't have to start from scratch in crafting a totally new strategy."

But the analysis also turned up some serious weaknesses that many newspapers need to address immediately before current—or potential— competitors see them and choose to exploit them. These included the lack of a cohesive vision for cross-platform delivery of news, the absence of an advertising sales strategy that addresses the digital-rate issues, and the need for a well-thought-out and executed plan to free up investment funds by eliminating legacy costs associated with the print edition. That is why newspapers need a three-pronged strategy for eliminating inefficient costs, rebuilding the customer base, and aggressively pursuing new revenue opportunities.

Facing a Cyclone: Developing a Three-Pronged Strategy

"Follow your customers and follow the money." That is the standard advice given to industries facing the "gales of creative destruction." But newspapers face a number of unique challenges in pursuing that strategy.

A newspaper, of course, has two types of customers, and the relationship between the two is complicated to say the least. Advertisers—not readers—actually furnish the majority of the revenue, yet without readers, there would be no demand for the advertising. So while the audience for the print edition is declining and younger readers are moving online, a newspaper cannot simply abandon the physical paper and follow their readers online without losing the majority of their advertising revenue, which is tied to the print edition. And because the rates for digital advertising are a tiny fraction of the price that similar display space commands in the print edition, any additional advertising revenue created by attracting a larger online audience is not sufficient to support the level of journalism most papers currently provide. Therefore, there is no financial payback for following customers online.

This leaves newspaper publishers with a conundrum: do you follow your customers or guard the money you currently have? Many community newspapers have been stuck in neutral, propping up an antiquated printing and distribution system while waiting for a sustainable digital revenue model to emerge. The problems with waiting for a new revenue model to materialize, however, are numerous. First, it assumes there will be one model that will fit all communities. In the predigital era, when community newspapers were a de facto geographic monopoly, that was the case.

But not so now, when newspapers face a slew of potential competitors that vary by market. On the other hand, attempting to implement what worked in other markets not only ignores the realities of individual markets but also often leaves advertising departments flailing about and wasting valuable time. Finally, while they remain focused on the revenue issue, publishers are doing nothing to address the other two potentially lethal assaults that creative destruction has inflicted on their cost structure and customer base.

For community newspapers everywhere, the next decade will be a period of transition. In most markets, the circulation of the print edition will continue to decline as readers age and die and are not replaced by a younger generation. But in many markets, some version of the physical paper will continue to exist for some time, perhaps in an abbreviated form or publishing schedule. Publishers have an option of managing that transition and tailoring it to meet the needs of their markets, provided they simultaneously pursue a three-pronged strategy that (1) sheds legacy costs associated with the print era; (2) builds community across multiple platforms: and (3) aggressively pursues new revenue opportunities.

By actively implementing this transition strategy, newspapers not only begin to follow their customers but also position themselves to follow the money in future years. In the meantime, publishers may come to realize that cross-platform delivery of both news and advertising is a tremendous competitive advantage over traditional rivals such as television stations and digital start-ups, both of which are primarily tied to a single platform.

Chapters 5 through 7 explore ways to implement all three strategies simultaneously. In the meantime, let's explore the strategic rationale behind each of the three legs of the strategy and examine how they build on current strengths. We will also acknowledge the weaknesses that many community newspapers must overcome if they are to thrive in the digital era.

SHEDDING LEGACY COSTS OF THE PRINT ERA

In order to "follow their customers" and build robust and engaging digital editions across multiple platforms, newspapers need to find money they can invest in new ventures. The barrier to entry that protected community newspapers in the twentieth century has been destroyed with the emergence of digital distribution. Yet at most newspapers, the cost of producing and distributing the print edition consumes more than half of all costs. So with profits declining, publishers need to produce the print edition as efficiently as possible. They need to shed outdated and inefficient legacy costs.

In recent years, newspapers of all sizes have laid off staff, centralized certain functions (such as administration or production), cut back on the amount of space devoted to news, and, in some cases, cut back on the number of days the print edition is published. But in many instances, the savings have been pocketed and not reinvested. As a result, the physical paper continues to wither, while the digital edition is starved for resources. This status quo approach also diverts management attention to issues of maintenance instead of transformation.

For publishers pursuing a three-pronged transition strategy, shedding legacy costs is the first essential step in initiating what economists call a "virtuous cycle"—one in which the funds from this endeavor are reinvested in building audience and community in the digital edition. In turn, this engaged audience attracts more advertisers who want to reach these potential customers. The increased revenue from these advertisers is fed back into the newspaper, improving the cross-platform delivery of news and information, which, in turn, attracts more readers and advertisers.

Therefore, "shedding legacy costs" is not so much about cutting costs as it is about coming up with a system for financing growth. That means publishers need to totally rethink both their orientation and management priorities, as well as their cost structure. They need to shed the broadsheet newspaper mindset and instead focus on building a robust cross-platform delivery system. Publishers should not underestimate how difficult this can be for the entire staff of the newspaper and for loyal readers.

For one thing, it goes against conventional publishing wisdom. Research in the latter part of the twentieth century concluded that companies that used recessionary periods to invest wisely in their core business—playing to win where they were strongest—were often able to outmaneuver their competitors who engaged in cost cutting. Using this logic, during downturns, newspaper publishers and editors should invest in the print edition since it remains the core business (or "cash cow"), producing most of the revenue and all of the profit. The problem with this business logic is, of course, that it ignores the changing media consumption habits of both readers and advertisers.

And there is an additional problem: the strong emotional attachment that both readers and employees have to the print edition. Compared to the physical paper, digital editions can seem to be very ephemeral substitutes. There is no press time to mark the end of the day, no permanence to the stories written, no sense of holding history in your hands. That is why Richard Foster, author of *Creative Destruction*, says that the commitment to "shed legacy costs" must be made from the top down by publishers who can anticipate and counter fallout and pushback from both employees and customers, as well as their own sentimental attachments to a symbol of a fast-receding era.

When a 2011 spring flood in central Vermont destroyed the press that printed both the *Rutland Herald* and the *Barre Times Argus*, general manager Catherine Nelson "went into overdrive," arranging to outsource the printing of both papers to a firm that prints more than forty newspapers and shoppers throughout New England. "Only when I walked through the empty press room a few weeks later," she says, "did it suddenly hit me: an era is over. It was something of an emotional moment—even though I had known for some time that we were heading in this direction and had begun planning for it, even before the flood."

Having adopted the cross-platform mindset, publishers then need to totally rethink their cost structure by asking this question: if we were creating this newspaper today, what skills would we need? This question should be asked of every department—the news and advertising staffs as well as the production and distribution arms. What sort of skills does a reporter or editor need in the digital age? An advertising sales representative? What implications does this have for new hires or for processes and procedures in the news or advertising departments that can be phased out?

Forward-thinking publishers take an expansive view of "legacy costs": it is any dollar expense or process associated with the "print-only" world. Can either of these be done more effectively or efficiently in a cross-platform, digital world? In chapter 5, we will discuss some of the insights gained and lessons learned from newspapers that have attempted to adopt a cross-platform approach, shedding the legacy costs of the print edition so they can invest in digital versions.

As we discussed in the previous chapter, there are three processes involved in producing a paper: creating content, aggregating it, and distributing it. The economics of distributing a physical paper prevent publishers from allocating funds to the two processes at which newspapers can excel in the digital era—that of creating and aggregating content, which attracts readers and then, in turn, the advertisers who pay the bills.

ESTABLISHING VIBRANT COMMUNITY
ACROSS MANY PLATFORMS

The next leg of the strategy—establishing vibrant community online—is, quite simply, about "following your customers." In the predigital age, the ability to pay for and own a printing press was a formidable barrier to entry for most community newspapers, keeping competitors at bay. Today, in the digital era, newspapers must rely on an intangible asset: the loyalty of its customers, which is the *only* "barrier to entry" that potential competitors must overcome.

Advertisers follow readers, so it is critical that newspapers must first train their sights on following readers into the digital space. To gauge the loyalty of readers, publishers and editors can use a simple measurement tool, designed by Frederick Reichheld, author of *The Loyalty Effect: The Hidden Force behind Growth, Profits, and Lasting Value* (1996). In the 1990s, after studying the customer base of a variety of industries, Reichheld observed that the loyalty of a company's current customers was directly related to its future profitability. Why? Because loyal customers buy more as well as sell more by essentially becoming a free "marketing department," recommending a product to their friends and colleagues. All this leads to more sales in the future. Reichheld's loyalty theory had tremendous impact on the bottom line in the predigital era. In the era of social media, his findings are even more profound, since the power of recommendation can take a newspaper's marketing effort viral.

The very good news is that most readers of community newspapers are exceptionally loyal to both the print and digital editions, as measured in surveys across more than a dozen markets. The bad news is that the audience for digital versions of most community newspapers still lags significantly behind the printed one. And the audience for the print edition is aging rapidly.

With more and more consumers toggling among multiple media platforms—their phones, tablets, and laptops—newspaper publishers have a shrinking window of opportunity to attract a new generation of loyal online readers and to convince current loyal readers of the print edition to sample the digital version. In order to accomplish this, they need to start thinking of themselves as a cross-platform medium designed to engage their loyal readers—regardless of whether they are on the website or holding a physical paper in their hands.

What determines loyalty? Readers told UNC researchers that they were loyal to newspapers that they perceived were "the most credible and comprehensive source of news and information" they "cared about." So in order to retain the loyalty of current readers and then attract new ones, editors need to understand what news their readers "care about." And the answer is invariably "local news." But are readers talking about *all* the news in the geographic region that the paper covered—"hyper-local coverage," as it is often called? Or something else?

In the predigital age, the newspaper created and aggregated content and "defined" its community, usually around geographic or political boundaries. In the digital age, large search engines and social-networking sites have supplanted the aggregation function and redefined community around special interests. Readers often volunteered that while they identified with the geographic community in which they lived, they also passionately cared about such topics as sports, parenting, or local politics. In other words, they also felt very connected to these smaller "communities of special interests"—often populated with friends and neighbors. It was not a case of "either/or"; it was, instead, a case of being connected to a geographic community *and* to at least one other community built around a special passion or interest. Many newspapers are already attempting to serve these communities in the print edition through the sports pages or the lifestyle and society sections. But they have failed to re-create similar "community" in their digital version, where they can use the interactivity and interconnectedness of the Internet to significantly enhance a reader's attachment to the newspaper.

Additionally, many community newspapers' websites often mimic the print edition—with a "home page" that is very similar to the front page, featuring news that will appeal to a wide variety of readers. The print edition assumes that readers will browse, searching headlines and flipping pages until they find something of interest. But online readers often are much more purposeful. They want to go straight to the topic or subject they care about.

In chapter 6, we will discuss how newspapers can create multiple, vibrant communities of readers online that build off topics already covered in the print edition. We'll also discuss the many digital tools that reporters and editors can use to create and aggregate new content for these online communities. Fully utilizing these tools requires a new mindset: newspapers in the digital age need to think of themselves as the "glue that binds" multiple communities to one another—the geographic community and others built around shared passions and affiliations. Historian Donald Shaw observes that for a medium such as a newspaper to reinvent itself, it must "use the new technology to find [ways] to reach [both] old and new audiences." In response to the introduction of television, for example, successful magazines began serving specialized niches or interest groups and then charging advertisers a premium to reach those audiences.

Like magazines, newspapers have a similar opportunity to build community (or communities) by creating "special pages" in the print edition and "online destinations." And as an added bonus, they also are able to offer advertisers the ability to target a message to an engaged audience that cares passionately about a subject.

Building vibrant community online has the potential to both strengthen loyalty with current readers and to attract new readers with like-minded passions. This, then, sets up community newspapers to participate in the third leg of the strategy: pursuing new revenue opportunities.

AGGRESSIVELY PURSUING NEW REVENUE

For many publishers, the "disconnect" with the reality they face in the marketplace occurs at this point. Even if they significantly increase readership of their digital editions—and more local businesses decide to advertise online—how do they make money when digital ad rates are so low? In order to "follow the money," publishers need to understand the history of "the rate problem" and how it can be corrected, as well as the marketing revolution unleashed by the Internet.

The "rate problem" actually harkens back to the dot-com era, when the goal for new websites was to "attract eyeballs" and "build traffic." These portals, followed in more recent years by the search engines, reach a mass audience, and the digital rates these online companies charge is based either on scale (a CPM, or "cost per thousand") or on "click-throughs" (the actual number of people who clicked on an advertisement). Most community newspapers initially set their rates using these same measures, which is why digital advertising brings in only a fraction (one-tenth or one-twentieth) of the revenue from the print edition.

In recent years, however, as Web marketing has matured, there has been a shift among a growing number of advertisers away from "mass audiences" and toward "engaged audiences," who are much more likely to notice advertisements adjacent to content they "care about." Needless to say, community newspapers are much better equipped to deliver "engaged" readers to local advertisers. In fact, they are probably the best medium for delivering an engaged audience to local businesses—better than local radio or television stations, as well as digital competitors. Therefore, publishers need to rethink and recalculate the actual value they can deliver to local advertisers and then retool their entire sales effort, adjusting their rates accordingly. But before they do, they need to also consider the implications of the marketing revolution unleashed by the Internet.

In the twentieth century, economists generally assumed that all media companies were playing a "zero-sum game." Since the amount of money spent on advertising (adjusted for inflation and economic cycles) stayed relatively constant, a new medium (such as television) benefited at the expense of the existing mediums (newspapers and magazines) by taking advertising dollars away from them. However, recent research has cast serious doubt on this notion of a zero-sum game—especially since the Internet has opened up a variety of new channels and a whole new type of marketing built around an interactivity and immediacy in advertising and marketing that was impossible in the twentieth century.

So while print advertising may have declined dramatically since 2000, there are other potential sources of new revenue for newspapers to pursue. Print advertising is likely to continue to be an important component of a local business's marketing effort. But there will be many other components—such as digital display ads, mobile messages, and event sponsorships—that can significantly enhance the effectiveness of a print advertisement in the newspaper.

That is why publishers need to be thinking of their newspapers as a cross-platform medium, and why they need to change the mindsets of the advertising sales representatives, retraining them to be true marketing consultants for local merchants instead of print "order takers." The *Naples Daily News*, circulation 45,000, serving a retirement community on the west coast of Florida, reorganized its sales force around specific business categories with the goal, says publisher Dave Neill, of getting its representatives to "operate at a much higher level of sophistication."

In order to move from selling space to selling solutions, advertising sales representatives need to become experts on the effectiveness of various mediums (print, online, mobile, and in person) and the ability of these various mediums to deliver the advertiser's message. So the *Columbia Daily Herald* in Tennessee has rolled out a "Platinum Plus" program that offers local advertisers a package of five digital and print platforms. In chapter 7, we will discuss in detail the many lessons learned by a variety of newspapers that are attempting to revamp their sales efforts.

Having retrained the sales force to understand the advantages of matching the medium to an advertising message, publishers then need to revamp rates and pricing across all three platforms (print, digital, and mobile) so that it more appropriately captures the value that advertisers receive. "Bundled" sales got a bad reputation in the early 2000s, when many newspapers gave away the online component. Recent research indicates that advertisers who use two or more platforms in tandem substantially increase the ad's effectiveness. Therefore, the pricing of cross-platform newspaper advertising needs to reflect the real value that a "bundled" sale of the print and online edition actually delivers.

Much of the growth in digital advertising in the first decade of this century came from search, which serves primarily one purpose: connecting consumers with products they are already inclined to purchase. But historically, advertising has served many other functions, from creating demand for a product to reinforcing the loyalty of customers. Repositioned as a cross-platform medium, most community newspapers are well positioned to provide all of these functions and better serve the advertisers in their community, matching the medium with the message.

The very good news is that newspapers are no longer playing a "zero-sum game" and consigned to the periphery as other mediums eat away at their print-advertising franchise. But newspapers need to aggressively pursue these new forms of revenue or risk being shut out of the market by competitors who get there first.

How Fast Must You Change? The 30 Percent Solution

Having realized the imperative for change, publishers next ask: how fast must I change? Understandably, publishers and editors often hesitate to commit to all three of the strategies outlined here at the same time. When there are no guarantees of success, it is very frightening to contemplate turning your back on your core business (the "cash cow") and instead investing in the "stepchild" that contributes only 10 percent or less of the paper's revenue.

But as Foster stresses, based on his experience in other industries—ranging from technology companies to financial-services firms—there is a very small window of opportunity. And surviving a cyclone and the "gales of destruction" it unleashes depends upon the ability of a newspaper to simultaneously achieve transformative change of cost, customer base, and revenue. Companies that fail to understand the imperative to act on three fronts simultaneously and continue business as usual—with only minor adjustments to strategy—are in danger of becoming irrelevant.

In his book *Creative Destruction*, Foster identifies three types of change: incremental, substantial, and transformative. In the late twentieth century, most publishers operating in a relatively stable business environment would make "incremental" changes year to year. These are the sort of routine up-or-down adjustments to either expenses or revenue that range from 3 to 6 percent. More recently, many newspapers have begun to make "substantial change" in their cost structure. Foster defines "substantial change" as laying off 10 percent or more of the staff, for example, to compensate for comparable revenue declines.

In order to survive creative destruction of their business models, Foster says, industries must strive for "transformative change." This involves adjustments to *both* the cost and revenue sides of the equation. Over a period of five to ten years, transformative change leads to a radical restructuring of the business model. Without a commitment to transformative change of their business models, publishers and owners are left to make cuts on the cost side—such as downsizing the staff—that will quickly weaken both the core business and the mission of the paper.

How aggressively must publishers pursue transformative change? During times of creative destruction, Foster advises that change must keep "pace with the market" in order to stay competitive. His proxy for "the market" is the S&P (Standard & Poor's) 500, composed of the world's 500 largest companies in terms of market value. Over the latter half of the twentieth century, the average "lifespan" of companies on the S&P 500 dropped from fifty years to a mere sixteen years. This means that there is an average annual turnover of 6 percent in the companies listed on the S&P 500. It also suggests that "the market" is turning over—or changing—at a rate of 6 percent annually. So to "keep pace with the market," Foster says, a publisher should strive to transform the newspaper's business model—both costs and revenues—at the same rate.

Put another way, this means that in order to keep pace with the market around them—and to preclude obsolescence at the hands of competitors—newspapers need to have in place a strategy that aims for an average annual 6 percent decrease in costs, coupled with a matching increase in new revenue. Therefore, at the end of five years, newspapers should aim for a 30 percent change in both costs and revenue.

In order to achieve this "30 percent solution," publishers need a near-term strategy that is both focused and disciplined. So while the tactics may vary by market and community, community newspapers will need to aggressively pursue all three strategies simultaneously, shedding outdated legacy costs whenever possible while also rebuilding community online and pursuing new revenue opportunities.

"I am constantly shifting and measuring and maneuvering," says Santa Rosa's Bruce Kyse. "To stay on top of things, you have to constantly ask,

'What drives business?' I try to eliminate costs that don't drive business and follow the money." Clark Gilbert, CEO of Deseret Media and publisher of the *Deseret News*, believes the pace of change will, if anything, accelerate: "I tell publishers all the time that I think the business model is going to evolve a lot faster than you think. That's why we need to stay in a constant state of reinvention."

For Whiteville's Les High, the realization that he needed to accelerate the pace of change came "when I looked at everything I wanted to do, and realized it could not all be additive—that I had to come up with the money from somewhere. That's when I came to understand why I had to do all three at the same time." He also realized that "decreasing costs and increasing revenue an average of 6 percent a year sounds doable at first glance. And then you realize you have to do it every year for the next five [years] if you're going to meet the goal of a 30 percent reduction in costs and a 30 percent increase in revenue. That means you have to really get serious and be aggressive."

This, then, is the mandate for change: the marketplace realities, including the rapidly changing media habits of both readers and advertisers, are working against newspapers. The industry has suffered three potentially lethal blows from the Internet, which has attacked its cost structure, its customer base, and its revenue potential. Instead of investing in the core business—the print edition—newspaper publishers need to respond to the challenges they are now facing by following their customers into the online world. By following their customers, they are also following the money.

The road map to recovery laid out in this book assumes that all newspapers, regardless of size and location, are on the first leg of a journey from the print-only world they inhabited only yesterday to tomorrow's destination, which will vary by community and market served. The first stop on the journey involves moving from print-only to cross-platform (print and digital) delivery of news and information that readers care about. Over the next decade, some community papers may move on to digital-only delivery. Others will conclude that cross-platform delivery is profitable and a key point of differentiation between them and other local competitors.

In his turn-of-the-millennium business classic *Good to Great: Why Some Companies Make the Leap—And Others Don't*, Jim Collins, former Stanford University professor, observed that great companies are like hedgehogs,

What Should I Do Now?

How does the publisher of a newspaper take the first step and formulate both a game plan and a timeline for weathering the "cyclone" of creative destruction? As a director at McKinsey & Company for twenty-two years and author of *Creative Destruction: Why Companies That Are Built to Last Underperform the Market* (2001), Richard Foster frequently advised executives in technology, health care, and financial services who were facing threats similar to those confronted today by newspaper publishers and executives. And the question was always the same: "What do I do about this now?"

Q. Why is transformative change so difficult?

Although I'm very comfortable with numbers, I don't think that is all there is to business. I'm fascinated with the psychology of an organization, and how it changes, depending on what stage the company is in. In the first two stages—foundation and growth—the mentality of founders is very outward as they try to figure out how the landscape is changing and how best to serve new or potential customers. As successful companies reach the third stage—dominance—the view starts shifting inward as companies naturally begin defending their legacy. By the fourth stage, there usually has been a handoff to the next generation of leaders in the company and cultural lock-in has set in. In this stage, executives often fail to see potential competitors on the periphery, who could eat their lunch, because they are focused on the existing business and marketplace.

Q. How does a CEO signal that change needs to occur now?

Change needs to begin at the top. Unfortunately, senior management often does not function as a "team" with common goals and accountability, but rather as a working group of individuals, each responsible for a separate business division and each with separate goals and incentives. The best way around this is for the publisher to call the managers together on Monday morning, so to speak, and say something like this: "We are not going to leave here until we decide to shut down, or at least stop funding, 10 percent of our current costs over the next year, focusing on our legacy costs. At the same time, I want to hear proposals by next week for at least three acquisitions or alliances or investments that will accelerate our progress down the right path, very specifically focusing on the revenue side."

Q. One caution in all this is that the new business model has not yet been firmly established. So how do you proceed to place bets and monitor change?

There are two key "tipping points." The first comes when your customers change. Senior management needs to have a dashboard for monitoring how their customers' behavior is changing to accommodate a disruptive technology. So at that Monday morning meeting, the CEO needs to ask: "Have we lost—or are we in danger of losing—customers who drive advertising revenue? If so, how do we get them back?"

Q. Of course, the issue is that customer behavior may tip before you've figured out a new business model.

The other key way to understand and monitor these transitions is to "follow the money," as they say. The second tipping point occurs when the economics start to work in favor of the attacker. Then the attacker can cut prices and drive the defender back until the defender's balance sheet is consumed and it is bought out or forced into bankruptcy.

Anticipating tipping points can only come if the executives have knowledge of the existing and potential (attacking) new business models, and a clear understanding of what they are looking for—in other words, irreversible changes in customer behavior or economic power. I end by reminding executives that if they do not lead, the next owner will. (Excerpted from "The News Landscape in 2014: Transformed or Diminished? Formulating a Game Plan for Survival in the Digital Era")

"simple dowdy creatures that know 'one big thing' and stick to it." A company determines that "one thing" by asking three questions:

- What can you be the best in the world at?
- What are you deeply passionate about?
- What drives your economic engine?

For most newspaper editors and publishers, the answers to the first two questions come easily: they care passionately about providing their readers with the news and information that is most important to them—and they are the "best in the world" at creating and aggregating that content. Now they need to decide how they will "drive [the paper's] economic engine" in the digital age. They must commit to decreasing their costs and increasing their revenue by 30 percent over the next five years, or else they will not "keep pace with the changes in the market" and risk falling by the wayside.

Newspapers that survive and thrive will have an ability to regroup, reimagine the possibilities in this changed world order, and then rebuild. As media historian Donald Shaw points out, "History always allows leaders options, whether they use them sensibly or not."

PART II Implementing a New Strategy

News stories traditionally answer five questions, the "Five Ws": who, what, where, when, and why. On the other hand, economic models have their own essential building blocks. . . . What information becomes news depends on a different set of five Ws, asked in the market:

- Who cares about a particular piece of information?
- What are they willing to pay to find it, or what are others willing to pay to reach them?
- Where can media outlets or advertisers reach these people?
- When is it profitable to provide the information?
- Why is this profitable?

—James T. Hamilton, *All the News That's Fit to Sell: How the Market Transforms Information into News* (Princeton University Press, 2004)

So far, we have reviewed the changes washing over the landscape and developed three strategies that all newspapers must pursue if they are to adapt to change. Now we turn our attention to the challenges of implementing these strategies, especially for the nation's community newspapers.

As many publishers and editors have observed, often in exasperation, creating a strategy is often the "easy" part. Implementing a new strategy requires a whole host of different leadership skills—those of working with and motivating people to set off on an unexplored pathway, of setting up appropriate benchmarks to monitor progress and adjust course when necessary, and of making really tough decisions about where to divest and invest.

As we explore these issues, we'll check in with newspapers around the country that are adapting and see what lessons their publishers, editors, and ad directors have learned. Specifically, at the end of chapters 4 through 7, we'll focus on what is happening at the *Whiteville News Reporter*, as managing editor Les High puts together a leadership team and then sets about shedding legacy costs, building community across multiple platforms, and pursuing new revenue opportunities. Acknowledging that "no path is ever straightforward," High has been very transparent and honest in sharing the paper's stumbles along with its successes in the hope that "our experiences can benefit other community newspapers."

CHAPTER FOUR
How to Lead Change

Community newspapers are currently facing a life-threatening shock to the ecosystem that supported them over the last century. In order to survive, they need to adapt—and quickly. But having realized the imperative to change, publishers and editors are often surprised at how difficult it is to enlist others at their newspaper to follow them as they head off into uncharted territory.

Why is change so difficult? Thousands of books—written by CEOs, Ivy League professors, and business consultants—have pondered that question. "There's a joke I tell on myself," says Clark Gilbert, a former Harvard Business School professor who in 2008 became the CEO of Deseret Management Corporation, which publishes the *Deseret News*. "I tell my former colleagues that it's a lot easier to lay out a strategy on a PowerPoint slide than it is to do it in real life. I vastly underestimated the amount of cultural work that would be needed to turn around a company. I now believe that a good strategy is, at best, only 49 percent of the solution."

According to Ronald Heifetz, founder of the Center for Public Leadership at the John F. Kennedy School of Government at Harvard University, all organizations face two types of challenges: technical and adaptive. Technical challenges can be fixed with current knowledge and institutional know-how. For example, a component in the printing press breaks. The unit is repaired or replaced, and life at the newspaper returns to normal. Adaptive challenges, however, are much more difficult for an organization to address, Heifetz says, since it "involves both conservation and innovation. It's about understanding what we want to preserve from our history, while also moving people and organizations into the future. Innovation is about tinkering until you figure out a model that builds off the lessons of history. Without learning new ways—changing attitudes, values, and behaviors—people cannot make the adaptive leap necessary to thrive in the new environment."

In training to be a psychiatrist before he joined the faculty at Harvard, Heifetz learned that "the deeper the change and the greater the amount of new learning required, the more resistance there will be. For this reason, people often try to avoid the dangers, either consciously or subconsciously, by diagnosing and treating an adaptive challenge as if it were a technical one." The sort of adaptive change that community newspapers must currently embrace is very difficult to organize and lead, he says, because it "requires ongoing experimentation—keeping people in the game over a sustained period of disequilibrium."

Gilbert says he "spends at least 60 percent of [his] day, not building strategy, but building culture" as he attempts to lead "dual transformations" of the 162-year-old *Deseret News*, owned by the Mormon Church, and the Deseret Digital Media division, which he created when he assumed leadership of the Salt Lake City–based company. "I feel a tremendous stewardship for all the media in the Deseret group. But we have to think differently in both divisions."

Similarly, Charles Broadwell, publisher of the 200-year-old daily *Fayetteville Observer* in eastern North Carolina, serving residents of ten counties and the large military community stationed at Fort Bragg, has become the consummate juggler of multiple "experiments" as he attempts to guide the paper's employees through this era of adaptive change. "We have to get off the island we built for ourselves," says Broadwell. "We have to try some stuff. And when it fails or has outlived its purpose, we have to move on. That is perhaps the hardest lesson to learn, because we are used to holding on to things."

In recent years, the *Observer* has started a magazine for army officers, built a "social network" for "military moms," and contracted to print dozens of other newspapers and magazines throughout the Southeast, "so the press room stays busy 24/7." All the while, Broadwell is constantly reassessing what goes into the paper and onto the website, fayobserver.com, which has almost 600,000 unique visitors monthly and is currently receiving a major facelift so it is better suited for mobile access.

"Adaptive change forces people to question and perhaps redefine aspects of their identity; it also challenges their sense of competence," writes Heifetz in his 2002 book, *Leadership on the Line: Staying Alive through the Dangers of Leading*, cowritten by Marty Linsky. "No wonder people resist."

Richard Foster of Yale University's School of Management has noticed that the psychology of people at a company invariably changes depending on where the organization is in its life cycle. In the early stages, when the company is growing rapidly, everyone tends to be very outwardly focused and customer driven, he says. But once the company becomes dominant in its market, growth naturally slows and the strategy switches from offense to defense. No longer focused on growth but rather on preserving and maintaining profit margins, the company loses touch with changes in the environment. He calls this phenomenon "cultural lock-in," as employees assume that what worked in the past will continue to work—if only company leaders would just stay the course and persevere.

But if community newspapers are to adapt to a rapidly changing world, publishers will need to follow the examples of Gilbert and Broadwell. Despite the natural resistance to change, they must move quickly, as Heifetz points out, to nurture "a new strand of DNA" in their newspapers since "the benefits for those around you are beyond measure." There is a "real nobility" to the mission of community newspapers, he says. "Communities learn and evolve over time. And each generation in a community requires mechanisms, like newspapers, that create forums of engagement. Without them, you lose the bonds that hold a community together and allow it to renew its richness."

Instead of prescribing a step-by-step guide for implementing strategy, this chapter focuses on the psychology of leading adaptive change and how publishers and editors can follow a process that begins with putting together a team—a "guiding coalition"—of people within the organization who can help them nurture the "new strand of DNA." That is the first and most critical step, since members of this guiding coalition become partners as well as advocates for change. Next, publishers and editors will need to establish outwardly focused, broad-based measurements of progress that can be understood by everyone in their organizations. These measurements need to go beyond the standard financial measures or Web-based analytics used by most community newspapers. Finally, we'll conclude with some thoughts on how publishers and editors can successfully "manage themselves" as they lead their papers—and their communities—into the future.

Reaffirming the critical mission of community newspapers, understanding why they need to change, and crafting both a new vision and a new strategy are important first steps on the road to a new future. But the journey is only beginning.

Leading Change: Choosing a Guiding Coalition

Business consultants often mistakenly believe that it's easier to lead change at a mission-driven organization like a newspaper. "If anything, it is harder," says Heifetz, drawing on his own experience advising politicians as well as those in industry and the nonprofit world. "People sign on because they believed in the enduring mission. And now it appears the mission is in jeopardy."

Publishers and editors looking for insights into how people on their newspaper staff will respond to the prospect of change might want to consult one of the business classics, published in the *Academy of Management Review* in 1978. "Organizational Strategy, Structure, and Process" identifies three types of "personalities" in a typical company: prospectors, defenders, and analyzers. Each has a different reaction to and perspective on change.

Not surprisingly, "prospectors" focus on adapting to the changing environment and are adept at "finding and exploiting new product opportunities." "Defenders," on the other hand, are naturally inclined to "seal off a portion of the market" and attempt to protect the company's main franchises during times of turbulence. "Analyzers" look for ways to "minimize risk while maximizing the opportunity for profit" and often play a key role in resolving the different approaches and strategies of the other two types. All three types are needed to ensure the smooth functioning of a newspaper. But during times of transition, publishers need to understand what contribution each can make and then assign roles and responsibilities accordingly.

Defenders are important because they remind the prospectors of what is important (the mission of the paper) and what must be protected at all costs. However, defenders must not prevent prospectors from stepping out and exploring new territory (especially when it does not jeopardize the mission). By the same token, analyzers are critical for determining whether the prospectors might have struck gold or the defenders are being too cautious and protective of the print edition.

To allay the fears of those who worry about whether the *Fayetteville Observer*, in its haste to adapt to a radically changed environment, is losing sight of its mission, the forty-eight-year-old Broadwell asks of every new proposal put forward by his management team: "'How is this going to serve our readers?' This has been our home, literally, for 200 years, because we've always asked that question first." As community newspapers implement a three-pronged strategy of eliminating costs while growing both their customer and revenue bases, defenders can be deployed—as they are at the *Observer*—to protect the interests of loyal readers and advertisers of the print edition. Prospectors, on the other hand, should focus on how to reposition the newspaper as a true cross-platform medium with both its readers and advertisers. Analyzers are the ultimate decision makers, assessing whether the various "experiments" undertaken by the prospectors are allowing the newspaper to "follow its customers and the money."

Leaders of adaptive change can be either prospectors or analyzers. If a publisher elects to be a prospector, he needs to make sure he has a strong analyzer on his "team" who can make sure the transition to digital is handled expeditiously but prudently. If the publisher is the analyzer, she needs to make certain that she gives the prospectors the mandate and ability to aggressively pursue and affect change. Most of the publishers in the UNC study were most comfortable casting themselves as "analyzers."

Having decided what role he will play, a publisher then needs to recruit and create a formal leadership group composed of prospectors, defenders, and analyzers. This group is often referred to as a "guiding coalition." Guiding coalitions or "change management teams" composed only of the publisher, editor, and advertising and circulation directors often fail in achieving transformative change, says longtime business consultant Jon Katzenbach, who has studied teams in a range of organizations, including newspapers. That is because membership is automatic and the contribution of each member is often defined by, and limited to, the role he or she is assigned in the company. In contrast, teams that successfully navigate adaptive change are usually composed of a small number of people (usually no more than five to seven) who are chosen because they have complementary problem-solving and technical skills.

As any publisher on the front lines will attest, there are basically three types of problems that community newspapers need to solve in order to adapt to the changed environment. First, there is the entrepreneurial problem, requiring that the news and advertising departments develop "a concrete vision of the new target customer and the specific goods or services it will offer." Once the entrepreneurial problem has been solved, newspapers then need to tackle the engineering problem, adapting the current technology "so that it can produce the new goods and services." Finally, the administrative problem must be resolved so that the newspaper formulates and implements new processes and procedures that nurture a "new DNA" and "enable the organization to continue to evolve."

Contrary to what many people believe, says Katzenbach, coauthor of *The Wisdom of Teams: Creating the High-Performance Organization* (1993), members of a guiding coalition do not necessarily have to "get along." In fact, teams that always "get along" are often very unproductive since tension is inevitable when dealing with the three interrelated organizational problems (entrepreneurial, engineering, and administrative) that must be solved during times of disruption in the marketplace. He also recommends choosing members for the guiding coalition who represent a diversity of perspectives as well as skills. Not only are the team members responsible for implementing a new strategy for the newspaper, but they also must assist the publisher in enlisting broad-based support among employees and customers.

Therefore, effective guiding coalitions are composed of members from both the formal and informal "table of organization." The formal table of organization includes the editor and advertising director, who are ultimately responsible for implementing the changes in their departments. The informal one includes other "influential" persons who have the ability to sway the opinions of peers—a top salesperson or a star reporter, for example. An additional benefit, says Katzenbach, is that those drawn from the informal table of organization are more likely to be "prospectors" than those in management, who tend to be "defenders."

As Harvard's Heifetz points out, leaders of "adaptive change" must win over both "hearts and minds" of various stakeholders by identifying why change is important to that particular group. During times of immense disruption, tension between defenders (who are intent on preserving the legacy of a newspaper) and prospectors (who are focused on adapting to the changed environment) is natural. Properly managed, such tension ensures a successful transition to a new business model. "The role of a leader of adaptive change is to regulate the disequilibrium," says Heifetz. "That's why you need a forum and an environment to surface conflict, challenge norms, and create a sense of urgency—but a *productive* sense of urgency."

That is why the first critical step for a publisher or editor is to identify and nurture a "guiding coalition" of carefully selected colleagues who bring to the task different perspectives and skills and, in the process, begin to chart a new path for the newspaper that is respectful of the past but focused on the future.

Leading Change: Measuring Your Progress

After choosing members for the guiding coalition, publishers next need to put in place a system of measurements that allows everyone in the newspaper to know whether progress is being made and how they, individually, can contribute to the change.

As we discussed in chapter 3, faced with creative destruction, community newspapers need to employ three strategies simultaneously. They need a three-pronged approach that addresses the cost side while still serving the various "special-interest communities," or niches, that reside in the geographic region the newspaper serves—the soccer mom, the sports enthusiast, or the local town politico. They also need to differentiate the newspaper from the competition—positioning it as a cross-platform medium—which then allows the advertising department to charge for the true value they are actually delivering to local businesses. With these three plates spinning at all times, publishers need to have in place a system for monitoring and adjusting *each* of these strategies.

"Why do organizations have difficulty implementing well-formulated strategies?" asks Harvard University professor Robert Kaplan in *The Strategy-Focused Organization: How Balanced Scorecard Companies Thrive in the New Business Environment* (2001). "One problem is that strategies—the unique and sustainable ways by which organizations create value—are changing, but the tools for measuring strategies have not kept pace." As he points out, most companies measure a strategy's success using primarily financial yardsticks. There are several problems with that. First, financial statements are backward looking, reflecting the newspaper's performance during the previous month or quarter. And second, they tend to measure the value of tangible assets but not the value of a company's intangible assets—the loyalty of its customers, for example.

Kaplan recommends asking four questions before implementing a strategy:

"If we succeed, how will we look to our shareholders?" In order to "to keep pace with the market" and avoid being overtaken by "the gales of creative destruction," a newspaper must strive to simultaneously decrease costs and increase revenue by 6 percent annually. In order to achieve this, a publisher must have a system in place that prioritizes savings and investments.

"To achieve my vision, how must I look to my customers?" Both advertisers and readers are heading online. Therefore, there must be some measurement of whether newspapers are "following their customers" by keeping pace with their changing media consumption habits and preferences.

"To satisfy my customers, at which processes must I excel?" In order to pursue new revenue, advertising departments have to totally revamp their sales processes. News departments may also need to rethink their editorial strategy and move toward a "digital first" emphasis. Therefore, newspapers need to be tracking the loyalty of both readers and advertisers.

"To achieve my vision, how must my organization learn and improve?" The newspaper needs to evolve into a cross-platform medium that serves both

readers and advertisers well. Therefore, advertising departments need to be periodically surveying local businesses to learn of their experiences with the paper and to get their recommendations for improvement. Similarly, the news department needs to be tracking how many new readers it is attracting to the paper's online community pages and learn what it can do to keep them coming back.

Establishing a system of measurement for all four questions helps publishers and those in the guiding coalition track progress against specific benchmarks. *Santa Rosa Press Democrat* publisher Bruce Kyse, for example, does a systematic three-month review of important benchmarks focused on Internet revenue and traffic, as well as cost savings. Similarly, Clark Gilbert has established in-house "quality metrics" for the news stories that appear in the *Deseret News*. He and the editorial leaders score themselves on major stories on a daily and weekly basis, with others in the company joining in on a monthly basis.

Most editors in the UNC study were already monitoring basic Web analytics and were aware of what types of stories drove "traffic" to their digital sites. Most publishers had a good handle on what had driven down their profitability in recent years and were acutely aware of the rate problems with digital advertising revenue. But, using this data alone, it is often hard to get the "bigger picture" and understand how well a newspaper is performing against its competitors or attracting a new generation of readers. Many of the papers had not conducted proprietary market research in the previous decade because it was very labor-intensive and expensive.

Fortunately, the digital age makes it possible to obtain reliable and timely reader and advertiser feedback and trending information. The UNC team used a simple four-part process for gathering additional information that publishers of even the smallest papers can use to establish a baseline from which to judge progress.

First, relevant data from local, state, and federal government agencies (such as the U.S. Census Bureau or the North Carolina Department of Commerce) were gathered and used to build a profile of the community that a newspaper served. The newspapers then looked at broad indicators—such as employment statistics and retail sales—and compared them to trends in other cities and counties in the region and state. Although initially time-consuming, once this initial profile has been done, it can be updated relatively easily on a yearly basis. And as an added bonus, this market research can serve another purpose: it can be turned into stories that put the quality of life in a community into perspective for the paper's readers.

Second, a brief online survey (of ten to fifteen questions) was posted on the newspaper's website to gather information about the readers of the digital edition. Depending on the information that the newspaper needed, these surveys were structured so as to collect information on changes in readers' media habits, their engagement with content, or their consumer purchase patterns (so that the newspapers could have up-to-date market information to share with local advertisers). Because readers knew in advance that the survey would take only a couple of minutes, there was a high response rate. In addition, almost half of all respondents in these surveys provided answers to the open-ended question: What else would you like for us to know?

Third, one-on-one interviews were conducted in each market with ten to fifteen readers who subscribed only to the print edition and said they had never looked at the newspaper's website. The readers were chosen by calling every hundredth person on the subscriber list and inviting them to come into the newspaper office for a half-hour interview. A student interviewer, not associated with the paper, would ask each of the participants the same list of twenty-five questions. In return for their time, readers were given a coupon worth between $10 and $15 that was good on purchases at a local merchant. These interviews were especially important in determining what features in the print edition should be preserved at all costs.

Fourth, half-hour interviews were conducted with ten to fifteen current or former newspaper advertisers in each market. The publisher provided a list of twenty-five to thirty local businesses, grouped into three categories: longtime advertisers, high-priority prospects who had never advertised, and those who had left or significantly decreased their spending with the paper. The student interviewers then called each of the advertisers and arranged a time to interview them at their businesses, working from an identical list of twenty questions. These interviews helped newspaper publishers better understand the competitive landscape as well as how they could respond to changing advertiser needs. (Examples of all of these surveys can be found on the instructional website that accompanies this book, businessofnews.unc.edu.)

While many of the publishers and editors admitted to feeling "nervous" about what sort of responses they would get to the surveys, the researchers found that in most communities, there was a tremendous reservoir of goodwill toward the newspaper, especially among readers, and enduring loyalty among longtime advertisers. By and large, customers appreciated being asked their opinion. Readers volunteered suggestions on improving the content in the digital edition. Advertisers often provided valuable marketing intelligence on a competitor's sales tactics.

These simple surveys not only established a nonfinancial baseline, but they were also helpful in identifying some "leading indicators" that publishers and editors could monitor in the coming years. These leading indicators included tracking the loyalty of both readers and advertisers, their engagement with content, and their changing media preferences. Such leading indicators—shared on a routine basis with the entire organization—help employees understand their role in the transformation and how they can help. Or, as Harvard's Heifetz would say, it allows broad-based ownership of the problem, which is essential if community newspapers are to adapt and thrive.

By tracking the loyalty of readers and their engagement with the content either on a semiannual or annual basis, editors can more easily determine whether they are successfully building vibrant community online. By tracking the loyalty of advertisers, publishers and ad directors can determine whether the paper is "following the money" and aggressively pursuing new revenue. And by tracking the changing media habits of the paper's readers and advertisers, publishers and editors can more wisely manage the transition between print and digital by "following their customers"—instead of getting out ahead of them or falling too far behind. This insight could help them more efficiently shed legacy costs associated with the print edition.

For Jule Hubbard, managing editor of the family-owned *Wilkes Journal-Patriot*, the responses from advertisers in the North Carolina mountain community that his paper served "were hard to hear." He learned that several merchants were considering defecting to competitors because they didn't believe the digital edition of the paper—a PDF of the print version—offered them the sort of audience or dynamic, interactive environment they wanted for their online ads. With that information in hand, Hubbard approached his father and uncle, the owners and publishers of the paper, who were both in their eighties and had resisted investing in the website. "It was hard for them to hear, too," he says. "But it ultimately opened up a really productive conversation. I think they basically realized that I was assuming the risk. I said, 'Look if this fails, it is on me, not you. But if we do nothing, it is on all of us.'"

Leading Change: Managing Yourself

Hubbard works with five other members of his family at the *Wilkes Journal-Patriot*. "That means I have to get all of us in the boat together, rowing in the same direction. And that takes time and perseverance," he says. The key to successfully leading change at a newspaper of any size is holding steady over months and years during a period of tremendous uncertainty. "In your efforts to lead a community, you will often be thinking and acting ahead of them," says Heifetz, who has spent the last two decades advising leaders in political, business, and nonprofit organizations on "managing themselves." Heifetz concedes: "Patience is a not a virtue typically associated with people passionate about what they are doing—and especially for editors and publishers who are used to having daily deadlines to meet. But holding off until the issue is ripe may be critical for mobilizing people's energy and getting yourself heard." So when he speaks to publishers and editors, Heifetz's message is clear: you are selflessly committing to a cause larger than yourself; however, in doing so, you open yourself up to criticism and second-guessing from the very people you have to motivate day-to-day.

In large organizations, leaders are often in danger of being too disconnected from day-to-day management. However, given the small size of their staffs, many community newspaper publishers and editors have the opposite problem: they are *too* connected. "I can look out on the newsroom and see everyone," says Fabiola Pomareda, managing editor of the Spanish-language weekly *La Raza*. Pomareda supervises four reporters. "So, if someone is off, it affects us all."

Therefore, Heifetz recommends that publishers and editors make it a point to "get up on the balcony" at the end of every day so they can understand where everyone at the paper is "coming from," because "sustaining your leadership . . . requires first and foremost the capacity to see what is happening to you and your initiative as it is happening." From the balcony, he says, publishers and editors can detach and watch "the grand waltz" that is occurring on the "ballroom floor" below. "Find out where people are at and listen to the song beneath the words," he says. "If you ask someone how he is doing, and he says OK, you can tell a big difference between a bright emphasis on a K and a sad emphasis on an O." Notice who is participating and who is sitting it out. Focus on the "influential" members who can sway others, and read them for clues.

Heifetz also strongly advises publishers and editors to seek out "confidants"—someone they trust—and invite them to come up on the balcony with them periodically. It can be a publisher or editor at another paper who is also leading adaptive change, or it can be someone very vested in the paper's success. At the family-owned *News Reporter*, editor

Les High and publisher Jim High schedule twice-yearly bird-hunting trips outside the state "so we can reconnect as father and son, and also discuss long-range plans, without the distractions of the office."

Confidants "help a publisher reflect on his own loyalties—to an organization's history and to its people," says Heifetz. "Confidants help you figure out whose water you're carrying, who you need to disappoint and how you go about disappointing them. There is always loss in adaptive change. We want to conserve the best, but we also have to innovate and move on. Disappointing people is one of the most emotionally challenging aspects of being a leader."

Being up on the balcony periodically detached from action also allows publishers and editors to think politically. They need to find partners who can help them achieve their strategic goals. "Finding partners is sometimes easier said than done. Partnering on an issue means giving up some autonomy," Heifetz warns. However, partners provide protection, help create alliances, and improve "the content of your ideas." Partners can be prospectors, defenders, and analyzers. What's important is that they are committed to making a change and enlisting others to sign on. That's why publishers and editors also need to know where the resistance is coming from and keep the opposition close, as well. "People who oppose what you are trying to accomplish are usually those with the most to lose," says Heifetz. "It's also true that the people who determine your success are often those in the middle, who resist your initiative merely because it will disrupt their lives."

With adaptive change, Heifetz warns there are winners and losers. "Surely, we would all prefer to bring everyone along," he says, "and we can admirably hold up this ideal. Unfortunately, casualties are often a necessary by-product of adaptive work. Few people enjoy hurting or making life difficult for old friends and colleagues. [But] if people simply cannot adapt, the reality is that they will be left behind. Some people simply cannot or will not go along. You have to choose between keeping them and making progress. There is too much at stake."

Acknowledging this, says Les High, is "perhaps the hardest part of my job. I see people who contributed a lot to this paper over the years but may not be able to do what is required in a few years." That is why Heifetz advises publishers to actively "orchestrate the conflict," controlling the temperature and pacing the work. Adaptive change occurs in fits and starts. It is very uneven. New behaviors need to be learned, new values and attitudes adopted. And in the end, adaptive change can

Leading a Newspaper "From the Balcony"

Ronald Heifetz, founding director of the Center for Public Leadership and King Hussein bin Talal Senior Lecturer in Public Leadership at Harvard University's John F. Kennedy School of Government, has written extensively on the risks and rewards of leadership. In his role as advisor to numerous political and governmental leaders around the world—from prime ministers to governors and mayors—he has developed a keen appreciation for the historic and unique role of newspapers in helping communities, large and small, adapt to changed circumstances.

Q. Why is implementing a new strategy so difficult for any organization?

Leadership is about connecting a community's history with the present reality and then adapting so that a community can move into the future successfully. You can't take all of history with you. Some of it has to be lost, and losses create resistance. For a publisher, leadership is really a service contract that you make with the newspaper and the community you serve. It's about helping both organizations build a culture of adaptability.

There are two difficult realities that leaders trying to help an organization adapt to change have to confront. First, there will be people who will want to keep things going as they currently are. That's only human. We're comfortable with what we know. And second, in order to successfully adapt to a changed environment, an organization has to conduct a lot of experiments before it can identify the right DNA necessary for survival. It's trial and error, and there are a lot of failures. Innovation doesn't come cheap. So for the person leading change, there is a tremendous amount of risk, a lot of being called "crazy."

Q. In your lectures and writings, you advise leaders of organizations that they must routinely "get up on the balcony." What does that mean, exactly?

I've known great mayors who loved people and spent time on the street, checking in with constituents constantly. But they didn't do as well as a governor or senator because they got trapped by the bureaucracy and never connected with the people. Whether you're working in a small organization or a large, you, as a leader, need to retrieve and then process information from relevant people. "Getting up on the balcony" is simply a mental way to regain perspective on what you've heard and witnessed.

It's not the same as separating yourself from the organization and the work of adaptive change. Rather, it is an exercise that allows you to see individual people in the context of the organization and the progress you are collectively making in terms of adapting to environmental challenges. In order to interpret what you are seeing, you need to start by zooming out and considering the arc of change on a timeline. How far has the organization come? What is still left to be done? And then you need to zoom in and consider the behavior of individuals and departments within the organization that you are witnessing in relation to the immediate challenges you confronted that day. Getting up on the balcony is about regaining your orientation.

Q. How often should a publisher or editor aim to get up on the balcony?

It needs to be a daily discipline—much like setting aside time for physical exercise or meditation. It is the time you set aside at the beginning or end of the day to consider what you witnessed. Especially on newspapers, publishers and editors tend to focus the majority of their "management time" on getting the paper out. There's always another deadline tomorrow. So, they're embedded on the dance floor, operating at a microlevel with everyone else, focused on the present. So the balcony becomes a sanctuary—a time and a place to reflect so they don't lose perspective and stay focused on the future.

Getting up on the balcony is also about generating a daily discipline in your own life that enables you to maintain your poise, so you can provide a source of calm and hope. You want to create a sense of urgency in an organization about the need to change, but you want to direct that sense of urgency and make it productive. So when your paper encounters failure, as it inevitably will, you can say, "This is containable. What did we learn? You can see that I'm not panicked. I have faith in us."

only take place when publishers and editors give the work back to their people and let them own the problem. "For a strategy to be successfully implemented, it has to be a widespread process that involves getting people to realize the need for change and then inventing the change," he says. "Adaptive change involves a lot of failures and a lot of organizational learning about what will ultimately work and get us to survive and thrive in the new environment." That's why at every stop along the way, publishers and editors must make the vision tangible, reminding people of the values they are fighting for and showing them how the future might look.

"We're still morphing," says Broadwell, the fourth generation of his family to be publisher of the *Fayetteville Observer*. "In 1995, when I was editor, we were one of the very first newspapers to establish a website. But now I think we're just getting to a sense in all parts of this newspaper that you [the readers] are valuable to me, regardless of how you receive your paper. That's the vision and the message I try to convey about the future. We've been a mainstay here and have a 200-year-old legacy to uphold—of serving this community through war and peace. It's the passion and the motivation that keeps me going—even when we are not sure where we are heading."

Adapting to a new environment is difficult for everyone in a newspaper, especially one with a long history and a distinguished legacy. That's why leading adaptive change is "to live dangerously," as Heifetz puts it, because "you challenge what people hold dear—their daily habits, tools, loyalties, and ways of thinking—with nothing more to offer perhaps than a possibility. . . . Each day brings you opportunities to raise important questions, speak to higher values, and surface unresolved conflicts."

It can be lonely work—which is why publishers and editors leading adaptive change at their newspapers need partners and confidants who can help them "get up on the balcony," where they can more clearly determine how to pace to the work, when to ask the probing question, and how to resolve the creative conflicts that are bound to occur. The rewards for successfully managing yourself through the dangers of leading change are great for publishers and editors of newspapers because, says Heifetz, "every day you have the chance to make a difference in the greater community you serve. There's more than just your own history at stake—it's your paper's role as an anchor, the preserver of a community's social capital that has been built up over generations."

The Whiteville Experience Getting Started

When profit at the *News Reporter* declined significantly in 2009, Les High initially attributed the dip to the ongoing recession that had gripped Columbus County and the rest of the region that year. High had worked at the family-owned paper since 1984, when he graduated from college and returned home to become a photographer, working his way up to managing editor.

His father, Jim—who in 2009 was in his late seventies and still active as publisher in the day-to-day management of the company—had brought the *News Reporter* back from the financial brink in the 1950s (after it had won the Pulitzer Prize) by investing in the paper, giving residents of Columbus County credible and comprehensive coverage of all the news and information they cared about. His formula for reviving the paper then was the same one that he and his son continued to use during all the temporary downturns in the economy that occurred in the latter half of the century. But after making the short-term adjustments to the paper's budget that had been successful during previous downturns, Les realized by the end of 2009 that the economy was not bouncing back. Also, there appeared to be a fundamental shift occurring with some of the paper's longtime advertisers—specifically realtors and car dealers—who were moving online.

The *News Reporter* had been one of the first small, nondaily newspapers in North Carolina to establish a website (whiteville.com) in 1998. A decade later, the website was still breaking new ground with a Twitter feed for breaking news stories. Under the stewardship of photographer Mark Gilcrest, it was attracting roughly 1,000 unique visitors a day, who viewed the postings of stories and photographs and often commented on them.

But while the website was a source of pride for the news department, it was a source of anxiety and worry for the advertising director, Mickey Greer. Despite several efforts to boost the number of advertisers on the site, the digital rate was so low that online revenue amounted to less than 5 percent of overall revenue for the paper. Print advertising, on the other hand, which was paying the bills and keeping the lights on, had declined significantly in 2008 and 2009. This threatened the *News Reporter*'s ability to continue its aggressive investigative reporting. "We had to pay $22,000 in legal bills this past year to get access to some public records," Les said in 2009. "When we were making 20 percent margins, there was no problem paying this. But with margins trending toward break-even, you have to weigh carefully whether it's worth it—especially if you don't know if you will prevail in court."

Complicating matters was the fact that two potentially strong competitors for whiteville.com had emerged: a proposed website that would focus on in-depth coverage of local prep sports and a television station fifty miles away that had suddenly started covering breaking crime stories in Columbus County (perhaps tipped off by the Twitter feed). Both sports and crime were two news franchises that the *News Reporter* had traditionally owned.

As he considered how he might respond, Les felt constrained financially. He and his father, who had politely rebuffed earlier offers to sell the newspaper, worried whether the *News Reporter* could remain independent for much longer. More than two-thirds of community newspapers in North Carolina were already owned by chains, many of which were headquartered in other states and owned by private equity firms that valued profit margin over aggressive public affairs journalism. As he worked his way through an analysis of his newspaper's current business model and the trends in the marketplace, Les realized he needed to make a significant strategic shift to accommodate the changes and reposition the *News Reporter* for the digital age. Because he was worried that he might alienate loyal subscribers to the *News Reporter*, he had been very reluctant to add much original content to whiteville.com. Surveys conducted with online and print readers convinced him otherwise. Indeed, he learned that many print subscribers were also reading the online edition, and that some of the most popular features on the website were those that did not appear in the paper.

This led to two conclusions. First, the *News Reporter* needed to begin adding more reader-participation features that would take advantage of the interactivity and timeliness of the Web while also strengthening the loyalty and engagement of current readers and attracting new ones. And second, Les realized the *News Reporter* should start envisioning the two editions as complementary and intertwined.

In a similar fashion, the advertiser surveys convinced Les that the *News Reporter* also needed to revamp its strategy of selling the print and digital editions separately. Greer was very worried about protecting the print edition, which continued to provide more than 60 to 70 percent of total revenue. Only one of the paper's three sales representatives was assigned to aggressively sell the digital edition. Yet many of the paper's longtime advertisers said they would like to see the *News Reporter* offer them more marketing options online. In order to get the return on the investment that would be needed, Les realized that he would need to rethink the current rate structure and the advertising staff would have to be retrained. That could not be done overnight.

As he analyzed the current trends in revenue and cost over the last five years—and then projected how much they would need to change over the next five in order to achieve a 30 percent decrease in costs and a simultaneous 30 percent increase in revenue from new sources—Les realized that he would, indeed, have to come up with a three-pronged strategy that would simultaneously reduce costs associated with the print edition, build community online, and seek out new revenue opportunities. "I realized it couldn't all be additive," he says. "We couldn't afford to invest in the online edition without making sure we were producing the print edition as efficiently as possible."

After arriving at this conclusion, Les High conferred with his father, Jim, who was still using an old manual typewriter to bang out editorials. They agreed that Les would take on the job of crafting a future vision and would, in essence, form a "guiding coalition" of others at the newspaper to help him lead the change. As he considered other important stakeholders in the company who needed a say, Les focused first on Greer, who was rightly concerned with protecting the print advertising, and Gilcrest, who in essence was the website editor. If the site was to be more than a one-man operation, others in the newsroom needed to also "own" it. Les considered both men to be defenders who would make sure that during this period of adaption and disruption the paper remained true to its mission and to its loyal customers.

What Les High felt he needed most on his leadership team was a "prospector type" who could envision the website five years out and then work with him to analyze and recommend a strategy that would protect the core business but also allow the newspaper to keep up with the times. He identified a couple of younger, recent hires, but they did not have the stature of either Greer or Gilcrest. Then, as luck would have it, his sister, Stuart, who had spent the previous twenty years in Charlotte, announced that she was ready to return home and help with the paper.

In the early 1990s, Stuart had worked in the marketing department of the *Charlotte Observer* before "retiring to raise a family." She conceded she would be on a steep learning curve, but Les felt she would be perfect. She would work to protect the family business, but she was not encumbered with defending past practices. He and his father appointed her director of special projects, making her the critical link between the news and advertising departments.

Stuart—who voiced a strong commitment to the historic mission of the paper—proved very adept at understanding the concerns of the defenders. And because she had no obvious agenda other than focusing on the future, she was able to elicit ideas from other prospectors in the newspaper and then work with Les to fit these suggestions into the three-pronged strategy framework. In short order, Stuart would become a proselytizer and prospector, as well as a day-to-day manager of change.

As he looks back on the decisions he made in 2009 and 2010, Les realizes there had been several key "turning points." The first came as he processed the results of the reader and advertiser surveys—along with the five-year financial trends—and realized both the imperative for change and "the strong support we continue to enjoy from the community. The reader surveys confirmed that our readers and advertisers understood what the *News Reporter* meant to this community—and that we had their support for changing."

The second big turning point occurred with the arrival of Stuart, who brought an outside perspective but also knowledge of the family's history with the paper. "It is essential when you are going through this that you have someone you can trust," says Les. "Someone who can point out things you missed, give you honest feedback on your own performance, and support you when you have to make the difficult decisions." Stuart's arrival freed Les to assume the role of an "analyzer" who could objectively prioritize the various initiatives and monitor their success once they were implemented. She would become not only a valued partner but also a "confidant" who could help him "get up on the balcony" often.

CHAPTER FIVE
How to Shed Legacy Costs

When Catherine Nelson returned "home" in 2006 to central Vermont as general manager of the newspaper company where she had gotten her professional start, the region's economy was already trending downward. So she immediately set about revamping the cost structure of the company's two daily papers—the Pulitzer Prize–winning *Rutland Herald* (circulation 12,000) and its sister paper in Barre, the *Times Argus* (circulation 7,000).

Nelson, who had more than two decades of experience with daily and weekly community newspapers published by the Harte-Hanks and Lee Enterprises groups, brought to the task a firm belief that "you do not want to touch the newsroom until the very end because it just doesn't make sense to attack what you do best." So in the first year, she "tried to understand the archaic ways we were still doing things—and in some cases, it was the only way we had ever done things."

Together, the circulation of the two newspapers—both of which had been published on a daily basis for more than a century—had grown to include homes in eight of Vermont's fourteen counties. Distribution routes stretched across all of the central and southern part of the mountainous and rural state. "We've always seen these two newspapers as . . . state papers, as well as community papers," says CEO and publisher John Mitchell. "And in Vermont [with a population of 650,000 residents, fewest of all states except Wyoming], you have to be both since what happens on the state level affects people in the community personally and directly."

But as Nelson looked at the spreadsheets, she realized that "we were providing a great service to our readers all across the state—your newspaper on the doorstep every morning—but with rising fuel costs and an aging fleet of trucks, the act of getting the paper delivered was pulling resources away from what the two papers did best—covering what was important to the state of Vermont and its residents." By outsourcing to a trucking firm, she was able to cut the distribution costs in half.

Next, Nelson began "taking advantage of technology" by consolidating and centralizing numerous business functions, such as administration and billing, and creating hybrid positions, such as a joint director of technology and circulation—"which makes sense," she explains, "because we're moving toward digital delivery of the paper to more and more of our readers." Print circulation of the *Rutland Herald*, for example, is half of what it was thirty years ago. Simultaneously, Nelson also began preparing to outsource printing of the papers. Therefore, when a flash flood in 2011 destroyed the press in Barre that printed both papers, "we were able to find an alternative printer and never miss a delivery because we had already taken advantage of cloud computing and moved many production functions, such as layout and design, to the 'cloud.'" Recently, she has cut rent and maintenance costs for the Barre building in half by moving the newsroom of that paper into smaller quarters.

Through her aggressive efforts, Nelson has cut more than 20 percent in production and distribution costs, and the payroll of the two papers has dropped from 200 to eighty full-time employees. "Catherine not only has a solid head for business and a clear vision for how to use technology to produce a paper in the twenty-first century, but a gift for dealing with people and explaining why it's important that we take these tough measures," says Mitchell. "She understands that the newsroom is the heart and soul of what we do—and without funds to support the news operation, we are not very relevant to our readers or our advertisers."

In the rolling Sandhills region of North Carolina, famous for its longleaf pine and world-class golf courses, David Woronoff, publisher of the *The Pilot*—a twice-weekly, family-owned community newspaper (circulation 13,500)—is also attempting to weather the storms of this transition by cutting costs "where we add the least value." In 1996, when he was thirty years old, he convinced four others—including his uncle, who had recently sold the state's second-largest paper, the *News and Observer* of Raleigh, to McClatchy Newspapers, Inc.—to purchase the ninety-year-old paper, which serves the upscale resort and retirement communities of Southern Pines and Pinehurst. Business was booming, and as a result, "the midweek issue was so big (with advertisements), we had to go to press two days early to get the paper out on time," he says.

So the new owners spent $3 million purchasing a state-of-the-art press and expanding the news and production facilities in downtown Southern Pines. In 1999 *The Pilot* began publishing three days a week—Wednesdays, Fridays, and Sundays. Over the next decade, Woronoff launched an award-winning website, rolled out free Wi-Fi service for residents in the community, and began publishing three upscale monthly lifestyle magazines for the residents of Southern Pines, Greensboro, and Wilmington and telephone directories for two counties in the area. He purchased a design company and a local bookstore, and he began contracting to print other publications, including programs for Atlantic Coast Conference championship events. But despite Woronoff's aggressive strategy to diversify revenue and grow the business across multiple platforms and venues, the sharp decline in newspaper advertising beginning in 2009 took a toll on the publishing company's bottom line and prompted him in the spring of 2013 to consider how to bring costs for producing the paper more in line with the revenues it has produced in recent years.

In the weeks leading up to his decision, Woronoff debated "how best to serve the community. We could cut news staff and continue publishing three days a week. But would we be serving the community better if we published three editions, full of stories produced by the wire services?" In the end, he concluded that "if we exist to serve the community, then we need to preserve the staff that produces the content." So, like Catherine Nelson, he looked first for savings in the printing and distribution of the physical paper, "where we added the least value." That is why, he explained to readers in a column, the newspaper was cutting back publication from three days a week to two.

"There are no easy decisions about where to cut costs," observes Woronoff. "On the one hand, you're messing with readers' and advertisers' habits, routines, and expectations. On the other, you are undermining the livelihood of loyal staff members, who depend on the paycheck." Yet as he explained in his column, newspaper publishers need to make these tough calls because industries that fail "to adapt to shifting currents" will be swept away.

With print advertising returning to 1950 levels, newspapers everywhere have struggled in recent years to adjust their costs downward to match the new revenue reality. Some, such as the *Deseret News* in Salt Lake City, have followed the lead of many "metro" dailies and cut back significantly on staffing in the newsroom—and have necessarily scaled back coverage of certain areas. Others, such as the *Rutland Herald* and *The Pilot*, have sought to preserve their newsrooms' staffing at all costs and find savings on the printing and distribution side first, even if that means disrupting readers' routines and preferences.

As every economist who has studied the newspaper industry stresses, given the competitive situation newspapers now face regarding readers and advertisers, publishers can no longer expect to achieve annual profit margins that routinely exceed 20 percent. That was a function of the de facto monopolistic status community newspapers enjoyed in the predigital era. Investor Warren Buffett, who has recently purchased several dozen papers in small cities and towns, believes that a 10 percent margin is still feasible in many markets. But in order to achieve that sort of margin, publishers need to come up with a long-range plan for reducing costs and "right-sizing" their newspapers' cost structure for the digital age.

Yale University's Richard Foster, who has spent the last three decades studying companies that are struggling to adapt to a disruptive innovation, found that businesses that survived made it a priority to aggressively reduce "legacy costs" associated with their traditional business model. "No one wants to kill the goose that laid the golden egg," says Foster. So the "goose" is kept on life support, resulting in a drain on the financial resources of the company that diverts funds that could be used for transformation of the business. Even more concerning, it becomes a strategic distraction for management.

In order for a company to be able to invest—and ensure its survival—leaders in the company must first figure out where to divest emotionally and financially, says Foster. Therefore, shedding all manner of legacy costs—including processes, systems, buildings, and people—associated with producing the print edition is the first, most critical step in transitioning community newspapers from a print-only world to a cross-platform one. Unless newspapers have an aggressive plan for doing it, they will not be able to free up funds to invest in following their customers into the digital realm.

In order to keep pace with the significant changes that are currently occurring in the industry, community newspapers need to have a long-term goal of shedding costs at an average annual rate of 6 percent. This translates into a 30 percent reduction of costs by the fifth year—no small feat. To accomplish that goal, publishers must look to trim expenses in the areas where they spend the most: the actual production and distribution of the print edition, as well as the payroll for all the employees who create the paper. The decisions in both areas are exceedingly difficult because they strike at the core of a newspaper's legacy in the community it serves and affect the livelihoods of loyal employees. But Foster warns that unless publishers focus on freeing up funds and resources that can be reallocated to the future, they are simply prolonging the eventual "death" of the newspaper. That, he says, is the real cost of not having an aggressive plan to shed legacy costs.

Divesting: Reducing the Costs of Distributing the Paper

In a digital era, the cost of distributing a story—or an entire newspaper—over the Internet is minuscule. This puts a real premium on creating unique content that differentiates a community newspaper, setting it apart from competitors so it can attract a loyal audience and, in turn, charge both readers and advertisers more. Therefore, it is understandable that many community publishers will first want to divest legacy costs associated with the printing and distribution of the physical paper, while attempting to preserve—or even strengthen—staffing levels in the newsroom and advertising departments, which are responsible for creating the content that attracts readers, and then selling the newspaper's audience to local businesses.

To calculate how quickly and aggressively they must shed printing and distribution costs, publishers should employ what is called "zoom-out, zoom-in" strategic thinking. First, a publisher needs to zoom out to understand the trend lines and key drivers of the current business model and determine what cannot be controlled. For example, print circulation of most community newspapers will continue to decline in future years since the print readers are aging and not being replaced by younger ones.

Then a publisher needs to zoom in and ask "what if?" What if the circulation of the print edition dips below a certain point and, as a result, the preprinted insert business disappears or shrinks substantially? What if a key advertiser defects? What if the aging printing press needs a major repair? By asking "what if?," publishers can understand critical tipping points that require immediate and significant cost reductions. For example, many community newspapers that publish twice a week would need to cut back to weekly relatively quickly if they were to lose the preprint insert business.

Costs related to printing and distribution are relatively easy to identify and quantify. Savings are usually accomplished in one of three ways:

- The printing and/or distribution of the paper can be outsourced to another publishing company, saving the upfront capital expenses of purchasing new equipment as well as the payroll involved. As in the case of the *Rutland Herald* and the *Barre Times Argus*, outsourcing also potentially allows the newspaper to "downsize" to a smaller building and save on rent, taxes, utilities, and maintenance.

- The size of the print run is cut back by eliminating distribution to outlying areas or shrinking the size of the print edition by moving features online. This option saves primarily the cost of newsprint, it but could also potentially generate some payroll savings related to either the printing and distribution of the paper or the creation of the content.
- The number of publication days can be scaled back, as in the case of *The Pilot*. This option, the most drastic of the three, saves on newsprint and other nonpayroll expenses, plus the cost of personnel involved in producing and distributing the print edition.

Of the three options, outsourcing is the most seamless to readers and advertisers. In many instances recently, the decision has been made by "corporate" to consolidate the production and distribution of several newspapers in a group to achieve "efficiencies." In the case of independently owned newspapers, outsourcing usually occurs when an aging press or insert machine breaks down. This forces a financial analysis as to whether the newspaper can justify the purchase of a new one. Ray McKeithan, general manager of the *Washington (N.C.) Daily News*, faced such a decision in 2009. "We had lost a substantial portion of our display classified in the recession, and I knew we had to reduce costs," he says. As he made his calculations, McKeithan said he realized he could *only* justify the significant funds needed to buy a new press *if* he believed the *Daily News* could contract with other publishers in the area to print and distribute their publications. "You'd have to come up with a plan to keep the pressroom humming 24/7," he says.

That is the economic dynamic that is occurring throughout the newspaper industry as printing and distribution is being centralized among a few regionally located newspapers or firms with state-of-the-art presses and truck fleets. Outsourcing of the *Daily News* to another publishing company forty miles away resulted in significant cost savings, says McKeithan, and "it was seamless to our readers since the paper was still delivered at the same time."

A flood in the pressroom prompted the *Rutland Herald* and its sister paper, the *Barre Times Argus*, to outsource printing to a firm that exclusively provides this service to forty other papers in the New England area. "But even if the flood hadn't occurred, we would have ended up outsourcing sooner, rather than later," says general manager Catherine Nelson. "A press is a depreciable asset. Plus, you have to calculate the payroll costs of manning the press forty hours a week. That is why every newspaper should be recalculating the costs versus the benefits of outsourcing at least once a year."

Additionally, Nelson points out that with the press gone, a newspaper can often "significantly reduce the amount of space you need for the remaining departments." With the press bay empty, the 24,000-square-foot newspaper building in Barre was recently sold to a developer, and the staff moved into a 3,000-square-foot office space nearby. Nelson anticipates that the *Rutland Herald* will also "downsize" to a smaller building over the next two years.

Publisher John Mitchell, who had worked out of the Barre newspaper office for forty years, admits to being "sad—especially when the developer told me he was bringing in the machinery to tear down the inside walls [of the Barre building] that my father paid an architect to design for the newspaper when he purchased the building in 1973. But we have bills to pay—including more than $100,000 in legal fees related to getting access to public records. We've fought that up to the Supreme Court because I've always believed that's the role of newspapers in democracy, and that's what our readers expect from us. We have to have the money to do the things our newsroom has been known for."

While outsourcing printing and distribution and downsizing office space are usually seamless to readers and advertisers, the next option that many publishers consider—decreasing the distribution footprint or the size of the paper—are not. "I am constantly trying to keep a balance between cutting product, cutting distribution, and cutting staff," says Bruce Kyse, publisher of the *Santa Rosa Press Democrat* from 2005 to 2013, who reduced overall staffing of the paper by almost half. He managed this by going to a collect press run, cutting distribution to outlying areas and reducing the size of the daily paper by eliminating features and sections from the print edition.

At first glance, reducing the size of the paper by moving certain features online would appear to save only a small amount of money and have the potential to unnecessarily antagonize loyal print readers, who suddenly feel like they are getting less. As a recent Pew Report noted, a third of those polled said they "had stopped turning to a news outlet because it no longer provided them with the news they were accustomed to getting."

However, as Kyse points out, if a community newspaper editor has a good handle on how readers' habits are changing, he may actually be able to save a significant amount. And as an added bonus, he may be able to entice print readers to sample the online edition, thereby building loyalty to the digital version as well. "I'm like most daily newspaper publishers" he says. "Almost half of my revenue comes from the Sunday paper. And I think the trend lines are clear—both in terms of readership trends and profitability of individual publishing days. So over the next decade, I think you'll see a lot of papers cutting back publication from seven days a week to the three, four, or five days a week that are profitable."

Kyse emphasizes the importance of reshaping readers' expectations during this time of change. "So when I think about eliminating features from the print edition," he says, "I'm trying to train my readers for that time in the not-too-distant future when the physical paper won't be produced and delivered on that day. I'm trying to build up the Sunday paper, adding features to that paper, even as I'm eliminating classifieds, for example, from the Monday paper and possibly even the Tuesday paper." In addition, the Santa Rosa paper has introduced new circulation packages. "Already more than 10 percent of our subscribers are getting the paper on a reduced schedule—like five times a week, instead of seven," says Kyse.

Many editors worry constantly about "alienating" current loyal readers of the print edition if they move any print features online—or even suggest in the print edition that there is additional original content available on the paper's website. But as discussed in chapter 2, even in rural and urban areas that are poorly wired, most readers of newspapers say their media consumption habits have changed dramatically in recent years—and that they are accessing the Internet much more frequently. Dozens of one-on-one interviews with subscribers to the print editions of community newspapers suggest this fear of alienating current readers may be overblown. Those longtime customers who read *only* the print edition told researchers that they like the routine of reading a physical paper. They are not inclined to drop their subscriptions, nor will they hold it against papers that begin offering new or richer content online.

Regardless of whether they decide to move certain print features online, editors need to constantly reassess what sort of news and information is valued and used by readers and then update content in both editions to reflect changing media preferences. Obituaries, for example, are the most-read feature after front page stories in many community newspapers. Many longtime print readers said they would be inclined to visit a newspaper's digital site to view a "memorial slide show" of a friend who has died. This suggests that community newspapers might be able to entice some longtime print readers to "cross over" and sample the digital edition if they carried expanded "multimedia" obituaries on their websites.

Editors of the *Wall Street Journal*, for example, were able to shed a significant legacy cost in 2006 by reducing the amount of newsprint devoted to daily stock listings while also creating a richer interactive online experience for readers, providing them with contextual and trending information as well as up-to-the-minute stock prices. Because the daily listings had been a standard feature of the paper since its founding in 1896, they had huge symbolic importance. But they had outlived their relevance and usefulness to readers, who could easily get more up-to-date stock prices online.

As the *Wall Street Journal* experience demonstrates, timely and interactive features are especially well suited to the digital edition of most community newspapers, and many loyal readers will actually appreciate the opportunity to engage more fully with a subject that interests them. The key is matching the content with the medium's capabilities and changing reader habits. Also, as Kyse points out, by moving content online and enticing readers to sample the information there, newspaper publishers can begin training readers and advertisers for what he and many others assume is inevitable: "daily" papers that are printed and distributed three, four, or five days a week instead of seven.

Nevertheless, calculating exactly when and how much to cut back production of the print edition requires Solomon-like wisdom stripped of emotional attachment since, literally and symbolically, the identity of most community newspapers is tied to the physical entity and not the more ephemeral digital one. The printed paper has often existed in many communities for a century or more and is viewed by both readers and advertisers as the official record of all that has occurred—from the historic to the mundane. There is a publishing rhythm that the entire community knows well. For customers, there is a sense of loss and a disruption of long-standing routines that consist of setting aside time in the ebb and flow of daily life to read the paper. Can a newspaper be a "daily" if it is only printed and distributed three days a week? How well is the newspaper serving the community and keeping citizens informed on the days it does not publish?

Having decided to cut publication days instead of reporters and editors, David Woronoff began examining the profitability of each of the three days that *The Pilot* was printed. "I looked at the feasibility of turning around long-standing trends," he says. "With the loss of real estate advertisements on Friday, I just didn't see a way to turn the profitability around on that issue any time soon." There was "some ego in my decision [to cut back publication from three days to two] since I had to announce to the community that we were having financial trouble." But he concedes that publishers of nondaily newspapers have a much easier decision than those of dailies. "I'm not sure it disrupts reader routines that much to drop from three times a week to two, or from twice a week to weekly. But if you are a daily, you are fundamentally changing the nature of the product you are producing."

As Santa Rosa's Kyse explains, most daily newspapers are profitable only three or four days a week based on the advertising they receive. Wednesday and Thursday profitability is usually driven by the grocery ads. Friday and Sunday profitability is the result of retail display advertisements, slick preprinted inserts with coupons, and some display classified ads. At many papers, this means the Sunday edition accounts for more than 50 percent of total advertising revenue.

In 2010 at the *Daily News*, McKeithan and then-owner Ashley "Brownie" Futrell wrestled with how to further reduce costs once they had outsourced printing and distribution of the paper. Several large daily papers—most notably the *Detroit News* and the *Detroit Free Press*—had recently decided to "follow the advertising dollars" and cut back to three-day-a-week home delivery of the paper. Like most daily newspapers, the *Daily News* was profitable only three days a week, but McKeithan and Futrell never considered that option because "it was too radical." They focused instead on the two least profitable days: Saturday and Monday.

"It was a reader-driven decision," says McKeithan. "Friday is typically a big news day—high school games, meetings, and events—so the Saturday edition usually has a lot of news of interest to our readers. Monday was a slow news day, and that's how we decided to eliminate print distribution on that day." Still, even after the decision had been made, Futrell, who had been publisher since 1975, agonized over it, wondering aloud "if we could still call ourselves a 'daily newspaper,'" says McKeithan. "It was a very difficult decision for him to make. He felt like he was changing his contract with the community."

And he was. In recent surveys conducted in various communities around the country, nothing caused loyal readers of the print edition more angst than the prospect of cutbacks in delivery of their paper. If this occurred, readers said they expected that the newspaper would compensate by adding local content to both the existing paper and the website. When he announced the cutback in publication from three days to two, Woronoff told readers that *The Pilot* would be adding eight to ten pages of local coverage to the Wednesday and Sunday issues and rolling out improvements to its website, including new video capabilities and more coverage of *both* national and local news and sports.

In contrast, the *New Orleans Times-Picayune*, in the first weeks after cutting back publication from seven to three days and laying off 100 employees, followed a different path that precipitated an uproar from its loyal print readers—and a competitive response from a newspaper in neighboring Baton Rouge. In the first four months after the conversion, the *Times-Picayune*'s website, nola.com, featured a much higher percentage of national wire stories on the days when the paper was not published, according to an analysis of content by topic and source. Initially, stories written by staff reporters that focused on local politics and public affairs were more than twice as likely to run in the print editions as on the website. However, four months out, the analysis found that the number of stories related to local politics and government had dropped by half in the print edition as well. "The website is still mysteriously frustrating for those who are interested in accessing the information we used to get in the *Times-Picayune*," Jed Horne, a former editor there who now works at an online investigative news site in New Orleans, told a *New York Times* reporter in the spring of 2013.

Heartened by the adverse reader reaction to the *Times-Picayune*'s cutback, the owner of the Baton Rouge paper decided to start publishing and distributing an edition in New Orleans. A year after announcing it would cut back to three days a week, Advance Publications, which owns the *Times-Picayune*, reversed course and returned to seven-days-a-week publication—printing and distributing a tabloid-sized paper on the other four days to supplement the broadsheet on Wednesday, Friday, and Sunday.

McKeithan "wishes we'd thought more about enhancing the Monday website" before dropping Monday publication of the *Washington Daily News* in 2010. "We added a lot of national stories and wire stories. But for the reader, the core of what we do is local news. I really wish we'd planned to have a special, expanded Monday Web edition. If we had, I think there would have been much less of a sense of loss—and more of a sense that we were going with the times." And that is perhaps the most important lesson that publishers of papers from the *Washington Daily News* to the *New Orleans Times-Picayune* can take from the experience of those who have attempted to shed legacy costs by cutting back on their printing and distribution expenses. Instead of simply pocketing the savings, they, like Santa Rosa's Kyse, need to stay focused on the future and look for ways to help current readers of the print edition embrace the digital edition as well as the print version.

During this time of transition from the print-only world to the digital era, newspaper publishers and editors need to know their readers. They need to remember what sort of stories customers expect to find in both the print and online editions. It's what attracted them to the newspaper to begin with and what keeps them loyal during a period of immense confusion and disruption of routines and reading habits. Or as Woronoff points out: "It's about remembering where we add value. Our local reporting and perspective on community issues and people is what sets us apart. That's true whether you're talking about the e-edition or the printed version."

Investing: Rethinking Staffing for a Cross-Platform Medium

Shedding legacy costs not only disrupts the "contract" that a newspaper has with its readers; it also permanently changes the paper's relationship with its employees. Publishers quickly realize this when they begin to look at the second-largest expense for most newspapers: the payroll. When dealing with staffing issues—especially in the news and advertising departments—shedding legacy costs is as much about transforming the culture of a company as it is about reducing costs. The dilemma then becomes how to best bring about the transformation.

There is the aggressive path, which involves laying off a significant number of employees associated with the legacy business in an attempt to "right-size" the company. Harvard Business School professor Clark Gilbert chose the aggressive course when, in 2009, he was named CEO of Deseret Management Corporation, owned by the Church of Jesus Christ of Latter-day Saints. Between 2008 and 2010, the 162-year-old *Deseret News* lost a third of its display advertising and more than 70 percent of its classified advertising revenue. To compensate, in 2010 Gilbert laid off almost half of the newsroom staff—fifty-seven full-time and twenty-eight part-time employees—in one fell swoop. In the "transformation age, you have to get a steep reduction in content cost," he explained. "You can't do everything. So I am getting out of anything I'm not best at."

While in recent years, many other metro papers have reduced staffing in the news department by a similar percentage, Gilbert believes the *Deseret News* "was able to get on with the transformation much quicker by doing one round of steep layoffs, up front and at the beginning. At other newspapers, the cuts have come have come over a period of several years—and maybe there's been three or four rounds of announced layoffs of 10 to 20 percent each time. By the second year, everybody is demoralized and just waiting for their number to come up. No one is focused on the transformation." In deciding which news and advertising employees he would retain with the *Deseret News*, Gilbert "looked for people who were very good at what they did, open to new ideas and willing to take feedback. You had to meet all three qualifications. You had to be good, but willing to learn a new way."

While many in the Salt Lake community, as well as the larger journalistic community, have worried that Gilbert is risking the venerable print franchise with this aggressive reduction of news staffing, Gilbert replies: "I feel a tremendous stewardship toward the *Deseret News*. I have a whole set of initiatives built around transforming it. But when you have revenues at 1950 levels, you've got to have a 1950s cost structure." He believes a significantly downsized print edition can survive, oriented around such "beats" as family and faith. "Based on the research we've done, I believe we can be a national newspaper—serving people around the country who care about these issues but aren't being served by other national newspapers, like the *New York Times*, for instance."

Still, he is hedging his bets by pursing a two-pronged strategy. At the same time he has been restructuring and repositioning the print newspaper, Gilbert has been creating and aggressively building a competing division within the company, Deseret Digital Media, which houses the legacy websites of both the *Deseret News* and the television and radio station KSL. This division, which has been growing revenues an average of 44 percent a year, now has 100 employees—and competes directly on the advertising revenue side with the print division.

"I have to manage a dual transformation," Gilbert says. "I have to lead both Transformation A—the *Deseret News*—and Transformation B of the Deseret Digital Media." Unlike Clay Christensen, his former Harvard Business School colleague and mentor and author of *The Innovator's Dilemma: When New Technologies Cause Great Firms to Fail* (1997), Gilbert does not "believe you have to destroy the legacy business in order to transform the business. That's my biggest break with Clay. Too many people have given up on print. I do believe you have to 'right-size' the legacy operation—and then you also have to set up an independent (and competing) digital unit. Failure to set up an independent unit [such as the Deseret Digital Media] guarantees failure." Currently, 25 percent of the revenues at Deseret Management Corporation come from the digital division, 35 percent come from print, and 40 percent come from broadcast, with the latter providing a significant financial cushion for the company as Gilbert manages "dual transformations" of the print and digital side.

Since most community newspapers do not also own broadcast operations—and therefore cannot rely on the sort of steady income stream that this division provides for Deseret—many publishers will not be able to follow the "dual transformation" model and will opt for an alternative approach. Instead of setting up an independent digital unit that competes with the legacy print business, they will attempt to transform the newspaper culture from inside out—from a print-only orientation into a cross-platform mindset. Adopting this more-conservative approach will inform how they then make choices about how to reduce payroll costs.

With newspapers repositioned as cross-platform mediums, the skills required of reporters, or advertising sales representatives, are very different from the ones needed in a print-only world. Successfully navigating this period of disruption and transition between print and online requires employees of community newspapers to be willing to acquire new skills and to "experiment" and change course when necessary. This means that, in addition to a financial analysis of printing and distribution costs, publishers who follow this alternative (less aggressive) strategy of shedding legacy costs need to do an "inventory" of their employees' current skills and knowledge. Next, they need to project what skills and knowledge are needed to produce editions across multiple platforms, including print, online, and mobile. And then they need to come up with a five-year plan for transforming the staff in both the newsroom and the advertising department.

Since 2009, managing editor Fabiola Pomareda and her staff of four reporters at the Spanish-language weekly *La Raza* have had to "learn how to do audio and video" when the paper implemented a five-step initiative that dictates how stories are written and posted: online first and print edition last, with different content in each iteration. Web versions, for instance, carry enhanced audio and video elements done by the reporters.

The advertising department offers a "360-degree solution" that allows businesses to purchase five different mediums, including the print and digital editions, mobile, and event sponsorship. *La Raza* publisher Jimena Catarivas has to understand "what drives the purchase decision" of the smallest local advertiser—the tailor or lawyer—as well as the large national advertiser—the consumer-product company. Both Pomareda and Catarivas are committed "lifelong learners," and both have learned to be flexible, adjusting both news and advertising strategies based on feedback they get from readers and advertisers.

That is the financial consideration that publishers need to constantly weigh as they consider ways to shed legacy costs and realign personnel:

Where can our community newspaper add value and enhance the experience of both our readers and our advertisers? That is where they need to invest while reducing costs in other areas. For the most part, "the industry has been very ingenious about cutting costs," says Rick Edmonds, media business analyst at the Poynter Institute. "But I worry that we are reaching a tipping point—especially when we're raising circulation prices. We're playing with fire if we are not providing more news."

Woronoff at the independently owned *Pilot* calculated where his newspaper could add the most value and concluded it was in the creation and aggregation of content and not in the distribution of content, where he trimmed significant costs. But he is also simultaneously pursuing transformational change in the newsroom. When his longtime editor retired, he hired a digitally experienced replacement, realizing that *The Pilot* needed reporters and editors who "are comfortable in both worlds"—print and digital. "While I don't foresee the print edition disappearing any time soon," he says, "I have to assume the digital edition will play an increasingly important role in the delivery of community news."

Similarly, the *Rutland Herald* recently eliminated two positions in the newsroom—the chief photographer and a sports editing position—but is adding four new positions, including two reporters to the twenty-one-person newsroom staff. In addition, general manager Catherine Nelson has reorganized and consolidated the dispatch and design departments so that the consolidated department of four people now does the layout for both news and advertising. "You want the editors focused on editing and not on layout. And you want the reporters focused on creating content for every platform," she says.

As both Woronoff and Nelson point out, reporters and editors in the cross-platform era need to be able to find new digital opportunities for existing print content and then present that digital content so that it engages readers, using video and audio to tell a compelling story. They also need to understand the newspaper's target audiences and know how to use new digital tools—such as mobile and social networking—to reach potential readers and reinforce loyalty with current readers.

UNC–Chapel Hill professor Ryan Thornburg—who worked previously as a digital editor at the *Washington Post*, the *Congressional Quarterly*, and *U.S. News and World Report*—has consulted with dozens of news organizations in recent years, helping journalists adjust to a new world. First, he says, whenever there is a vacancy, editors of community newspapers "want to hire the right new people—reporters who can mine data, young people with an improvisational ability who automatically say 'yes and.' But, these new hires need to know more than the new technology. They need to respect and manage the community connections that the paper has built up over decades." That, he says, is why editors need to also make sure they do everything possible to bring along the stalwarts on the news staff—"the historians," as he calls them. He has found that "a lot of these people are opposed to the vocabulary but not to what needs to be done. In many ways, they're already doing it for the print. They just need to think about how they extend it and enhance it for the digital edition."

Thornburg advises editors to take "reporters resisting the transition out to lunch and try to get them to remember why they went into the business. Help them find the excitement and passion they had on the first day and not see the future as a threat." If they can't be excited, he concludes, "they need to find another job" because in most newsrooms, editors simply cannot afford to have reporters who can only do print.

Publishers need to take a similarly unemotional look at their advertising sales staff, says Jed Williams, director of consulting at BIA/Kelsey, who has advised numerous publishers of news organizations, ranging from AOL to the *Deseret News*, on how to incorporate digital into their legacy operations. "Spurring long-term growth requires more than mere sales change," he says. "It requires full-on sales transformation. Ultimately, it's about having the right people on the bus." Newspaper sales representatives, he says, need to be able to advise advertisers on how to use various mediums—print, digital, and mobile—to best advantage. They must know how to calculate and convey to the advertiser the "true" value (or return on investment) of using more than one platform. In addition, they need to understand the newspaper's target audiences and know how to design ads that engage readers. Publishers must "not only be willing to hire sellers that understand digital, but they must also train and incentivize appropriately to spur on their success," says Williams. "Without training, sellers walk into an unprecedented competitive battlefield for local advertising dollars with little armor. Without reward, many will fall back on what they know: selling high-margin legacy products that have paid the bill—but won't much longer."

As Mark Palmer, publisher of Tennessee's *Columbia Daily Herald*, points out, newspapers need to consider how to "set advertising salespeople up for success, in order to change behavior." This involves everything from revamping the rate card and the incentive plan to providing structured training (all of which will be discussed in more detail in chapter 7).

In addition, Catherine Nelson says, newspapers need to get "the right person" to lead the transformation in both the news and advertising departments. The *Rutland Herald* has recently hired a new editor and a new vice president of sales and marketing. Rob Mitchell, son of John and the third generation in his family to assume the title of editor, has spent the last decade or so "learning the ropes" at various community newspapers in California and serving as director of digital media and state editor at the *Rutland Herald*. The paper's new advertising director is coming from outside the company because, explains Nelson, "we've redone the rate card so that it stresses cross-platform sales, and we've invested in extensive training. And while more than half the ad staff is moving in the right direction, we need to accelerate the pace. But the biggest challenge we face is the one most newspapers face. The first response to a new program is often: 'We tried it several years ago and it didn't work.' Sometimes you need someone with an outside experience who has done it differently and successfully and will approach the challenge differently."

The "business of producing a good newspaper has always been about getting the right people in the right job," says John Mitchell, owner of the *Herald*. "But it's even more critical now when the very survival of a newspaper is at stake." As Yale's Richard Foster stresses, "Shedding legacy costs is about freeing up funds to invest in your future." Both divesting and investing—that is the only way for publishers of community newspapers to stay on top of creative destruction and navigate the disruption that is occurring in the market.

The dual transformation that Clark Gilbert is attempting with the Deseret media group is very different from the strategies that the publishers of the *Rutland Herald*, *The Pilot*, and *La Raza* are pursuing. Only time will tell whether all four publishers have placed their bets correctly for the communities that their papers serve. But all have understood the imperative for community newspapers to move aggressively in reducing their costs during this time of disruption, uncertainty, and transition.

"I've been doing this for a long time," says Nelson, who has more than three decades of experience managing newspapers. "And often people come up to me and say, 'Your industry is dying.' And I respond, 'For too long, our industry was too slow and too boring. All that has changed. It's a challenging time, but it's also a very creative time, and that makes it an exciting and interesting time for people who are open to new ideas, believe in the value of newspapers, and want to help the industry solve problems and evolve.'"

The Whiteville Experience Tackling the Tough Issues

The realization that he needed to "get serious" about reducing costs associated with the print edition came gradually to Les High. "It took at least two years for me to understand what the full scope of 'shedding legacy costs' really involved," he says. He credits his sister, Stuart, who had joined the paper in fall 2010 as director of special projects, with finally "connecting the dots" for him and his father, Jim, and creating a sense of urgency. As Les readily concedes, when "the recession first hit" in 2008, his primary concern had been retaining subscribers to the print edition—not building readership of whiteville.com. As revenues from classified advertising plummeted, the *News Reporter* had relied increasingly on the preprint insert business to fill the gap, which would be in jeopardy if the circulation declined significantly below 10,000.

Although the website was almost twelve years old at that time, it had largely been treated by reporters in the newsroom as the "baby" of its founder, staff photographer Mark Gilcrest, who singlehandedly created and posted the content for the site. Surveys conducted in the spring of 2010 found that readers of both the print edition and whiteville.com were exceptionally loyal. The results were reassuring—and also eye-opening, especially as it concerned whiteville.com.

Half of the readers of the website were also subscribers to the print edition, who viewed the website as complementary to—and not competitive with—the print edition. They expected to find material on the website that was not in the print edition, such as slide shows and videos of the Friday night football games. On the other hand, those who read only the print edition said they liked the routine of holding the physical paper in their hands. They were not inclined to drop their subscriptions, nor would they hold it against the *News Reporter* if the paper began offering more online content that was not in the print edition as long as the physical version continued to carry the "news and information I care about."

These findings prompted Les to realize that, in the eyes of many readers, the website was rapidly becoming an "equal sibling" with the print edition. It also prompted him to begin "thinking about how we could create new content" that could run in both the print and online editions and increase readership of both. But there was also a disconcerting trend in the reader surveys that, at first, escaped Les's notice. The subscribers who read both the print and online editions were, on average, twenty years younger than those who read only the print edition. The average age of print-only readers was sixty.

Stuart was the first to understand the significance of that difference. Shortly after she began working at the *News Reporter*, she noticed a publishing-day ritual that puzzled her. On the Mondays and Thursdays that the paper was published, the carriers would come into the pressroom, pick up a paper, and flip immediately to the page where the obituaries were printed. "After watching this for several weeks, I suddenly realized they were checking to see if any of their customers had died," she said. She relayed this insight to her brother. "I realized that even if we retained every loyal print customer we currently had, the circulation would gradually decline," says Les, "because, as our loyal print readers age, they aren't being replaced by younger ones."

Faced with an inevitable long-term decline in print circulation, Les began to consider how he might reduce costs associated with the print edition and use the savings to invest in expanding content in the online edition and other areas, such as a local magazine. He looked first to see if he could shed legacy costs associated with the actual printing and distribution of the physical paper. Outsourcing was not an option. In fact, the *News Reporter* had benefited significantly in recent years as other area businesses—including two newspapers—had outsourced their printing to the Whiteville paper. Roughly 20 percent of the *News Reporter*'s total revenues came from these printing contracts. He worried about moving regular print features online: "I don't want to do anything to alienate my loyal print readers. For the money saved, it is safer to just continue to give them the same paper."

That meant the only way Les could shed significant printing and distribution costs was to cut back publication of the *News Reporter* from twice to once weekly. "That was drastic and would disrupt loyal reader habits," he says. "So I only want to do that as a last resort—if it meant that we can stay profitable and live to publish another day." A quick back-of-the-envelope calculation convinced him that he would need to consider this "last resort" if the *News Reporter* "lost the preprint insert business or if we lost several of the outside printing contracts we currently have. Either of those two events would be our tipping point [into unprofitability]."

With a clear understanding of what levers he could—and could not—pull in the printing and distribution area, Les then turned his attention to the second-biggest expense: payroll. Here, he ran straight up against the same personnel issues many small, family-owned businesses encounter, including those involving all manner of benefits.

Through his dedicated stewardship, Les's father, Jim, had turned around the financial fortunes of the *News Reporter* in the 1960s. Jim felt the paper needed to "set an example for the community in how we treat loyal employees." This meant that, among other things, the *News Reporter* still paid 100 percent of the health-insurance premiums for its employees. "When you cast your eye on payroll, you begin to realize how we see ourselves in the community," says Stuart.

Many on the *News Reporter* staff had joined after graduating from college or high school and were considered "pillars of the community"—including advertising director Mickey Greer, who had signed on in 1980 after completing a business degree at Wake Forest University; and Bob High, the legendary chain-smoking crime reporter who had first signed on in 1953, right after the paper had won the Pulitzer Prize. After reporting stints in various cities, including Houston, he rejoined the paper in 1987. Bob, who looked like he was straight out of central casting, was recognized as the "historian of record" for the county. He was also known to be a mean story machine, knocking out as many as forty deadline crime articles on Monday morning for that day's paper.

Both Stuart and Les considered it essential that "stalwarts" such as Greer and High remained with the paper "since their history and knowledge were invaluable. They were the face of the newspaper in the community. And they had been there for Dad and the paper." But as the newspaper had begun to add content to both the print and online editions—creating community pages and selling "sponsorships" of the pages to local merchants—Stuart had also realized that "we need to develop a new mindset and different skills." So, working closely with UNC, she and Les began offering and attending training sessions for reporters and the advertising sales staff at the paper on Friday afternoons, "helping them and us learn how to think and act differently." They also made it a point to involve both Greer and Bob High in their discussions about the future of the newspaper and seek their opinions and input often.

But even with such training, Stuart realized, "there was a capacity issue. Most people were working flat out doing content for both editions. We also needed some new hires—people who didn't have to be retrained to think differently, because when we get overloaded, we naturally try to go back to what makes us comfortable, which is to focus on the print edition only." As she discussed her concerns with her brother, they realized that they needed to rethink everything, including staffing in every department. Les realized that this was going to be a difficult transition for his father, since it went to the heart of the legacy he felt he had created—that of treating the employees of the *News Reporter* as lifelong members of the family.

Les began signaling that his own attitude had changed by modeling the behavior he wanted from reporters, posting every story written for the print edition simultaneously on the website. In doing so, he wanted to signal that "everyone at the paper needs to own the digital edition. The days of 'letting Mark handle it' were over."

Realizing that the "day when we would be totally digital might be much closer than I had imagined just two years before," Les also sought the counsel of another experienced editor and publisher of community newspapers who could help him totally rethink his cost structure and assess the skills his employees would need to transition from a primarily print orientation to a cross-platform mentality. "Could I go down two people in production today and use the money to hire new reporters who knew how to produce news stories for both editions?" he wondered. "The sports editor is nearing retirement. How do I look five years out and envision what sort of replacement I should be looking for?"

Considering how to reduce the legacy costs associated with the *News Reporter* required Les to put aside emotional attachments. Rather than investing in the "goose that laid the golden egg"—his natural inclination—he was forced to consider how best to divest and focus instead on channeling limited resources into the "gosling" website, which may or may not produce another golden egg. Added to that was his realization that he would most likely be forced to make tough personnel decisions about loyal employees.

But until the moment that he found himself "asking the tough questions," Les admits he had not really "absorbed what was at risk if we didn't reduce costs: all that the *News Reporter* stood for over the last three quarters of a century that my family had owned it. Everything we wanted to do couldn't be additive. We had to cut back somewhere. Painful as it was, that was the reality."

CHAPTER SIX

How to Build Vibrant Community
on Many Platforms

What do readers of community newspapers want? They say they want "local news." But what exactly does that mean in a digital era? Is "local" a geographic definition? Or does it refer to a set of "special interests and affiliations" residents of a community share with each other?

And how should newspapers respond? Should they go "hyperlocal" and provide information that readers can access on a microscopic level, such as a city block? Provide context and analysis to breaking news or policy issues that affect a region? Or focus on covering the special interests and passions of people in the community, such as high school sports or religion or family values?

The journalistic decisions about how to build and nurture community that newspaper editors and publishers face are not without precedent. In response to the introduction of television, the most successful magazines in the latter half of the twentieth century turned away from a strategy of providing "general interest" news and information and instead pursued a "niche" strategy, focusing on serving "communities" with specialized interests—sports, entertainment, family, religion, or business, for example.

But most community newspapers cannot simply mimic the magazine strategy and "go niche" without abandoning their historic mission of helping people in geographic proximity to one another understand how their actions affect others and how they can band together to influence public policy and improve the quality of life for all residents in the area. Therefore, in the thirteen years that he has been publisher of the *Fayetteville Observer*, Charles Broadwell says he has come to view "community as a three-layer cake." First, "there's the city of Fayetteville and the longtime residents who care about *everything and everybody* local. Next, there's the [ten-county] Cape Fear region, which is tied to Fayetteville as an economic hub—so we try to provide coverage of regional issues and trends. And then there is Fort Bragg. We try to create a sense of 'home' for the 50,000 soldiers and their families, and help them connect with the community, to each other, and to their mission."

The 200-year-old *Observer*—an early Web pioneer, establishing fayobserver.com in 1995—was also one of the first newspapers to establish a vibrant online community of readers built around a special interest and shared affiliation: Fort Bragg. From the early 2000s through 2009, this "community page"—called "Military Life" and aimed at the "military moms" left behind when their spouses were deployed in Iraq or Afghanistan—often attracted as many unique daily visitors as the fayobserver.com home page. As the two wars have drawn down and "Facebook has come on big," the *Observer* has "pulled back somewhat" on military moms and is now focused on creating a community experience—with a magazine and a website—for officers and their families, many of whom have transferred into the area since 2011 as two large commands previously based in Georgia have been consolidated at Fort Bragg. In creating communities, either those built around geography or special affinities and affiliations, "you have to go where you can add value," says Broadwell, balancing the community's "needs" with the limited resources many newsrooms face.

Across the continent, in California's wine country, the *Santa Rosa Press Democrat* has also taken a multilayered view of community. In the mid-1990s, Bruce Kyse, who was then the executive editor of the *Press Democrat*, oversaw the rollout of the first newspaper website for wine consumers, WineToday.com. Since he became publisher of the *Press Democrat* in 2006 after a stint in "corporate" with the newspaper's owners, the New York Times Company, Kyse has dealt with "business falling off the cliff" and juggled transitions among three different owners. (The New York Times Company sold the *Press Democrat* to the Halifax group in early 2012, which, in turn, sold it to a group of local investors less than a year later.)

But even as he has cut staffing levels almost in half, Kyse has funneled limited newsroom resources toward creating a number of digital communities focused on readers' special interests and passions. The paper has established eleven separate sites—in addition to pressdemocrat.com—for readers who might have a special interest in areas such as business, entertainment, prep sports, professional football, parenting, very local neighborhood news, or civic affairs. Most of the sites can be accessed directly or off the home page of pressdemocrat.com. Content on sites such as SantaRosaMom.com is reader generated. Other material, such as the stories on WatchSonomaCounty.com or 707Entertainment.com, are produced by the paper's reporters.

"Unfortunately, with revenues down, we have to live with reduced staffing," says Kyse. "So in the newsroom, with these digital communities, we have to stay focused on where we can create value for our readers, and that is on producing products—both in print and digital—that they can use and engage with. This then attracts advertisers to those products."

A smaller staff, however, should not change the quality or depth of the paper's news reporting. "By the same token, we need to continue to aggressively and fairly report on public-policy issues that will affect the quality of life in the community going forward," Kyse continues. "The new owners live here and care about what is happening in the community. But residents here also are wondering what sort of influence they may have since this new group of investors includes a state lobbyist and a developer. So that means we have to keep the same sort of balance and perspective in our coverage of issues as before, devoting as much attention to these policy issues as we did in the past, and then be very transparent about how our editorial decisions are made. It is about engaging the readers and retaining trust across all these products."

As both Kyse and Broadwell suggest, editors face two challenges as they attempt to build vibrant community across multiple platforms. In the case of nurturing geographic identity, they need to provide balanced *context* to stories, not only reporting about events but also explaining why readers should care about a trend, issue, or policy even when it is not always apparent that they should. In the case of nurturing communities built around special interests, they need to *connect* readers with the content, with each other, and with the paper around passions and interests they share.

This chapter explores how editors can tap into a new, expansive notion of "community," taking advantage of the tools available—including digital applications, mobile, and social media—so that the newspapers can still be the "glue that binds" together residents in a community, regardless of their different interests, passions, and affiliations.

While building vibrant community across multiple platforms is but one of the three strategies that newspapers need to pursue in order to thrive in the digital age, it is a *critical* link between the other two—those of shedding legacy costs associated with the print era and pursuing new revenue. Funds freed up from shedding legacy costs need to be funneled into building vibrant communities of readers across multiple platforms so that newspapers are then able to aggressively and profitably pursue new revenue opportunities with advertisers who want to reach an engaged audience. By building vibrant community based on geography as well as special interests, newspapers ensure their continued relevance to both readers and advertisers during this period of transition and disruption.

Building Loyalty, Building Community

"Build traffic." That's the advice that most consultants give editors seeking to boost readership of their newspaper's website—and with good reason, since the number of visitors to many community newspaper websites still lags behind print circulation. But simply focusing on the number of "page hits" or "unique visitors" to a website does not ensure that a newspaper is actually building a vibrant community of readers online. Nor does it necessarily allow a newspaper to play to its journalistic strengths of providing unique content that can engage readers at first glance and then keep them coming back for more.

While readers' media habits and preferences are changing dramatically, many continue to express strong loyalty to their community newspaper. And that is very good news for newspapers as they consider how to build strong community in the digital era. Research over the last two decades has determined that there is a strong correlation between the loyalty of customers and the future profitability of a company. There are several reasons for this. Loyal readers of newspapers can increase visits to a site because they are likely to "recommend" it to friends. A "recommendation" or a "like" is an especially powerful marketing tool in an era of social media, where links or comments on stories can be easily shared and "go viral," introducing a new generation to a newspaper's site.

Loyal readers are also more engaged with the news and information on a site, making them much more attentive and receptive to advertising that appears adjacent to it. This reader engagement allows savvy publishers to increase their digital rates based on the extra value they are delivering to advertisers versus other digital competitors. In short, loyal customers can usually be counted on to sell more (by recommending content to friends), buy more (come back more frequently), and pay more (attach a higher value to the content). So for most community newspapers, the key to future success is to focus not on building "traffic" but instead on building loyalty, which leads to greater reader engagement.

Fortunately, determining the loyalty of a reader is a relatively simple matter, thanks to Fred Reichheld, a longtime partner at the consulting firm Bain & Company. He determined that one question could provide valuable insight into the strength of an individual customer's loyalty for affordable products such as a newspaper. That key question is: on a scale of 1 to 10, with 10 being highest, would you recommend this newspaper to a friend? To account for grade inflation, Reichheld set a high bar for loyalty. Only those customers who answered 9 or 10 were classified as loyal. Those answering 7 or 8 were viewed as "fence-sitters" in danger of defecting to another product but also potential converts. Those who answered 6 or lower were defined as "detractors" because they might hurt sales by bad-mouthing a product.

This reader-loyalty gauge was tested at several large newspapers in the late 1990s and early 2000s. Results revealed, not surprisingly, that readers of both the *New York Times* and the *Wall Street Journal* were very loyal to their papers and frequently "recommended" stories in the paper to their friends and colleagues, which in turn cultivated a new generation of readers. While Reichheld's loyalty test does not produce the sort of statistical accuracy that many pure researchers strive for, it does provide a very accurate trending report and allows editors to construct a useful profile of their loyal readers and their interests.

Using this question—as well as other questions that sought to determine what sorts of "local news" readers valued—research conducted in more than a half dozen markets found very strong loyalty to *both* the print and online editions of most community newspapers. In fact, reader loyalty to some small community newspapers, such as Whiteville's century-old *News Reporter*, often exceeded the strong reader loyalty that national newspapers like the *New York Times* enjoyed.

In most communities, there were three types of "loyal" newspaper readers: those who read only the print edition, those who consumed their news by visiting the digital site exclusively, and those who toggled between the print and online platforms. More than half of the readers of the online edition were also frequent readers of the print edition—and they were the most loyal. They expected the online site to "complement" or "add to" coverage in the print edition and to provide "more up-to-date" news, as well as material not in print, including transcripts of county commissioner meetings; photo slide shows of the Friday night football game; charts and graphs illustrating a community's progress over time; and lists of births, garage sales, crime, real estate transactions, and other local events. ("I like to be able to turn to my husband and say, 'Can you believe the Smiths' house sold for that?'" said one reader.) Furthermore, they expected their newspaper sites to be dynamic and interactive so that they could communicate with the editors—and other readers—on a routine basis.

The loyalty of those who read only the print edition was also very strong, though for a very different reason. Their weekly or daily routine was built around reading the paper, which they considered "a ticket to community membership." They read the newspaper cover to cover, attempting to scan all the photos and headlines. The good news: they liked the routine of reading a physical paper and volunteered that they were unlikely to drop their subscriptions as long as the print edition continued to carry the sorts of news and information they had read over the years. The bad news: they tended to be much older than online readers, and as they age, they are not being replaced by younger readers, hence the declining circulation of most print editions.

The loyalty of online-only readers of community newspapers, while strong in most markets, was the weakest of the three. Typically, online-only readers reported that they visited the site to learn about breaking news or to "catch up" on stories or reader-participation contests they had "heard about" from someone else—a neighbor, friend, or office colleague. If they happened to discover another story that caught their attention, they would tarry on the site and perhaps visit it again. Therefore, it is very important that newspaper editors understand what types of stories will attract a new generation of readers while reinforcing the loyalty of current readers.

Our research found that loyalty to a community newspaper strongly correlates with whether or not readers agree with this statement: "This newspaper is the most credible and comprehensive source of news and information that I care about." If the readers did not "care about" the news provided, they did not engage with the content. Therefore, if editors understand what topics current and potential readers "care about," they can focus on becoming the "most credible and comprehensive source of news and information" about those particular subjects. By building out content in these areas in both the print and online mediums, newspapers could enhance the loyalty of current readers of both editions and maybe even entice loyalists who currently read only the print edition to sample content on the digital version. In addition, by grouping content about these topics on a "community page" in the digital edition, newspapers could potentially attract a new generation of loyal readers who consume only the online version.

Probed as to what sorts of news and information they "cared about," readers volunteered that they had an insatiable appetite for all sorts of community news. This included stories on "quality of life" issues in a community, such as student scores on standardized tests or employment trends. But it could also include a calendar of "family-friendly" events, recipes contributed by some of the community's better-known cooks, or simply photos of a neighbor's child.

In other words, readers of both the print and online editions cared about issues related to the geographic community where they resided *and* to their own special interests. These other "communities" that they "cared about" could be built around affiliations with the local church, civic club, or some other association, such as the *Fayetteville Observer*'s community of "military moms." Many of these communities were also centered on shared affinities, passions, and interests, such as prep sports, religion, cooking, parenting, or local politics. Many readers indicated they had several overlapping "local" passions and "belonged" to several informal "communities of special interest."

In her book *Can Journalism Be Saved? Rediscovering America's Appetite for News* (2010), Northwestern University communication professor Rachel Davis Mersey notes that "people use media to craft their identities and the media reinforce people's identities. . . . The takeaway is that the best media create what we can call an identity experience." This "social identity theory," as it is known, helps explain why loyalty is so important in the digital era (when we tend to form social networks of people who have our same "likes") and why editors need to reevaluate how they cover and present "community" news in the online realm.

Therefore, community newspaper editors in the twenty-first century need to craft an editorial strategy that allows them to both go "broad" (take an "expansive" view of what is "local news") and go "deep" on the topics that engender a "sense of belonging" to smaller subsets of communities built around affiliations and affinities. Like the *Santa Rosa Press Democrat* and the *Fayetteville Observer*, most community newspapers in the digital age need to be both a "general interest" publication that reports on the top stories of interest to people who reside in a certain geographic area and a "special-interest" publication that reports on the topics that engender the most passion, loyalty, and engagement among the various subgroups of people who inhabit the larger, geographically defined community. The savviest editors will figure out how to reinforce the "ties that bind" between these smaller "communities of special interests" and the larger community—defined by geography—so that the newspaper can continue its historic role of informing citizens about important public-policy issues that affect the quality of life of all residents in a neighborhood or region.

Building Geographic Community

There are two ways for editors to think about nurturing a sense of geographic community among their readers. They can go "hyperlocal," providing news on the city-block or neighborhood level. Or they can attempt to give a "bird's-eye view" of the community, providing analysis of and context to the underlying political, economic, and social trends that may not be visible at the street level.

Much editorial attention over the last decade has been focused on how to improve "hyperlocal" coverage since readers of community newspapers often volunteer that they "care about" what is happening in their own backyard (to their family members and neighbors). "I feel like my local newspaper covers everything in this community—every birth, death, and leaf that falls," said one reader of a rural newspaper in West Virginia. "I love seeing pictures of people I know and reading about them."

Readers should also "care about" people they don't know who live in the same geographic vicinity, but often they don't realize that they should. Stanford University economist James Hamilton calls this tendency one of "rational ignorance." Readers choose not to read stories about public-policy issues, for example, because they believe the outcome does not affect them or that they are powerless to influence the decision making. They fail to see the interrelationships of residents in a community to one another and how the consequences of an action can affect everyone in the geographic community, either directly or indirectly.

The best community newspapers have historically provided both types of local news, even if their readers did not volunteer that they "care about" stories that focused on broad political, social, or economic trends. The Spanish-language weekly *La Raza*, for example, covers what is happening in the many Chicago communities and neighborhoods where Latino immigrants live, as well as big policy issues, such as immigration and health-care reform, that affect the quality of life of the entire city. For two centuries, "newspapers have been a 'mass' medium covering issues that affected a broad swath of people, with seemingly dissimilar interests, in a geographically defined area," says media historian Donald Shaw. "It is very important that newspapers continue to provide that unique journalistic perspective—or they lose the ability to inform about issues that ultimately affect the quality of life in a community."

This type of journalism—one that explores and analyzes issues that affect and influence a geographically defined community—is what the Pulitzer Prize–winning author Alex Jones at Harvard University refers to as the "food supply of democracy." Economists call such journalism a "public good" because it is a "product" that benefits everyone in a community, since informed citizens help craft better policies. Yet unlike national defense or street lighting, for example—which citizens typically pay for through taxes—readers have not paid much at all for this public good. The economic reality of newspapering during the twentieth century is that advertisers, who provided the majority of revenues, indirectly funded the news operation and "agenda-setting" public-affairs journalism.

With newspaper advertising revenue declining dramatically—and readers splintering virtually into communities of special interests—it is imperative that newspapers in the digital age get readers to value "public-affairs journalism." Unfortunately, many of the public-affairs stories in community newspapers are "meeting stories," describing the "most important" issues discussed and voted on—at a town council meeting, for example. The stories are not written to help individual readers understand why they should "care about" a policy or how it affects them personally. As a result, readers say that the front pages of most newspapers are "unfriendly" and don't have stories "that interest me personally."

Magdalena Pantelis—editor and founder of informancjeusa.com, a Web-based news organization that focuses on U.S.-centric issues that affect Polish immigrants—is tackling this issue head-on in her new role as general manager of the 105-year-old *Polish Daily News*. "Unfortunately, many people in the Polish community in Chicago still care more about what's happening in Poland than issues that are occurring here in the city or the state or the country that affect them personally," she says. "For example, we recently did a story on sequestration, which has huge implications for people here—and it got only 150 hits" on the newspaper's website. Her formula for turning this around is based on her years as a television reporter in Poland and Chicago and, more recently, her experience at informancjeusa.com, which typically received 3,000 hits a day and is now merged with the *Daily News*. "You have to focus on key words—in the headline and first sentences of the story—that grab people's attention. You have to bring it down to a personal level and actually say, 'This is why you should care it affects your pocketbook or your health or your legal status.'"

Many editors and reporters on traditional mainstream newspapers, though, are so disconnected from the many "subcommunities" within the larger community that they are unable to even discern what issues and trends people should care about, says publisher Dave Neill. "In most communities there are invisible communities. In Naples, for example, when I arrived, the Hispanic and Haitian communities were largely ignored in our news pages—and we had zero relationship with the religious community. Connecting with these communities involved a concerted effort of reaching out, asking people in these communities to tell you what they cared about, building up trust and then reserving space for people who had never had a voice. That is what helped [us] from both an editorial and business standpoint [to] reinvent [the *Daily News*]." But while a focus on "key word" tagging and "reaching out" to neglected communities is important, editors and reporters at community newspapers also need to provide context to "dull" policy discussions by analyzing data and trends—explaining to readers their interrelationships with other residents in a community "who might seem unrelated to us—but really aren't."

"What binds southeastern North Carolina?" publisher Charles Broadwell asked in a recent column in the *Fayetteville Observer*. "Think of our highways, our history, our shared economic future. And our rivers, from the Cape Fear on down." What binds seemingly unrelated residents of a region together? The physical infrastructure, its shared political and social history, its economy, and its environmental ecosystem, which today's citizens share and must pass on to tomorrow's generations. "A good newspaper is an anchor in the community," says Harvard's Ron Heifetz, because its journalists understand their role in keeping track of the underlying trends that define not only a community's past but also its future.

Historically, data analysis of trends has been one of the more expensive and time-consuming reporting tasks. Fortunately, there is more information available than ever before for journalists who know where to look and a growing number of digital applications that help them analyze the data and then create compelling public-policy stories—on both the hyperlocal and regional level—that readers "care about." One such tool with promise is OpenBlock, a computer program that, when connected to the Internet, takes large sets of government data and displays it as a map and timeline that any reader in any geographically defined area—such as a city block or a zip code—can use to find individually relevant news. Located on a newspaper's website, OpenBlock can be an easily accessible data dashboard for readers, allowing them to search or browse various types of important and interesting public records—such as arrest reports, school-performance data, new business incorporations, real estate transactions, building permits, and restaurant inspections.

But just as important, OpenBlock and similar digital applications can become the seed from which many types of contextual and analytical trend stories sprout, providing reporters and editors with a dashboard that allows them to mine digital public records for the kinds of news stories that might not be readily apparent. Each week or month, the newspaper can feature proprietary trend stories that originate from analysis of the data. Once a quarter or once a year, the newspaper can set the agenda for debate of public-policy issues by hosting a conference of local and regional officials to discuss broad quality-of-life issues such as economic growth, health care, safety, and education.

"By itself, displaying public records on a map won't rebuild a newspaper's house and create local 'news' that readers automatically care about," says Ryan Thornburg, former digital editor at the *Washington Post* and now a UNC–Chapel Hill professor who received a grant to explore whether OpenBlock could be streamlined and used by both readers and reporters of community newspapers, large and small. "But reporters and editors can take the data and dig deeper than the busy reader has time to do and provide more context than a computer algorithm is able." In the process, newspapers help readers understand *why* they should "care about" this particular trend, what it means to them personally and to others in the community in which they live.

As Al Cross at the Kentucky-based Institute for Rural Journalism and Community Issues points out: "It is all about a mindset among editors. Most readers of community newspapers don't read a big metro daily. The only regional and national news they're getting is from television—and that's mostly useless—about breaking news elsewhere. In this interconnected world, you just can't live in a world that stops at the county line. Editors need to help citizens be part of the larger polities of the state and the nation."

Connecting residents of rural communities and inner-city neighborhoods with the larger geographic community in which they reside is especially important, says Mary Kay McFarland, director of West Virginia Uncovered, an organization of roughly three dozen community papers in that state. "West Virginia has one of the lowest broadband penetration rates in the country. And with the terrain in this state, it's pretty easy to stay down in the valley and never know what's happening on the other side of the mountain," she says. One of McFarland's main goals is to help editors and reporters learn how to use the digital tools available to them so "they can mine the data, do the reporting, and tell compelling stories. With the low broadband rate here, most newspaper reporters have much better access to the Internet than their readers. So they need to be constantly thinking about how to tap into the information that's available to them and then make it accessible for readers."

Video is an especially effective medium for promoting or summarizing longer "take-out stories" in the print edition or for "reaching and engaging a younger audience," says the West Virginia University professor. "And they [younger readers] are the very ones carrying mobile phones and likely to forward the video on. So in connecting readers with important issues, editors need to think about using all mediums to best advantage."

At the *Rutland Herald*, editor Rob Mitchell is using an application he developed that allows readers to take "a photo with your mobile phone of things in your community that need fixing—such as a crack in a sidewalk or a dangerous pothole." Readers then digitally tag the location and post this on a map of the city housed on the paper's website. "It is both a form of crowd-sourcing and using the paper as a platform for solving community issues and bringing these issues to the attention of a public servant who can solve the problem," he says.

From applications such as OpenBlock to video, the Internet has provided community newspapers with a host of new tools that reporters and editors can use to rethink the way they tell a compelling story and build geographic community across multiple platforms. In an age when we can connect virtually with people on the far side of the globe, the historic role of community newspapers—of explaining how we are still connected politically, economically, and socially to neighbors we know and those we don't—is still as important as ever. Therefore, the best community newspapers will embrace both imperatives, going hyperlocal while also providing readers with context and analysis of the important trends in a geographically defined community. As they consider how to use the digital tools to reinvent public-affairs reporting, newspaper editors and reporters, says Thornburg, "should be aiming to help individuals solve the

Using Digital Tools to Enhance Public-Affairs Reporting

Ryan Thornburg has worked as a digital editor at the *Washington Post*, the *Congressional Quarterly*, and *U.S. News and World Report*. As a UNC professor, his primary focus is on using new digital tools to improve the quality of public-affairs reporting in news organizations. In 2012 he was awarded a Knight News Challenge grant to see if a data-mapping application called OpenBlock could be used by community newspapers to enhance their reporting on policy issues by providing context and analysis to government data.

Q. What was the original promise of OpenBlock, and how did that change?

Originally, it was all about transparency and presentation. By the time Adrian Holovaty and his team launched the original OpenBlock application at Everyblock.com in 2007, governments had already been building databases and digital maps for more than a decade. Computer-assisted reporting—finding stories in troves of digital government data—wasn't new, either. But Everyblock.com—which focused on mapping government data down to the level of a city block—was part of a vanguard of Web applications that would begin to allow journalists to share the data with readers in a visually compelling way. But after Everyblock.com was sold to MSNBC.com in 2009, the site moved quickly and permanently toward user-generated content and away from visualizing public records.

Q. What is your goal?

I have turned back to that original promise of digital government transparency. Rural news organizations thrive on community minutia, and in expansive rural areas it makes sense that citizens would benefit as much—if not more—from this kind of geographic filter as urban citizens. But the real value of OpenBlock isn't just in creating automated content for a county map. Once that data is in hand, reporters and editors can use it to begin digging for the print stories that add context to the digital data.

Under the very best scenario, the context provided by computerized data alone is limited to who, what, when, and where. The "why and how" is still most efficiently provided by human reporters and editors whose job it is to know their entire readership and the questions those readers would ask of the data if they had the time. Knowing that a car was broken into on my block is news. But what current, complete, and machine-readable public data gives reporters is the ability to put that break-in instantly and automatically into some basic context. Are there more or fewer break-ins than last year? More in my neighborhood than others? What time of day are they most common? And which models are the most frequent targets?

When I think about how reporters might use the data that OpenBlock provides, I think about how police agencies are using data not just to react to crime but to predict it. I want a rural reporter to be able to open up a Web browser and quickly see where the same data that runs OpenBlock might also help them determine where to look for accountability and explanatory stories that might actually pan out. That kind of deep digging has always been relatively low yield and high cost, but OpenBlock has the potential to make it much less expensive.

Q. Why is data analysis so important for community news reporters?

Research has found that loyalty to a newspaper is determined by whether readers perceive it is the most credible and comprehensive source of news and information they care about. As it was originally envisioned, OpenBlock does help newspapers become a comprehensive source of information that is geographically relevant. But what has always been the most interesting aspect of the application is the kind of context it can help provide once all those geocoded news items are plotted as points on a map. Giving context to an issue helps readers understand why they should care about it.

Launching OpenBlock requires news organizations with a legacy of tenacity—those who once demanded access to closed town council meetings—to now demand access to digital public records. Building vibrant community online isn't about abdicating responsibility to audiences or algorithms. It's about using new tools to provide a platform for civic and economic engagement in a community. (Editors can learn more about the product by following @openrural on Twitter, liking OpenRural on Facebook, or sending an e-mail to openrural@unc.edu.)

problems in their backyards and beyond by connecting and coordinating with others."

Building Special-Interest Communities

The interconnectivity of the Internet gives us the ability to escape physical boundaries and form virtual communities of friends and neighbors who share our concerns, our passions, or our affiliations with certain groups or organizations—such as sports, parenting, civic life, politics, or religion. We can connect directly with these "communities of special interests," bypassing the more "general interest" news that is typically on the home page of most newspaper websites.

Among readers, the Internet has created a "shift in priorities from the [geographically defined] community to the individual," says Northwestern's Mersey, who believes that newspapers have "effectively ignored individual-based needs." Recent research on consumer behavior has found "that people who find a product more useful are more likely to use it, and targeted products tend to be more useful," she says. "In fact, special media, including narrowly cast magazines, have performed relatively well by comparison to general-circulation media."

As Mersey points out, magazines, which pioneered the concept of catering to the special affiliations and affinities of their readers, have been rewarded with a loyalty that has endured over the last several decades. Despite the rise of the Internet, annual surveys reveal strong reader attachment to "special-interest" magazines today, regardless of age. Eighty percent of respondents in a recent Deloitte survey, which has tracked generational shifts in media consumption for the last decade, reported making time on a routine basis to read a "favorite" magazine. This included twenty-one-year-olds in the "millennial generation" and baby boomers who are pushing sixty-five. By fostering this engagement of devoted readers, many magazines have been able to gain pricing leverage with their advertisers, providing them with very efficient access to a highly targeted audience. Over the last decade, as the mass audience for television has fragmented, cable networks have also followed a similar strategy—branding themselves to appeal to certain target audiences—and enjoyed success with both viewers and advertisers.

Therefore, as they consider how to pursue new revenue opportunities in a digital world, newspapers need to view the creation of these communities built around either "affinities, affiliations, or affections" as an opportunity to enhance loyalty with *both* readers and advertisers. This means that, in addition to building vibrant geographic community online, newspaper editors must also consider how to build and nurture "communities of special interest"—most especially if they hope to attract a new generation of readers that are addicted to the interconnectivity and interactivity of the digital era.

The challenge for editors trying to build community based on geographic identity is that of getting readers to "care about" the journalism. In contrast, when building communities based on special interests, the journalistic challenge is figuring out how best to connect readers with the content, each other, and the newspaper, as well as with the advertisers who want to reach them. Readers already "care about" these topics; the paper needs to provide the appropriate forum for them to connect in as many ways as possible.

Creating "communities of special interest" involves a whole new way of thinking about how to create and package content for a cross-platform world for both print and online editions, as well as, potentially, specialty magazines and mobile applications. For example, among the large metro papers, the *Denver Post* has a colorful tablet application titled *Colorado Ski Guide*, with detailed resort listings as well as locally produced content on skiing. The *Minneapolis Star Tribune* has built an interactive children's health site with staff-produced material. And the *Boston Globe* has created an online community for start-up technology companies and venture capitalists with much use of social networking.

In a highly publicized example of building community based on an affinity for certain values or subjects, CEO Clark Gilbert at the *Deseret News*, owned by the Mormon Church, reorganized news coverage around six areas that extensive research identified were of special interest to readers of the paper: family, faith, educational excellence, media values, financial responsibilities, and care for the poor. "We want to own faith and the family the way the *Washington Post* owns politics," says Gilbert. "In the world of the Web when you are click away from something better, you have to be differentiated."

UNC reader research conducted in a half dozen geographic communities located in both urban and rural areas identified at least five subcommunities of "special interests" grouped around such topics as sports, family life, culture, the comings and goings in the daily community, and social life. Within these broad groups, passions often varied considerably by region of the country or by ethnicity. For example, in the rural South, many sports enthusiasts not only were passionate about local prep sports but also were huge fans of NASCAR racing. In Chicago, readers of ethnic newspapers tended to be passionate about following popular sports in their homeland, such as soccer or cricket.

Not surprisingly, social life was of special interest to teens and young adults, regardless of region or ethnicity. That is why Pantelis, the general manager, has added a section to the *Polish Daily News* that covers local concerts and events in a way that is "a little more gossipy—or lighter—than the other news stories" and has begun streaming live video of these events on its website, accessible for viewing over mobile phones. "There have basically been three waves of Polish immigrants to Chicago since World War II," she says. "Those who still read the print paper are fifty-plus years old and maybe came here for political freedom in the 1980s and before. The newest generation—those who have come in the last decade since Poland joined the European Union—tend to be much younger and professionally successful. They are very connected to the cultural scene and know the local Polish artists and musicians, as well as successful national ones."

For many newspapers, the easiest way to begin to create these communities is to establish "themed pages" or websites. While many of these special-interest topics often compete for space with more general news in the print edition of newspapers, in the online version—where space is virtually unlimited—coverage can be greatly expanded. The content should not be duplicative for two reasons. First, research has shown that visitors to the online sites expect to find additional material that "complements" what they may have already seen in print—a weekly pregame or postgame video interview with the local high school coach or additional stats from the Friday night games, for example. Second, online users expect to interact with others and with the content on the site. So editors should look to use the interactivity of the web—sponsoring weekly reader contests, for example—to attract new readers to the online community. (Examples and prototypes of some of these "home pages" for communities of special interests can be found on businessofnews.unc.edu.)

Taking it one step further, newspapers with circulations ranging in size from 50,000 (the *Santa Rosa Press Democrat* and the *Fayetteville Observer*) to 13,000 (the daily *Columbia Daily Herald* and the twice-weekly *Southern Pines Pilot*) have also created successful magazines for special-interest groups. "It's a matter of finding holes in your community and then figuring out how to fill the holes," says *Columbia Daily Herald* publisher Mark Palmer. "Our editors and advertising people are constantly talking to readers and local merchants. We ask four things of a new magazine: Is it needed? Will it be appreciated? What will be in it? And how often should it come out?"

Though the *Daily Herald* serves an economically struggling area south of Nashville, it is currently producing three magazines, including, says Palmer, "a profitable men's lifestyle magazine for the affluent suburb of Brentwood. It's the most affluent suburb in Tennessee. It has horse racing, polo—my friends joke about wanting to be in the centerfold. Before we went in, we asked, 'Who are our competitors?' And, much to our surprise, we discovered we didn't have any." In addition, the *Daily Herald* is also producing magazines that focus on health and real estate. "The health magazine serves a reader interest" Palmer says. "The real estate magazine is about helping our struggling realtors, who asked me point-blank: 'Where were you when we needed you—when GM [General Motors] closed shop and left town, and the housing market tanked?'"

Regardless of which platform they use—magazine, newspaper, or digital pages—editors of community newspapers need to know their readers well and be willing to shift as their interests and concerns change. "At the height of the war, many of the troops were deployed for more than a year," says *Fayetteville Observer* publisher Broadwell. "The spouses left behind were coping with being single parents and often getting used to living in a new place. We hired a really good blogger and started encouraging people to post photos and comments. And that 'community page' for military moms just took off." Referring to the *Observer*'s recent shift away from military moms to officers, he observes: "As newspaper journalists, we are not used to giving up stuff. But sometimes you have to build sand castles—and let them get washed away and build another. That's the world we're dealing with right now. Readers' interests change—and we have to follow them."

As Fayetteville's pioneering experience with military moms suggests, editors have to stay in touch with readers and keep track of how their interests and passions change. But by understanding those passions, community newspapers have the opportunity to significantly increase not only traffic to the digital sites but also reader loyalty to the paper and engagement with its content.

Using Mobile and Social Media to Nurture Communities

Most community newspapers have a Facebook page with thousands of friends. But few editors attend to those friends as diligently as Sallie See, the sixty-two-year-old editor of the West Virginia weekly *Hampshire Review* (circulation 7,000) in the town of Romney, which has 2,000 residents. The newspaper's Facebook page is always on her computer screen at work, and "most weeknights, I'm online after supper having a lot of fun with our readers." In her own posts, she does "a lot of cheerleading of local high school teams and community events like the Christmas parade." But she's also busy checking out postings on the Facebook pages of the newspaper's 4,200 friends. "It's the best way to stay on top of everything going on in this community," she says. "I can't tell you the number of photos I've used that I saw first on Facebook—like the picture of a house fire we used last week—or the reader postings that I've mentioned in my weekly column highlighting what people are talking about."

In Chicago, the Spanish-language weekly *La Raza* (circulation 150,000) relies primarily on social media and the online site to stay connected with its readers. Reporters post quick summaries of all stories on the paper's digital site and then promote the stories through social media. The vast majority of visitors to the paper's website access it through their mobile phones. "I see the mobile phone as a potential game-changer," says Pantelis, general manager of the *Polish Daily News*, who believes her website, informancjeusa.com, founded in 2009, was "ahead of our time." For many of Chicago's 1 million Polish immigrants, "a home computer is a luxury that they don't need in daily life. And suddenly smartphones appeared, and it has become the computer you can carry in your pocket."

"Even editors who serve rural communities that are not wired should be considering how to use mobile and social networks," says West Virginia's Mary Kay McFarland. "Many people in rural communities commute fifty miles or more to work in towns and cities that are wired. And when they are there, they can readily access the Internet through their phones."

The printed newspaper has historically been very portable—a medium that fit easily into a briefcase. But as Pantelis points out, until recently, consumers who wanted to read a newspaper's digital edition had to access it through a computer terminal. The proliferation of smartphones is revolutionizing how readers access news, and the simultaneous explosion of social networking is changing how they communicate with editors and reporters.

More than half of cell-phone owners use their phones to access the Internet, according to the most recent Pew Internet and American Life

Project. Almost 20 percent of Americans report that they now go online mostly by using their phone—and, when they do, many are on their Facebook pages. Between mobile and social media, journalists have many ways to both follow their customers online and nurture many types of community on many platforms. But research shows that most newspapers still lag behind in fully utilizing these digital innovations to nurture vibrant community.

"I tell every editor of a community news organization, if you're not into mobile yet, get in the game *now*," says John Clark, director of the Reese News Lab, an experimental digital news laboratory at UNC's School of Journalism and Mass Communication. The Reese Lab has focused on producing research that can be used by the news media both to understand how consumers are accessing news and to learn how to design websites that can be easily accessed by smartphones. In 2012 a team of students and professionals, for example, launched a mobile-friendly political news site called WhichWayNC.com, which featured original reporting about political issues that affect state residents, such as health care and unemployment. WhichWayNC.com used "a responsive design" approach, which meant that its website adjusted automatically to a user's device and screen size, resizing and adapting itself to meet the needs of that platform.

Responsive design is "probably the most efficient and economical approach for most community newspapers at the moment—it's certainly less expensive than designing two separate sites for computer and phone access," says Clark, who, as general manager of WRAL, one of the state's largest television stations, pioneered mobile video delivery of news. Mindful of the challenges that the news industry is facing as it attempts to adopt mobile delivery, the Reese team took detailed notes on how visitors to the site interacted with the material. What they found may surprise newspaper editors. Because screens of smartphones are small and readers can only see a few lines of text at a time, the reporters initially assumed that mobile visitors would not scroll to read long stories. But preliminary data suggests that mobile readers' willingness to consume long stories may not be as limited as initially feared. Mobile users tended to scroll to the end of a story at about the same rate as desktop users. On both platforms, an average of about one in five users finished a story.

However, the Reese Lab discovered that photographs, videos, and infographics posed a different challenge. The lab's photojournalists and designers struggled to produce visually diverse stories that would be comprehensible on a phone screen. They had to adapt their images to fit a vertical format and often had to simplify their work. "Actors in movies can use subtle eye movements or small shoulder shrugs to convey a particular emotion to the audience," said one photojournalist. "On stage, actors use grandiose gestures and make their body language as obvious as possible. That is because small gestures are lost to the people in the balcony. . . . We found that on a mobile screen, subtle motion disappeared." (For more information on the Reese Lab research project, News on the Go can be downloaded at www.reesenewslab.org.)

Currently, the Reese Lab is focusing on developing mobile applications that community newspapers could offer their readers and use to build community. As an example, Clark cites the *Dallas Morning News*, which has a SportsDay app that provides users with stories on fifty to sixty high school games and allows them to access weekly rankings and to engage in chats with journalists and other sports enthusiasts. Users pay $1.99 to download the app, and advertisers pay roughly $700,000 yearly to sponsor SportsDay content across multiple platforms, including print and the website. The free *Chicago Tribune* RedEye app, sponsored by an advertiser, focuses on providing commuters with transit information, as well as details on nearby hotspots and dining locations.

Smartphones and tablets allow readers not only to engage with news on the go, Clark points out, but also to share information through social networks with each other and editors of the newspaper about the places they visit and the things they see. Newspapers can use social networks (such as Facebook and Twitter) in conjunction with mobile devices to perform a variety of community-building tasks, including promoting content in both the print and online editions; enticing print readers to sample the online site; connecting reporters with readers and readers with each other; and, finally, building strong loyalty to special niche products that focus on sports, parenting, or politics and community affairs. Yet a recent survey of 144 news reporters and thirty-two editors at midsized newspapers and television stations in eight markets in the southeastern United States found that most papers have not developed a cohesive strategy for using social networks effectively and efficiently.

Although both print and television reporters found using social media to be relatively easy, television journalists used new media more often and in more ways than their print counterparts. The biggest factor in determining how a newspaper or television station used social media was whether the editors and reporters perceived their competitors to be using it. Among the many uses of social media, the most common use of Facebook or Twitter by newspaper reporters was to promote stories in the local paper. This was followed, in rapidly descending order, by communication with readers or viewers, surveillance of other organizations (such as governments), finding interviews, generating story ideas, and sharing opinions with readers.

Few of the news organizations surveyed had guidelines other than those concerning the frequency of postings expected for the day. In addition, there was a significant disparity between what editors perceive to be the value of using social media (generating leads on stories) and what reporters say they are actually able to accomplish (promoting stories). None of the reporters or editors used it as aggressively or skillfully as West Virginia editor See, who has managed to accumulate more than half as many followers on the newspaper's website as those who subscribe to the paper.

In contrast, many readers of community newspapers have developed very specific media strategies using social media. In both rural and urban markets, Twitter users are some of the most avid consumers of local news. Frequent visitors to online sites report that they are often checking their Twitter feeds for headlines on breaking news, suggesting that Twitter feeds and text messages can be used effectively to "break" news, update stories, and promote items in the print edition. But overuse of Twitter can also lead to reader fatigue. Loyal readers in one community expressed annoyance at Twitter feeds that were posted hourly, regardless of whether there was any "real" news.

While users of Twitter tend to connect with "headlines," users of Facebook reported that they want to connect with friends and family. This suggests that newspapers can effectively use Facebook to give the paper a "public and neighborly face," connecting readers to reporters and to each other. Even more important, reader feedback suggests that Facebook can be used effectively to build digital communities of special interests and strengthen the loyalty of current readers.

As Facebook has gained widespread acceptance, the demographics of a frequent Facebook user has begun to correlate more closely with those of a digital-edition newspaper reader. Frequent Facebook users in rural markets primarily consist of young and middle-aged adults. Carefully and strategically managed, a Facebook page for the local newspaper becomes a sort of "town square" similar to the editorial page in the print edition, where residents can meet to comment on issues big and small. In addition, it can connect the reporters and newspapers with the geographic community as well as to those digital communities with special interests. "Both social media—like Facebook and Twitter—and mobile are great tools," says Rob Mitchell, editor of the 12,000-circulation *Rutland Herald*, which has 9,000 Facebook friends and 3,500 followers on Twitter. "But as journalists, we need to remember that they are tools, and we need to use these tools to help us tell a story and cement connections with readers."

Mitchell's own strategy for using social media has evolved considerably in recent months. "I've moved from trying to inject personality into the *Herald* Facebook page to seeing it as an opportunity to educate our readers about what a journalist does," he says. "For example, I may write about why we got the facts wrong in a story—what we used as sources, what we verified. And I'll explain how a news story is different from an editorial that we have written on the same subject. We sort of assume people understand what we do, and even some of our most loyal readers don't. It's about transparency, which builds trust."

Mitchell "confesses" that even though he was digital media director before becoming editor of the paper, "I am like most journalists and tend to think, first, about the print version of the story. And I think that is okay as long as I think about the print version as the end result of a process that starts with posting the headline on mobile, followed by a posting, maybe with video, on the Web, where it can also be accessed by mobile. Then the story in the next day's paper puts the events of yesterday into perspective. And then, if it is a controversial story, or one that was hard to report, I'll follow up with comments on Facebook, explaining why we made certain decisions. Each of the mediums then becomes a tool for telling a part of the story, broadening the audience and connecting with different communities of readers." For Mitchell, it's about "using every available tool to connect with our readers—in print, on the Web, on mobile phones, and on Facebook and Twitter."

For See in West Virginia, Facebook is a way for the weekly newspaper to carry on a "conversation" with "anyone" in the small community of Romney who wants to chat with the editor. She stays on top of breaking news. "We had a fire on Sunday. I saw the posting on Facebook and I immediately had a story on the website with a photo, and then an interview with the family in the paper later that week," she says. "I like to blur the line between Facebook, the website, and the paper."

For Pomareda in Chicago, the cell phone is a way to reach an audience that the print edition might not otherwise reach. "Most Latinos in Chicago have a cell phone," she says. "So when I post a story, I think about the headline—and how I can attract those people who won't read the [print edition] to the website, where I will have a longer story and either audio or video."

For all three of these editors, the key to success is using available digital tools to build vibrant community across multiple platforms.

To Charge or Not to Charge?

Once they have committed to building vibrant community online, publishers usually confront a second dilemma: should they charge their readers for access to the online material? And if so, how much is it worth? Ironically, long before the Internet moguls taught readers that "digital news just wants to be free," publishers taught them to pay only a small fraction of what it costs to create, produce, and distribute a newspaper. Consumers always have a "reference price" in mind—and they will attribute little or no value to an item if the producer of the product does not help them understand how much value they are receiving, according to longtime business consultant Thomas T. Nagle, author of *The Strategy and Tactics of Pricing: A Guide to Growing More Profitably* (2006). The "reference price" established by many publishers in recent years is that consumers should pay fifty cents or less for a copy of the newspaper. That is why online efforts that ask news consumers to "contribute what you think this is worth" for certain stories largely fail. Put another way, this is the equivalent of being a musician, opening up your violin case on a street corner, and asking passersby to drop in a tip. You will receive small change and one-dollar bills unless consumers understand why the story has value to them.

A 2011 study sought to determine if online visitors to news sites would be willing to pay for access to various types of information. Only 10 percent said they would—and the price they would be willing to pay correlated with the typical newsstand price of many community newspapers. Asked what types of news they would be willing to pay for, they mentioned national and world news most often. But, as Stanford economist James Hamilton observes in his book *All the News That's Fit to Sell: How the Market Transforms Information into News* (2004), in reality, the most-read, "in-demand" stories in the online world are not traditional news stories or the public-affairs journalism that is the hallmark of strong community newspapers. Rather, it is "news" focusing on celebrity gossip, entertainment events, business decisions, and consumer purchases. Readers tend to seek out stories that they "find personally interesting," as well as "information that might help them in their jobs or [help them find] products they are thinking of buying," says Hamilton.

Reeducating consumers and getting them to use a new "reference price" for news involves a whole range of tactics. It involves explaining to loyal readers why they should "care about" a story on a controversial public policy or how they can use the information on a website. It also involves giving them a "face" at the newspaper to interact with—the editor and a reporter, who are available on Facebook or leading community forums on important issues affecting the quality of life in the community, such as the state of the local economy or the area schools.

Experience in other industries suggests that value-based pricing works *only* when community newspapers are focused on growing the loyalty of current and potential customers, since loyal customers are willing both to pay more (for the value they believe they are receiving) and sell more (recommending the paper to other potential readers).

This, then, enables publishers to lay the groundwork for pursuing a long-term "value-based pricing" strategy. Such a strategy envisions pricing a product according to the value delivered to a specific group. To do this, a publisher must first be able to segment customers into groups or communities and understand the value the newspaper is delivering to each group or community. Then he can begin a process of "educating" the consumer in a particular group as to the value the paper is actually delivering.

As John Clark of the Reese Lab points out: "I can see the potential of charging sports enthusiasts a monthly fee to access information about various teams [as subscribers to the *Dallas Morning News* SportsDay app now pay], or local parents paying to access a comprehensive calendar of events. I think the model of unbundling proprietary information and then charging a fee for access to it may well work in the newspaper's favor over the long term, especially if it has managed to build niche communities around in-demand information. We've only just begun to explore this territory."

While initially, many analysts predicted that newspapers would evolve toward a micropayment model—such as the one used by the music industry, in which consumers pay a nominal fee (ninety-nine cents) to download a musical tune—most of the newspaper industry has instead gravitated toward use of a "pay wall." With a pay wall, a reader has free access to certain material but must pay a subscription to access more proprietary material on a routine basis.

There are two types of pay walls: a "hard" one and a "soft or leaky" one. In 1997 the *Wall Street Journal* was one of the first major newspapers to charge for online content. It opted for a "hard" pay wall in which certain material—such as breaking news and front-page stories—was free, but only subscribers could access other proprietary stories that the staff had produced. In contrast, in 2011 the *New York Times* opted for a "soft" pay wall," known as a "metered model" in which readers can access a certain number of stories a month (usually ten to twenty) free of charge, regardless of the topic or subject matter. To access more than the set number, readers must pay for an online subscription. Following in the footsteps of the *Times,* several hundred newspapers—mostly larger dailies—now charge for online access to content, and the majority of these papers have opted for the metered model instead of the hard pay wall.

Deciding *when* to charge for online access is an especially critical calculation for many publishers of small community newspapers, since the traffic to their papers' websites often lags significantly behind the circulation of the print editions. Many small online newspaper websites currently do not draw enough visitors to merit any significant advertiser investment, unless the website is paired with the print edition. And charging for online access may well hamper efforts to attract either new readers or loyal print subscribers to online venues that hold the potential to grow advertising revenue. Similarly, publishers need to carefully weigh the pros and cons of *how* to charge—whether to employ a "hard or soft" pay wall. In order to charge for online content, says Rick Edmonds, media analyst for the Poynter Institute, newspapers must deliver content that readers value.

However, recent reader surveys in two markets in which newspapers with hard pay walls charged nonsubscribers for access to online material revealed that nonreaders—even those who expressed a preference for the types of "local news" that the papers provided—were largely unaware of what additional content was available behind the wall. This suggests that publishers who choose to adopt a pay wall need to determine what popular content remains free, thereby driving traffic to the site and, potentially, introducing new readers to additional proprietary content available for a fee.

At the *Wall Street Journal*, for example, editors made a decision early on to make certain "high-traffic" articles free to nonsubscribers—including many op-ed pieces and breaking news stories on the home page. The *Journal* editors reasoned that, since opinion blogs were readily available on the Web, the paper could be part of the larger debate if its opinion columns could also be e-mailed freely around the blogosphere. Similarly, in offering breaking news stories for free to nonsubscribers, the *Journal* editors acknowledged that in the digital age, "hot" news is not proprietary for long. Therefore, they deemed it more important to reinforce the paper's reputation for being "a credible and comprehensive source of news and information" when a hot news story broke. By putting all other proprietary information that they created behind the pay wall, the *Journal* editors were able to get their loyal customers to attribute a "value" to that information and pay for access to it.

Like the *Wall Street Journal*, the *Rutland Herald* (with a print circulation of 12,000) erected a hard pay wall in October 2010, allowing nonsubscribers access *only* to obituaries, wire stories, and letters and opinion pieces. However, after three months, "we also allowed them to access breaking news that we were reporting," says editor Mitchell. "The feedback from online readers was that 'you are cutting us off from what makes us a community.'" In the months immediately after implementing an online subscription, the number of unique daily visitors to the *Herald* website fell by almost half, from 11,000 to roughly 6,000. While three years passed before the number of unique visitors returned to the 2010 level, Mitchell considers the pay wall a success. "There have been a number of side benefits. We've been able to collect 40,000 e-mail addresses [which can be used for both marketing and advertising purposes]," he says. "We monitor what content we offer for free and the number of visitors every three months and will continue to make adjustments. Our philosophy is that if you want our content, it is not free. But we are also very aware of our responsibilities to provide information to people in the community who may not be able to afford to pay."

Three years after implementing an online subscription model, the *Herald* had almost 900 online subscribers paying $3.49 a week—which is roughly equivalent to what a subscriber to the print edition pays—and more than 500 online subscribers to its sister paper, the *Barre Times Argus*.

For an additional fifty cents a week, the *Herald* and *Times Argus* print subscribers could also receive unlimited access to the online material. "The additional income from circulation has definitely softened the blow from the economic recession—and allowed us to stay even on total revenue," says Mitchell.

In 2011 the *Fayetteville Observer* (with a print circulation of 55,000) began charging nonsubscribers for access to its online material using the metered system. Originally, the *Observer* offered nonsubscribers free access to as many as fifteen articles a month. That number has now been adjusted down to ten, "and we'll continue to monitor whether it should be adjusted again," says publisher Broadwell. With roughly 300 online subscribers, he terms the soft pay wall "a modest success."

As Broadwell points out, in making the calculation about whether to charge readers, it is also important to remember that circulation income has historically accounted for only 15 percent of revenue at most community newspapers, and, for the time being, there is often less potential in the online world. Even the *Wall Street Journal* and the *New York Times* are able to charge digital readers only a little more than half of what they charge for a print edition. However, he says, "we wanted to honor our print subscribers who were paying for the news. At the same time we didn't want to discourage new online subscribers and traffic to the site, so we kept the obits, blogs, and videos outside the pay wall. Our number of online-only subscribers is in the low hundreds, but using a metered system was a low-drama way to begin to establish some value for our content online."

Poynter Institute's Edmonds considers a "pay wall—properly tended—a good investment in the future. It gives newspapers an advantage as readers migrate to mobile and tablets for delivery of news. It is essential that the good newspapers begin to establish in the reader's mind a value for the content they create—content that is expensive to produce." Value-based pricing of content is an admittedly long-term strategy that involves reeducating readers to conjure up a "new" reference price that attributes a higher value to the journalism produced by local newspapers. But in an era when the cost of distributing content online is minuscule, proprietary content that readers value is what differentiates good newspapers from all others. And as Edmonds points out, the migration to phones and tablets has also given publishers the chance to rethink and reimagine the traditional business model and begin educating readers to more appropriately value the unique content they receive from a community newspaper.

Therefore, building vibrant community across multiple platforms is critical for publishers and editors of community newspapers who hope to re-create a successful business model in the digital era. Before they can follow the money—and aggressively pursue new revenue opportunities—newspapers must first follow their customers. Those customers, thanks to the Internet, now have a very expansive notion of community. That means that most newspapers will likely follow a path similar to the one laid out by the *Santa Rosa Press Democrat* and the *Fayetteville Observer* and come to see community as multilayered—built around local and regional issues as well as "special-interest" concerns.

Community newspapers must first look to be very local and give readers the news of what is happening in their own backyards. But as Al Cross of the Institute for Rural Journalism and Community Issues points out, they also need to honor their historic roots and be the tie that binds together residents in a geographic community to the world outside their doorsteps. That is not always the sort of journalism that readers volunteer that they "care about"—although they should.

The Internet has given editors new tools for thinking about how they can create and aggregate news so that it builds loyalty and engagement with content—tools that allow journalists to show readers exactly why they should care about news that happens in their geographic proximity. The Internet can also help editors build communities across multiple platforms (mobile, social networks, digital, and print) based on affinities, affiliations, and affections. These communities of special interest will vary by location, and that is why it is very important that editors know their readers.

Harvard Business School professor Robert Simon says the first—and most important—question that every chief executive officer should ask is: Who is my primary customer? For newspapers, the answer is: "the reader." Without the reader, there are no advertisers. That is why building vibrant community across multiple platforms is so important.

Most community newspapers continue to enjoy strong loyalty from current readers and have the opportunity to attract new ones by building on the strengths of their digital platforms—including interactivity, timeliness, and the ability to produce richer and deeper coverage of news and information. This is a very important finding, as editors think about how to pursue the final prong of the three-pronged strategy for renewal—that of aggressively and profitably "pursuing new revenue opportunities" with their advertisers.

The Whiteville Experience
Building Community Online and in Print

By the fall of 2010, Les High had become intrigued with the idea of creating "community pages" for both the print and online editions of the *News Reporter*, which he hoped would retain the paper's current readers and attract a new generation. But he had a number of concerns. He worried about how the news staff of five reporters could continue to cover all the important news plus produce additional material for the community pages. Who would be in charge of the community pages? Should the newspaper focus only on creating community pages for both the print and online editions, or should it follow the path of several other area newspapers and also produce a lifestyle magazine for Columbus County? And finally, who would tie together the various digital technologies—such as the Twitter feed, the Facebook page (with more than 4,000 friends), and mobile texts—to support these communities?

As he contemplated these questions, Les realized that he was really contemplating a "new" editorial strategy—one that would span multiple platforms, including print (the newspaper, plus a potential magazine) and digital (the website, mobile, and social networks). He also realized that he would need to embrace two notions of community: an expansive one based on geography and a more-targeted one built around special interests. "I wanted to make sure we continued to provide the same caliber of public-affairs journalism we'd been known for in Columbus County—and enhance it, using digital technology," he says. "By the same token, I want to stake out territory in areas like prep sports and crime that we've traditionally owned before a competitor attempts to."

Les began by using census data and regional economic and voting statistics, as well as information from the reader surveys, to identify six sizeable and overlapping "special-interest" communities (ranging in size from 8,000 to 25,000 people) within the geographic boundaries of the county, which had 55,000 residents. He gave a descriptive name to each of the communities so that the reporters could more easily relate to various groups.

Les estimated that the four largest communities established and named by the *News Reporter* were "Curious Citizens," "Sports of All Sorts," "Plugged-In Parents," and "Front Porch Neighbors." Readers who were part of Curious Citizens were residents who cared about such broad quality-of-life issues as the economy, education, and the environment. Largely Internet savvy, they liked knowing the details (such as could be retrieved from an OpenBlock application), as well as reading the types of analytical and contextual stories that reporters could produce from analyzing the data. Sports of All Sorts community members were roughly age twelve years and up and included both genders, skewing male in adulthood. They liked being the first to know the outcome of a game and were avid fans of all types of sports, including prep, local leagues, collegiate, and professional contests. With the large freshwater Lake Waccamaw nearby and the ocean only fifty miles away, they spent a lot of time and money on outdoor recreation, including hiking, running, fishing, boating, and hunting.

Plugged-In Parents, ages twenty-five to fifty-five, skewed predominantly female. Heavy users of social networking, they were especially interested in stories on local education and health care, as well as information on family-friendly events. This group contrasted with Front Porch Neighbors, who were generally residents forty and older who knew everyone in town. They were loyal readers of the print edition of the *News Reporter* and loved being in the know and relating little-known facts or details about a news story that they read in the paper. The two smaller communities—with approximately 8,000 members each—consisted of "Texting Teens," ages fourteen to twenty-two, who were heavy users of mobile devices and social media; and "Home-for-the-Holidays," former residents who grew up in Columbus County, live within 100 miles of "home," and visit family members regularly (often monthly).

With the fall 2010 arrival of his sister, Stuart, who was placed in charge of special projects, Les decided to focus first on creating community pages for the three largest groups—Sports of All Sorts, Curious Citizens, and Plugged-In Parents—all of which he estimated to have around 20,000 potential members. Working together, brother and sister followed a three-step process for creating "pages" for each community, first conducting an inventory of all "special-interest" content published in either the print or online edition, then organizing the content under community headings, and finally considering what additional material should be added.

Since Les did not want to distract the news staff from their primary responsibilities of covering everything from the town council to Friday night high school games, he developed these criteria for adding content to the three themed pages that the newspaper would create and roll out:

- Could the creation of additional content be easily worked into a reporter's routines?

- Could content currently being published in either the print or online edition—for example, a community calendar—be easily expanded and enriched?
- Could some of the additional content be written by external "experts," such as a local mother who would blog about parenting issues?
- Could the paper also become an "aggregator," recommending material that would be of interest to a particular community?
- Could the newspaper efficiently use new digital technologies, such as OpenBlock, to provide readers with more detail and context around issues that concerned them?

In conceiving each community home page, Les sought to make sure that the pages in both the print and online editions were not simply mirror images of one another. That way, the paper could use one edition to promote unique content in another. Because his primary goal was to build up readership of the digital edition, he opted—for the time being—not to charge for any online content. Les viewed the online "community pages" as providing potential readers with multiple "entry points" into the digital edition in addition to the home page. Because so many of the paper's readers have multiple, overlapping interests and passions (prep sports as well as parenting, for example), he also decided to link the various communities together with material on each community page referring to related content on other community pages, as well as the digital edition's "home page" and the print edition pages. For example, a story on the community home page for Plugged-In Parents could refer to standardized school test scores (which are detailed on the OpenBlock application by school and grade on the home page for Curious Citizens) as well as a story in the print edition about the most recent board of education meeting.

Les designed each of the community pages with new anchor features that run in both the print and online editions, plus additional material online that allows readers to interact with one another. (Prototypes and more extensive descriptions of all three communities are available for downloading on the website, businessofnews.unc.edu.)

- Sports of All Sorts, to be published in the Thursday print edition, had three anchor features that appeared each week: Athletes of the Week, a sports calendar, and a photo highlight of a game. Both the sports calendar and the photo highlights would be greatly expanded in the digital edition (which also featured video footage of the games), and there was a weekly football contest. In addition, the online Sports of All Sorts would have a subscriber Twitter feed that highlighted score changes in important games, two video "blogs" (five-minute recorded interviews with coaches on Thursday evening and Saturday morning) that served as a pregame rundown of what to expect in the Friday game, and a postgame assessment of what actually happened.

- Plugged-In Parents, to be published in the Monday print edition, had three anchor features: a parenting column, a recipe of the week, and a "High-Five" calendar of events, plus four sets of themed features on the local schools, healthy living, family fun, and hobbies. The themed features appeared monthly in the print edition but appeared weekly in the digital edition. In addition, the digital page had a parenting blog plus a variety of reader-generated content and interactive activities—including contests and question-and-answer forums.

- My Community (the page for Curious Citizens), to be published in the Monday print edition, focused each week on a specific public-policy issue, such as safety, education, the economy, and health. The stories, appearing in both the print and online editions and written by local reporters, placed in context the hyperlocal data available on OpenBlock, which anchored the My Community page in the digital version. The reporter compared trends in crime or student test scores, for example, to those in neighboring counties in the region and to the statewide average, explaining to residents why they should "care about" these trends and what they can do to address them. "It provides us with a new way to encourage dialogue and lead local community discussions about solutions to these long-term challenges," says Les, who is also hoping to moderate quarterly panel discussions with local and state leaders on topics that concern the community. These sessions would be broadcast live on the Web, and transcripts would be published in both the print and online editions.

The launch of Sports of All Sorts was timed to coincide with the beginning of the 2012 fall high school football season and was promoted each Friday on the front page of the *News Reporter*. Within one month of its debut, unique daily visitors to whiteville.com had more than tripled to

3,000. The most frequently clicked-through features in the online edition were Athletes of the Week and the football contest.

After scoring a win with the first themed page, Les and Stuart initially planned to launch the second community page—Plugged-In Parents—in the spring of 2013, followed by the My Community in the summer of 2013. But as they began to assemble material for the next two community pages, Stuart called a time-out. There were a number of issues she felt needed to be addressed before launching the next two pages. "We needed to work out who is going to be responsible for each page," she says. "As director of special projects, I was the point person on Sports of All Sorts. But as the pages take hold, they need to be handed off to someone in the news department who is responsible for the content. Plus, I realized that the reporters were approaching capacity. We needed to rethink the whole editorial process for creating and posting stories.

"There had been a real excitement in successfully launching Sports of All Sorts. The community loved it, the advertisers loved it—and the reporters were excited," she says. "But Sports of All Sorts was actually easy for us because we were already producing a lot of content in the print edition that we could simply expand in the digital edition. That wasn't going to be the case with Plugged-In Parents or My Community. A lot of the content would be totally new. And we needed to manage the editorial process differently."

Stuart also wanted to spend some time "sprucing up" the design of Sports of All Sorts, which was "kind of thrown together," and creating new video segments on individual sports such as golf, sailing, and hunting "to attract visitors to the site during the summer, when there were no prep sports." In addition, she wanted to explore how the paper could better promote and use its mobile capabilities and more effectively marshal its Facebook following. "These were afterthoughts the first season," she says, "and something we really need to utilize better now that we know the rhythm of the sports season and how this affects the community page." She was especially pleased that several teenagers had signed up for Twitter feeds on game scores. "Sports could be a real key to bringing in teenagers to the digital edition," she believes.

In early December, Stuart and Les decided to postpone the launch of the next two community pages until the spring of 2014 so she could address these issues. As Stuart began to focus on refining the community pages, Les suddenly had a new issue to contend with: a competitor decided to launch a magazine that focused on Columbus County. He and Stuart immediately turned their attention to creating the new quarterly lifestyle magazine that Les had been contemplating over the last year as he talked to other newspaper editors who had launched one recently. Named *954* (the number of square miles in Columbus County), the magazine debuted in April 2013.

"It's been said that competition makes you better, and the entry of an out-of-county publication into our market gave us the final push to start *954*," Les told readers. Editorially, the magazine—full of feature stories on county natives and unique local landmarks, as well as consumer tips on nutrition, fitness, and do-it-yourself projects—provided a great opportunity for the newsroom to begin "experimenting" with some of the content Les and Stuart envisioned would appear on the Plugged-In Parents page.

"Magazines are a bit of a different animal than newspapers," says Les. "Our staff was excited about the magazine because the writing and photography are done in a more-relaxed style, making for more artistic and creative license than the more straightforward style of newspaper journalism." Launching a community page for sports enthusiasts was "a significant first step in rethinking our future," he says. "It helped people in the newsroom see that whiteville.com could enhance our coverage of a franchise we had always owned. Plus, it set up the newsroom to create and launch a lifestyle magazine in a couple of months—something we'd never done."

Before launching Plugged-In Parents or My Community, Les "wanted to reflect on what we now knew and figure out what sort of resources would be needed in the newsroom to do these next two communities right. We have to rethink how we produced stories for the *News Reporter*, as well as whiteville.com and the new magazine."

Les began reorganizing the newsroom so that every reporter is responsible for producing content for *both* the print and online editions. In addition, he assigned individual reporters leading roles in producing and coordinating material for the community pages. In many cases, he said, it is trial and error. "You have to be flexible, and you've also got to get the reporters to 'own' the content they're producing." He was especially concerned that the two reporters responsible for the material for My Community "own" the contextual and analytical stories that would be featured on that page "since this is about really enhancing the public-service journalism that we've been known for." So he made certain that the longtime crime reporter and the government reporter ("both are great at getting the data and telling the story") work closely with UNC professor Ryan

Thornburg as he designed and refined the OpenBlock application, which would map public records.

"We always put stories in context when the news breaks," says Les, "but this is about routinely telling readers about the underlying trends that may not make the headlines but affect the quality of life in Columbus County. If we don't aggressively pursue that mission, then where does it get us to have created a series of disconnected communities built around individual interests?" Reflecting on what he and the news staff had learned from the experiences of the past year, he concludes: "I think we've learned that we have to pace ourselves. We can't do this overnight. This is a new way of thinking about creating, displaying, and distributing news. We've also got to stay flexible and respond to competition. Both Sports of All Sorts and *954* reached new readers and told our current readers that we're changing with the times. And we've all begun to realize that we have to reach out in as many ways as possible—through the *News Reporter*, whiteville.com, *954*, Twitter, Facebook, and mobile. I think we now realize that building a community of loyal readers across many platforms is going to be key to our success."

CHAPTER SEVEN
How to Pursue New Revenue Opportunities

For publishers seeking a strategy that will improve bottom-line prospects, the advice to "aggressively pursue new revenue" seems maddeningly simplistic and unfocused. The realization that no one seems to be coming up with the same solution only adds to the frustration. In the highly competitive media landscape that community newspapers now face, there is not just one way but many ways to pursue new revenue.

Sallie See, editor of the weekly *Hampshire Review* in West Virginia, must "spread as wide a net as possible to get the advertising dollars we need to run the paper. We'd starve if I focused only on the businesses in downtown Romney, so I approach the merchants across the county line that my readers patronize." The *Review* has also set up an in-house digital ad agency of sorts, having designed more than thirty websites for area businesses, all of which the paper now hosts on its server.

Across the continent, in the upscale community of Santa Rosa, California, publisher Bruce Kyse has also created an in-house digital agency at the *Press Democrat* that offers Web development, search optimization, and social media assistance to clients who are willing to pay more than $1,000 a month. "We are simply following the dollars and the needs of our advertisers in this market," says Kyse. "We have to develop this expertise to serve them well."

Meanwhile, in the Florida retirement community of Naples, *Daily News* publisher Dave Neill "reinvented" that daily newspaper's advertising sales effort by abolishing sales "territories" based on geography and replacing them with a structure built around business categories—including health and wellness, real estate, food, and transportation. Like Kyse, he believes that the key to revenue growth is to "operate at a much higher level of sophistication" for advertisers.

And in two very disparate communities in Tennessee and North Carolina, the *Columbia Daily Herald* and the twice-weekly *Pilot* have pursued a strategy of diversification. Serving an economically challenged area forty miles south of Nashville, the *Daily Herald* "operates in a world . . . [where initiatives] that bring in a few thousand dollars are valued," says publisher Mark Palmer. Therefore, the paper has developed a portfolio of seven online services and products; launched three "niche" print magazines focusing on health, men's lifestyle, and real estate; and developed a host of online opportunities for local merchants. David Woronoff, publisher of *The Pilot*, which serves the upscale communities of Southern Pines and Pinehurst, has created three slick monthly magazines, two telephone directories, and a local search engine, as well as design and printing businesses. Most recently, the paper purchased a popular local independent bookstore in downtown Southern Pines.

As these examples illustrate, the challenges—and opportunities—are different depending on the market. But while a willingness to aggressively seek out new opportunities is key to success in the digital era, publishers of community newspapers need to establish some strategic parameters if they are to *profitably* pursue new revenue. As Woronoff points out about his own efforts to diversify: "None of these investments come with the kind of fully allocated profit margins newspapers had in the predigital era—nor the income. To compensate for the print advertising loss, you have to diversify your revenue streams—*but also* choose wisely."

This means that publishers must prioritize and calculate which "opportunities" will yield the greatest return. To stay abreast of the digital transition currently under way, newspapers need to be diversifying their revenue streams by an average of 6 percent a year. Therefore, at the end of five years, newspapers should, at a minimum, have 30 percent of advertising revenue coming from the new sources. This is more than three times what most community newspapers currently receive from their digital editions. So there is tremendous imperative for newspapers to quickly adopt a whole new way of thinking and selling.

Most community newspapers face two significant threats to their current advertising base. In addition to rapidly declining print volume, they must also contend with depressed digital advertising rates. A recent study by the Pew Research Center concluded that for every dollar newspapers gained in digital advertising revenue, they were currently losing anywhere from $7 to $16 in print advertising. Simply increasing the volume of digital advertising is not sufficient to reverse the fortunes of most community newspapers.

While print advertising is likely to remain an important marketing tool for local businesses in many communities, it will be only one of several platforms—including digital, mobile, social networking, and event sponsorship—that a local merchant can use to get out a message. Therefore, publishers of community newspapers need to move aggressively to reposition the newspaper away from its print focus and toward one that emphasizes its cross-platform advertising capabilities. Simultaneously, newspapers need to address the "digital rate problem" by revamping the way the sales staff is pricing and selling advertising.

In order to accomplish these two goals, there are three key strategic advertising initiatives that all papers—regardless of size and location—need to pursue if they are to survive and thrive in a highly competitive environment. First, all members of the paper's advertising staff *must* understand how to match an advertising message with the appropriate medium. They need to become experts on the effectiveness of the various platforms (print, online, mobile) so they can advise local merchants on choosing the appropriate medium and then designing the message or advertisement to take full advantage of a medium's capability.

Next, the community newspaper needs to be repositioned as a cross-platform medium, and local merchants need to be educated as to how the various platform options work together to make advertising in the newspaper much more effective than the competitive alternatives. Simultaneously, publishers need to revamp their advertising rates to more appropriately value the reach, exposure, and audience engagement the newspaper is uniquely providing local merchants, especially when two or more platforms—print and digital, for example—are combined. Publishers also need to expand available marketing options.

Finally, on a day-to-day basis, the sales effort needs to be retooled and managed strategically. Sales representatives need to be transformed from print "order-takers and processors" to cross-platform marketing specialists. Accounts need to be prioritized so that sales representatives spend their time more efficiently. Without a strategic approach, the sales effort is likely to become diffuse, and the bottom line will suffer.

A 2013 Pew Research Center Report profiled "Four Revenue Success Stories," with each paper pursuing a different advertising strategy "tailored to the particulars of that market." The report concludes: "What worked in a wired California wine community might be a poor choice for a Florida resort destination. Customizing the business model for the community . . . is a key component of success."

However, regardless of which new revenue model a community newspaper ultimately adopts, a community newspaper's sales staff needs to understand how to best use various platforms to achieve a range of advertising objectives—from introducing a product or service to reinforcing the loyalty of existing customers. And publishers need to think broadly about the products and services that newspapers offer, including in-house digital agencies and "niche" products aimed at communities of readers who share "special interests." Successfully executed, this new sales strategy allows newspapers to build a bridge between the print and online editions, to regain the ability to charge advertisers for the unique value that a cross-platform newspaper is actually delivering to them, and to *profitably* pursue a whole range of new revenue opportunities.

A lot is riding on how newspapers navigate this period of transition between the print-only world of yesterday and the multiplatform world of today—not the least of which is the ability of the news department to have the funds necessary to produce quality local journalism.

The Perplexing World Your Advertiser Faces

It is clear that the landscape is shifting quickly. Both traditional and digital media are selling aggressively against community newspapers, and in many cases, they are doing it successfully. But before community newspapers can begin to sell differently, publishers and ad directors must first understand where the local merchant is coming from. If you—as a publisher or ad director—are confused about which revenue strategy to pursue, consider the dilemma of your local merchants who have been longtime advertisers in your community newspapers. They are being told daily—in the press and in conversations with other merchants—that they must "go digital" or "go mobile." They are bombarded with data and analytics supplied by online sales representatives that they do not understand. But they feel that they are going to be "left behind" if they do not get on the digital bandwagon.

Therefore, many longtime newspaper advertisers are considering allocating a portion of their marketing budget to online outlets "just to test the waters and see if it performs better." But they are not sure how to take the first step—how to identify the most appropriate digital channel for reaching their customers or how to design an effective digital advertisement.

In interviews with more than sixty advertisers in a half dozen rural and urban markets, UNC researchers found a reservoir of goodwill for and loyalty to their community newspapers among a majority of local businesses surveyed. But in many cases, that loyalty appeared to be much more tenuous than the loyalty voiced by readers of those newspapers, who overwhelmingly viewed their local paper as without peer.

Also, whereas reader loyalty to *both* the print and online editions of community newspapers was strong in almost all markets surveyed, a significant majority of advertisers expressed loyalty *only* to the print version. And in several cases, that loyalty came with reservations. Given what they perceived to be the advanced age of most print readers, roughly half of the merchants who described themselves as "longtime newspaper advertisers" expressed some concern about how much longer the print edition of the newspaper could continue to "bring feet through the door" of their businesses. "I know that I need to reach younger customers—those buying engagement rings and wedding rings and charm bracelets and all," said one second-generation owner of a jewelry store in a small town. "But I'm not sure how to reach them. Do they read the local newspaper anymore?"

Many local merchants said they had not considered advertising in the digital edition of the local paper because the advertising sales representatives almost always pushed the print edition exclusively. Online ads at many community newspapers are sold "separately" by a designated "digital" person or persons on the sales staff or are "outsourced" to an out-of-town vendor who comes into the market a couple of times a year. As a result, many sales representatives at community newspapers are ignorant about how to position and sell digital advertising in combination with the print edition, which still has the larger audience.

"When I asked last year about advertising in the digital edition, the salesman told me he would send around 'the digital guy,'" said the manager of an independent financial services firm. "Some guy I had never seen—I'm not sure he even worked at the paper—came in a couple of weeks later and tried to sell me a small ad that listed my firm and the contact information, the same sort of directory ad I could place in the local Yellow Pages. I passed."

Further complicating matters, local merchants said that many newspaper sales representatives failed to present a compelling reason to buy "space" in either the print or online editions of the paper. In contrast, they said, sales representatives for digital and mobile media, as well as "old" mediums such as billboard companies and radio stations, come armed with data and statistics on their reach and efficiency. They cite viewership numbers or syndicated research, which paint a demographic picture of the audience that will see the ad.

Community newspaper sales representatives, however, rarely provided data about either their print or online audiences. When they did, they tended to cite general circulation or Web statistics, such as household penetration in the local market or the number of "page hits" or "unique visitors" to the website—neither of which conveyed a compelling demographic portrait of loyal newspaper readers. They also did not give local merchants a rationale for the price of the ads and their value versus other mediums. Local merchants often described newspaper sales representatives as "order-takers and processors," selling ads the same way they have for the last twenty years. "I like the local newspaper guy a lot, but he's basically just very good at picking up my order and getting it into the newspaper correctly," said a local clothing retailer. "He never shares any numbers, except to tell me that my rate is going up every year or so."

In the absence of credible and compelling information and data, local merchants said they were often inclined to believe what a community newspaper's competitors said. "The television and radio guys at least pretend to be consultants and bring out the numbers to show you how your ad will reach the people you want," said a large area car dealer.

Then there are the local realtors, who have moved a significant portion of their marketing budget into digital outlets because of the technological advantages this medium offers versus the print edition of newspapers. "In an era when we can offer prospective buyers virtual home tours, newspapers are living in the Stone Age—offering us a page of advertising with small thumbnail photos of homes for sale," said a realtor who is part of a large nationwide chain. "Everyone knows those rows of small photos that run in newspaper ads don't move houses. It basically just pleases the seller, who sees his house in the paper."

Digital alternatives are also much more efficient, she said, since they reach "people who are already inclined to buy." Like realtors, many other local merchants also expressed interest in purchasing media that offered them "targeted" or niche audiences. "The vast majority of my sales come from maybe 20 to 25 percent of my customers," said a department-store manager in a small city. "If I can get those big spenders into my store more often, it helps my revenue numbers and the bottom line. That is supposed to be an advantage to digital: the online folks tell me I have a better chance of targeting the ad to the right person."

Yet, despite the frustrations, confusion, and reservations voiced by many merchants, there was also some good news for community papers in the advertiser research. Most merchants indicated they still allocated the majority of their marketing budget to the local newspaper since they believed—for now—that the paper was the most cost-efficient way to reach the widest possible local market. They also liked the engagement of a newspaper audience, believing this meant their advertisement was more likely to be noticed. "Unlike radio, where you don't know whether they're daydreaming or not, people have to pay attention when they are reading the newspaper," said one chain retail merchant in a small city.

Even though broadcast and online sales representatives shared data and information with them, most merchants still viewed the local newspaper sales force as more "trustworthy" than those with other mediums, such as the regional television station, billboard company, or online sites. "I personally know the newspaper advertising director and the salesman who handle my account," said one retailer. "I see them around town all the time, and the guy handling my account comes by every week or so to check on things and pick up the ad. Most of the other salesmen cover us as part of a big territory, and I see them maybe once a month or a quarter. We're just not a priority, like we are with the newspaper."

In addition, almost all local merchants indicated that they were still rooting for the newspaper's financial success. "Let's face it. I'm a resident of this community, too, and want to see the local paper succeed because it is important to this community," said one realtor, summing up the prevailing sentiment. "If the newspaper could come up with something I couldn't get somewhere else, I'd move advertising dollars back into the paper."

In sum, advertiser research indicates that there is a foundation on which newspapers can build during this time of disruption in the marketplace, as they seek to navigate from a print-only focus to a multiplatform one. Since most merchants still allocate the majority of their budget to the local paper, publishers and advertising directors will want to come up with strategies for prioritizing service and offering products that appeal to these advertisers. They will also want to build on the perception that the paper's staff is viewed as more "trustworthy" by training everyone in the sales effort to understand how to match the medium with the message.

However, with the dynamics changing dramatically, publishers need to act decisively to counter mistaken impressions in the marketplace and reposition the community newspaper as a twenty-first-century medium. This requires reframing the "story" about the value of advertising in a cross-platform "newspaper" and then totally retooling the newspaper's sales operations to *strategically* pursue new revenue opportunities.

Matching the Medium with the Message

Journalists understand that they need to convey information in such a way that they capture the attention of readers. Similarly, advertising directors and sales representatives need to understand that they need to be telling advertisers a compelling "story" about the audience the newspaper delivers and the value of using multiple mediums (print and digital) to build "share of mind" with the consumer. If publishers and advertising directors are to "follow the money" in the twenty-first century, they must understand the new media economics of the digital age.

The economic theory that prevailed in the twentieth century described what is known in economics as a "zero-sum game" in which the success of one medium comes at the expense of another. It was first articulated in 1965 by Charles Scripps, chairman of E. W. Scripps Company, who observed that, despite the introduction of two new mediums—radio and television—the amount of advertising dollars spent on media in the twentieth century seemed to have remained a "relatively constant" 2 percent of our country's gross domestic product. Because this "Principle of Relative Constancy," as it became known, assumed that the size of the "revenue pie" remained the same—and was dependent on growth or contraction of the economy and not altered by the introduction of new media technologies—it predicted a future of declining revenues for an existing medium, such as newspapers, when a new medium, such as the Internet, entered the market.

But in contrast to the twentieth century—in which video, audio, and print messages were pushed out in separate channels to captive audiences watching a television show, listening to a radio program, or reading a newspaper—the advent of the digital age has brought us multiple channels and a whole new type of marketing that features interconnectivity, immediacy, and interactivity across various channels and with consumers who navigate between them in real time.

Considering both the traditional (print, video, audio) and nontraditional forms of marketing that this new technology has allowed to flourish, initial research calculates that the amount of advertising dollars spent on media in the twenty-first century is more than double the 2 percent assumed in the twentieth century. And, even more important, it is growing, especially among "nontraditional" forms of advertising and marketing. For newspaper publishers who have despaired over the precipitous decline in print advertising revenue in this decade, this new insight offers a path to renewal—provided they embrace the notion that their community newspapers are cross-platform mediums and take an expansive view of additional content and experiences newspapers can offer both readers and advertisers.

Yet a recent report by the Pew Research Center suggests that companies are leaving money on the table by failing to fully utilize and capitalize on the new technology—and the cross-platform opportunities it offers. Most community newspapers that publish both print and online editions are well positioned to offer local merchants one-stop shopping for a variety of advertising services. This includes assistance with introducing a product, differentiating and attributing value to an existing product, and encouraging purchase and repurchase of a product or service.

In order to take advantage of the cross-platform opportunities, newspaper sales representatives need to be able to advise a merchant in terms of both choosing the most appropriate medium to reach the right audience and designing the message so that it uses the medium to best advantage. But first newspaper sales representatives need to understand the message, or messages, the merchant is hoping to deliver.

When asked what they hope to accomplish, most local businesses initially respond that they simply want to either "sell" a certain product or service or "get feet through the door." In other words, merchants are very focused on the transaction. Indeed, in the predigital world, most print advertisements in newspapers were intended to entice consumers to purchase a product or service by giving them information about where to buy it and how much it cost.

The interactivity and timeliness of the digital era puts local advertising "on steroids," enabling newspapers to offer a range of marketing "solutions" to their clients. In addition to encouraging purchase or repurchase of an item, advertisements can now directly connect consumers with businesses so they can conclude the transaction without ever leaving home. Search advertising, for example, serves primarily one purpose: connecting consumers with products they are already inclined to purchase.

But there is a whole range of functions newspaper advertising can provide prior to and after the transaction. For example, prior to purchase, advertisements can increase consumer awareness about a new product or service. Similarly, they can rekindle demand for, or attribute more value to, an existing or mature product or service, differentiating it from the competition. After a purchase, they can be used to build loyalty among current customers, who may recommend the product to friends, building awareness among a new set of potential consumers.

While print has declined, it still remains a very viable and enduring medium for a variety of messages. Advertisements in print editions of newspapers, for example, can be used to efficiently and effectively broadcast a message to a large audience. It can provide information about a product or service and where to purchase it. Online advertising can be used to engage customers prior to and after a purchase, and it can make the transaction happen, putting consumers directly in touch with the seller. Online can also be used effectively to segment an audience.

"Print to expose, online to close" is how one newspaper framed the solution to potential advertisers. That simple slogan indicates the power of using both mediums to best advantage. The print edition of most community newspapers still delivers a much larger daily audience than the digital one. However, the digital edition delivers a younger, more engaged audience—the very type of consumers most likely to purchase both big-ticket items (such as cars and houses) and smaller ones (such as groceries and clothing). Most newspaper digital audiences are also more tech savvy than print readers—and much more likely to have purchased items online recently.

The Chicago weekly *La Raza* offers its advertisers "a 360-degree solution" that includes mobile, website, print, and event sponsorship. "Each of these options reaches a different segment of the audience," says publisher Jimena Catarivas. "Mobile typically reaches people who don't read the print edition but access the website from their phones. Event sponsorship reaches people who read us in print and online, as well as people in the larger community who may not read us regularly."

As Catarivas points out, it is very important that a newspaper's advertising sales staff know and understand the differences in demographics and purchase habits of the various audiences that each of the mediums deliver so they know how to advise advertisers on how best to use the various platforms to either extend reach or double down on exposure to a message. That is why newspapers should consider doing a simple annual market survey that tracks spending habits of readers, as well as their loyalty and engagement with the two editions. (See businessofnews.unc.edu for an example of a simple reader survey.)

Being informed of the differences in audience that the two editions of one community newspaper delivered, a large regional car dealer in one rural market immediately began to see how he might use the paper to effectively craft a dual marketing strategy, placing advertisements for high-end sedans and luxury cars in the print edition. His typical customers for these cars were forty and older, much more in line with the print profile. Reasoning that many of his customers had teenagers and might be in the market for a third car, his print message also directed customers interested in compact and used cars to his dealership's ad in the online edition. That advertisement featured homemade video tours of a handful of some of the "top" cars on the lot, as well as a link to his site that had photos of all the used cars available. He reasoned that most of these online customers were younger—and more likely to browse online before purchasing.

This integrated sales plan used print and online to segment the audience and get the appropriate and most effective message in front of both audiences. In addition, the dealer then created messages that were appropriate for the two mediums. He felt that "elegant" black-and-white photos in the print edition spoke to consumers about the quality of high-end cars, such as a Lincoln or a Cadillac, while the homemade videos engaged a younger audience who expected "sight, sound, and motion" with online advertisements.

Perhaps because he had previously purchased advertisements on a regional television station, this car dealer was much more perceptive about matching the message to the medium than most local merchants are. In part, that is because many community newspapers have, until recently, offered online solutions consisting entirely of static online banner or directory-style ads, some of which have a link to the merchant's online site. When businesses don't have many users who "click-through" to their site from the online newspaper site, or customers don't mention the digital ad when they come into the store, the merchants assume no one saw it.

In fact, many people see the online advertisements, but they aren't moved to respond. The problem is with the message. It is a static message in a very interactive environment.

Most of the merchants surveyed in small to midsized markets recognize that they need to move beyond banner and directory ads, but they are uncertain how to do so. If the newspaper does not help them make this transition, someone else will—and pocket the money for these services. So it is in the long-term best interest of the newspaper to develop the ability to match the message with the appropriate medium.

Therefore, some community newspapers have begun to set up in-house ad agencies to help local merchants move beyond directory and banner advertisements. They can do this simply, as the *Hampshire Review* in West Virginia and the *Columbia Daily Herald* in Tennessee have done. Both newspapers help local merchants design their own websites and come up with marketing plans that utilize print, online, and social media. The *Daily Herald*, which is owned by Stephens Media, then hands off the ongoing maintenance to corporate headquarters, while the independent *Review* provides that service for a monthly fee.

"Most of my clients don't know how to do this," says Sallie See of the *Review*. "One advantage to providing this service is that I can charge them a monthly fee for all of it—and I usually put them on a one-year contract. That way I can focus on retaining them instead of having to make the sale monthly." The *Review* charges as little as $75 a month for its online advertising services. At the other end of the spectrum is the *Santa Rosa Press Democrat*, which charges its sixty-five clients an average of $1,000 monthly for a full range of digital marketing services, including Web development and search-optimization packages. At the end of the first year, the agency accounted for 25 percent of the paper's digital revenue.

But a full-service, in-house agency may not be a profitable venture for smaller, less-affluent markets. A recent white paper by the American Association of Advertising Agencies concluded that "digital advertising is more complex and more expensive to execute than traditional advertising." So another approach is for advertising representatives to identify and build a local network of design specialists to whom they can refer merchants. "With print advertising, we've always offered design for free. But creating digital advertising is much more time-consuming," said one advertising director. "So we plan to work with the local community college to develop this expertise."

A newspaper partnership with local designers has a number of advantages. It frees up the newspaper's salespeople to advise and consult on message and medium but also continue to make sales calls. More broadly, it also benefits the entire community since the newspaper is actually connecting small business owners (merchants and Web designers) and encouraging local commerce. A third approach is the least labor intensive and also provides a valuable client service: a newspaper can hold monthly workshops that instruct local businesses on how to create online advertising that matches the medium with the marketing goal, such as using supporting video or interactive participatory reader contests with online advertising.

Regardless of which type of design service a community newspaper chooses to offer its advertisers, it is vital that its sales representatives understand how to advise their clients on choosing *both* the right medium and message. In addition to creating an in-house digital agency, the *Columbia Daily Herald* has developed seven digital initiatives, including a Platinum Plus program that allows merchants to advertise in a package of five platforms—three in print and two in digital, including on the paper's website and in an e-mail blast to 8,000 subscribers. Among the print

Advertising as the Art of Storytelling

How can newspaper publishers help the advertising staff transition from selling space in the print edition to selling cross-platform marketing solutions? The first step, says JoAnn Sciarrino, an advertising executive with more than twenty-five years of experience, is to understand the capabilities of the various mediums and then use the appropriate mediums to help the advertiser tell a compelling and engaging story. Prior to becoming Knight Chair in Digital Advertising and Marketing at UNC, Sciarrino was executive vice president for BBDO North America, where she advised more than thirty global clients. Her recent research focuses on measuring the emotional connection between people and brands.

Q. Is Print Advertising Dying?

No, print is not dying, but it will settle down to a lower level than in the past. There is a prevailing belief in the media industry—and among publishers in particular—that print advertising is in a zero-sum game with online advertising, such that, for every dollar of print advertising lost, online advertising gains a dollar. This misconception is untrue, as total advertising has been on an upward trend due to the increase in channels and innovations in types of media.

Q. How different is this new world of advertising that newspapers face?

Empowered by technology and more mobile than ever, connected consumers move quickly in and out of hundreds of paid and "owned" brand connections a day. As an example, there are more than 1.1 billion active Facebook users. Sixty percent log in daily, 68 percent using a mobile device. They have an average of 200 friends and upload 350,000 photos each day. Marketers and advertisers have never had so many ways to connect brands to people, and yet had such difficulty in making meaningful connections through all the clutter. Despite these challenges, some brands are thriving, even on comparatively lower budgets. What are these marketers and advertisers doing for their brands that others are not?

These successful marketers are creating disproportionately higher levels of emotional attachment between people and brands through effective storytelling. Higher levels of emotional attachment between people and brands matter because it has been associated with higher financial performance.

Branded storytelling is the next generation and natural evolution to traditional advertising, and a domain that newspapers are in a unique position to leverage. Even though time spent with print media is flat, artful and effective storytelling is giving rise to new revenue opportunities that drive higher levels of emotional brand attachment. This is why I believe now will come to be known as the "Golden Age" of advertising. Advertisers are no longer one-way "story yellers"; rather, they are evolving to be some of the greatest storytellers of our time.

One recent example of effective storytelling that successfully matched the medium with the message is Maybelline and Blippar in the "Color Show Nail Lacquer" campaign, which engaged users to participate in a virtual nail show to select the perfect shade via integrated print advertising. The target audience was trend-setting females, ages thirteen to eighteen, who like to experiment with color. The print ads enticed readers to virtually "try on" forty different shades of nail polish on their own hand through a mobile app. Additionally, users could post the image of their virtual nail polish pictures to social media, enabling reach beyond paid media.

Q. As a publisher, what does this mean about the future role of newspapers in local advertising?

Newspapers need to have a deep understanding of the capabilities of each medium and how they work together to improve efficiency. For example, nearly a third of today's ROI (return on investment) from a print advertisement comes from having the print ad go viral and shared on other media. That means if you aren't developing ways to help your advertisers' [paid] stories go viral, you aren't helping them achieve higher returns.

Newspapers can begin to help advertisers by thinking about how the medium and the message can work together to produce the best stories. Even if newspapers don't have an in-house agency, the consultative thinking about what stories will drive emotional attachment between people and brands will add incremental value for your advertiser. Evaluate whether that static banner or directory ad your advertiser wants to run will drive an emotional attachment between the people and the brand. If not, show them how to build an emotional attachment with the brand through stories that clearly demonstrate shared values and shared experiences.

options are three slick "niche" magazines introduced beginning in 2009. "We only create products that we think will be good for the merchants," says publisher Mark Palmer. "And we track the profitability on everything. We have lower profit expectations for our digital products than for our print magazines. But we don't create anything that we don't believe will succeed. We owe that to our advertisers and our sales staff."

As the *Daily Herald* example shows, it is not the size of a paper that influences the options it is able to offer advertisers; rather, it is about the "mindset" of the sales staff. Community newspaper publishers who are able to change the mindset of their sales staff (from selling space to selling solutions) and then educate them on how to match the medium and the message to a merchant's sales goals have a tremendous advantage in the marketplace. In contrast to sales representatives of other mediums—which typically push only one platform—those from local newspapers can come to be seen as very credible "marketing consultants" who can offer a range of print and online options to local advertisers.

Moving beyond Print

In the advertising business, there is always a tension between reach (delivering a message to the widest possible audience) and efficiency (targeting the audience most likely to respond to a message). Community newspapers have traditionally positioned themselves as delivering the "mass" audience to local merchants. Increasingly, those merchants believe they need both "mass" and "niche." By using the various media platforms now available, advertisers can connect with consumers in both the broadest and narrowest sense.

"Two weeks ago, a new realtor in town came into the advertising department wanting to purchase an advertisement in the paper to announce his arrival in town. He was only thinking about buying an ad in the print paper," says Catherine Nelson, general manager of the *Rutland Herald*. "I spent about thirty minutes with him, asking him what he was hoping to accomplish and who he wanted to see the ad, and was able to put together a program for him on five different platforms—including our e-edition, our business journals, our paper, and our website. I saw him yesterday and he said the ad had reached everyone he hoped to reach and more. He said other realtors had come up to him and told him his ad appeared to be *everywhere*. He couldn't believe the exposure he'd gotten from one ad in the *Herald* on multiple platforms."

Recent industry and proprietary studies have found that advertisers who use two mediums to send a message can increase the effectiveness of their campaigns by as much as 50 percent. This suggests community newspapers have a tremendous competitive advantage if they sell digital *in combination* with their print offerings. By repositioning themselves as a cross-platform medium, they can offer their advertisers something most local competitors can't: effective and efficient access to engaged consumers across multiple channels.

Repositioning the newspaper as a cross-platform medium involves two important steps. The ad sales staff must learn how to help advertisers effectively engage and connect with the newspaper's readers on various platforms and in various venues (online and "offline"). Simultaneously, publishers and advertising directors must revise the advertising rates, taking a "value-based" approach to pricing of both the print and online editions—especially when sold in combination—and then set about reeducating advertisers as to the advantages of using two or more platforms in tandem to reach the various audiences that a paper is delivering.

In order to advise advertisers on how to more effectively connect and engage with consumers, sales staffs need to see the marketplace and the potential media options as the newspapers' readers do. Most readers of community newspapers—whether in remote towns or crowded cities—are increasingly comfortable engaging in conversations on multiple media channels, reinforcing and expanding their connections with their geographic communities as well as several largely "social" communities built around special interests and passions. In addition, in certain "offline" venues—such as a concert, a meeting, or a shopping mall—they are often online as well.

Therefore, "in a media-saturated world, persuading through interruptions and repetition is increasingly ineffective," concluded a recent article in the *Harvard Business Review*. "To engage consumers, advertisers must focus on where and when they will be receptive." The article outlined four separate channels—or venues—for connecting and engaging consumers in what it termed the "public, social, tribal, and psychological spheres." Community newspapers can use these "spheres" as a framework for helping advertisers connect with readers in a way that is both high-tech and high touch.

In "the public sphere," as the article calls it, customers are in transit, often heading to a specific destination, such as a grocery store, their workplace, or home. Such interactions often are solitary, involving only a single consumer with a particular medium. In the past, advertisers hoping to reach these consumers relied primarily on radio and billboards and "pushed out" a single message aimed at a mass audience. Mobile technology opens up a whole range of possibilities that newspapers can utilize to reach and interact with these consumers and to personalize the message using video; online newsletters and updates; text messaging; and targeted, geospecific coupons.

In contrast, consumers in "the social sphere" are intentionally, or unintentionally, interacting with one another—either face-to-face or through a medium such as the Internet. In its digital edition or through a Facebook page, a newspaper can make the interactions of readers with one another or with advertisers much richer and more meaningful by offering numerous opportunities for them to "meet" through online games, contests, and reader forums. In West Virginia, for example, Sallie See attempts to interact daily with the 4,200 friends that are on the Facebook page of the *Hampshire Review*, commenting on their posts and informing them of new stories and advertisers on the paper's digital site. The *Columbia Daily Herald* offers its readers numerous online contests, all sponsored by local merchants.

The *Polish Daily News* recently added weekly reader contests in an attempt to draw readers to the newspaper's classified advertising, carried in both the print edition and on the website. Unlike many other community newspapers, the *Daily News* still has a healthy classified business, carrying eight pages in the daily paper and an average of eighteen pages on the weekend. "Many immigrants are looking for either a job or an apartment in Chicago, and this has been the place Polish immigrants have turned to for a century," explains general manager Magdalena Pantelis. "We feel the key is getting a new generation to consult the website as well as the paper. And when we get them to the [redesigned] website, we're trying to engage them and let them see they can interact with it and with each other."

But not all of the interaction in the "social sphere" needs to be online. There are numerous "offline" opportunities for newspapers to connect readers and advertisers. Chicago's *La Raza* hosts cultural events that connect advertising sponsors with the city's Latino community. "But an important function is also to connect people in the Latino community with one another since many Latinos are recent immigrants and don't know many people here," says editor Fabiola Pomareda.

Having connected in the social sphere, consumers often deepen their interaction in "the tribal sphere," where they associate with people who have similar affiliations or affinities. Like the *Columbia Daily Herald* in Tennessee, many newspapers have focused on providing advertisers with an efficient way to target a niche audience by establishing print and online magazines and special pages focusing on such topics as health, sports, male lifestyle, and parenting. By creating special print and online publications or pages for these "communities of special interests," newspapers have the potential to increase reader loyalty as well as engagement with both editorial and advertising content.

In doing so, they pave the way for consumers to "connect brands with specific thoughts" or editorial content in the "psychological sphere." This last concept—of connecting psychologically, not with one another but with a brand message—is useful in helping newspapers consider how to move beyond offering the traditional "advertisements" that run in the print edition without regard for what content it adjoins. Taking a cue from other mediums, such as magazines and public television, newspapers can create and offer a variety of marketing opportunities that allow local merchants to be "associated" with certain content.

At its most basic level, this "association" with editorial content involves simply grouping articles by subject matter and charging a premium to an advertiser who routinely asks to be near—or adjacent to—certain topics, such as business or sports news. More elaborately, it involves identifying subcommunities—or "tribes"—of readers with special interests (such as sports or parenting), creating special cross-platform content for these communities and then offering "sponsorship" packages that allow an advertiser to reach a targeted, engaged "special-interest" community across various media channels. As an example, an advertiser who sponsors a community page for sports enthusiasts might be entitled to be associated with any or all of the following content: weekly pregame and postgame video blogs by local football coaches, mobile text messages that update game scores, sports contests on the newspaper's Facebook page, and a yearly preseason breakfast with the coaches, moderated by the sports editor. (For more examples of sponsorship packages, see businessofnews. unc.edu.)

As the various media options—and channels for reaching consumers— have multiplied, many local merchants no longer distinguish between advertising and marketing expenses. "I used to divide my marketing expenses into two buckets," says a local retailer in Chicago. "One was for 'advertising,' mostly in the local newspaper. The other was for 'marketing'—you know, sponsoring local events. Now, with social networking and all, there are so many ways to promote your business. So now I just have one expense line for all marketing expenses."

"One expense line" for all marketing and advertising expenses: that is the way both national and local advertisers are increasingly allocating their advertising dollars. So at the same time that publishers are training their sales staffs to understand how to engage readers with an advertiser's message in a variety of venues, they need to be reeducating advertisers as to how to get a better return on their marketing dollars by using the various print and digital platforms that a community newspaper offers.

But first they need to reset pricing expectations for these nonprint options. While many newspapers have "pushed" digital advertising by hiring online specialists or contracting with local vendors to sell it, most have not adjusted their digital rates, which are a very small fraction of those for print advertising. Therefore, publishers talk about getting only "dimes" or "nickels" for online advertising compared with "dollars" for the print edition. The fact that the number of "visitors" to many community newspaper websites is less than half the number of readers of the paper's print edition only exacerbates the problem. So the digital revenue—priced on a low CPM (cost per thousand) basis—is minuscule at most newspapers because of the small size of the audience.

To escape the digital pricing problem, newspapers need to move away from selling and pricing their print and online options as separate advertising mediums and instead move toward focusing on the value of the audiences that the newspaper is offering on its various platforms. "Four years ago, we realized we were selling against one another," says *Santa Rosa Press Democrat* publisher Bruce Kyse. "By sending out two sales representatives—one for print and one for the digital side—we were coming across as a two-headed monster to area businesses. We can't compete. We have to sell the value of both our print and digital products."

Longtime pricing consultant Thomas Nagle has worked with a number of newspapers over the last two decades—including the *New York Times* and the *Wall Street Journal*—on revamping their advertising rate cards to appropriately capture the value the newspapers are delivering in their print and digital versions. He lays out three steps that newspapers can use to strategically align the value of cross-platform advertising with the price that advertisers should be willing to pay. First, publishers and advertising directors need to calculate the cost to a local merchant of advertising in competitive media. In most communities, this includes print and broadcast media, such as magazines and radio, as well as digital options, including those offered by traditional outlets. Next, they need to identify all factors that differentiate their newspaper from these competitors. This includes the reach of a community newspaper across various print and digital platforms, the engagement of readers with the editorial content, the timeliness of the material, and the ability to segment an audience based on its special interests. After determining the values of these "differentiating factors," newspapers then need to add them up "to determine the total economic value—what a fully informed, economically rational consumer" would pay. Using this process in conjunction with the insights gained from reader and advertiser research, publishers can begin to devise a rate card that more accurately captures the value delivered to local advertisers who use two or more mediums to connect with readers.

As recent research has shown, use of two or more mediums increases the efficiency of advertisements by 50 percent or more because an advertiser is much more likely to reach additional consumers as well as expose consumers who have seen an ad previously to the message again, increasing the chances they will recall it. Repeat exposure is often necessary to move a consumer toward purchase of a product. This means that local merchants who purchase both the print and online editions of community newspapers are receiving two quantifiable benefits. Approximately half of the visitors to online editions say they "rarely or never" read the print edition. Therefore the advertiser has reached new customers with his online message, but he has also increased exposure to the advertisement with the other half of digital edition readers, who are also frequent readers of the print edition and are seeing the message for the second time.

In addition, the latter group—those who read both the print and online editions—tends to be very loyal to the newspaper. Loyal readers are much more likely to be engaged with the editorial content, which will make them more likely to notice and engage with adjacent advertising messages.

Even when the smaller audience of many online newspaper editions is taken into account, then, the value of an advertisement that runs in both the print and online editions of most community newspapers is at least 50 percent greater than an advertisement that runs in the print edition only—due to the increased reach, exposure, and reader engagement that the digital medium offers. By pricing the combination print and online rate at a 20 percent premium, newspapers are still offering advertisers exceptional value while significantly boosting the 5 or 10 percent digital add-on rate that most community newspapers charge.

How to Think about Cross-Platform Sales

As senior analyst and director of consulting for BIA/Kelsey, Jed Williams has led strategic consulting projects for a number of media companies, including AOL, the Associated Press, Deseret Media, Google, and Time Warner Cable. A master's student at UNC from 2008 to 2010, he was a project leader in the initial phase of the Community Newspaper Project and has continued to advise newspapers of all sizes on how to build and execute successful cross-platform sales and marketing strategies for their advertisers. His insights have recently been cited in the *New York Times*, the *Wall Street Journal*, and Bloomberg, among others.

Q. How can newspaper sales staffs reinvent and retool to adapt to the digital age?

With newspaper sales, there's often a lot of hand-wringing about whether the root problem lies in design or personnel. In other words, is this about the quality of the product being sold or the type of person selling [it]? Product selection and bundling strategy are obviously critical, especially with growing competition from digital pure plays. That is why newspapers need to reposition themselves as cross-platform advertising mediums.

But it is also a people matter. Do you have the right people on the bus to make an authentic transformation? First and foremost, an advertising salesperson must understand the value each platform offers. They must understand, innately, how online and mobile advertising work, why they work, and how those two combine with print to increase advertising effectiveness.

Q. What implications does this have for the portfolio of marketing products and services that newspapers should offer?

Increasingly, advertisers aren't willing to fork over the lion's share of their advertising budget to merely rent real estate on a newspaper's website or in their printed editions. They have more options than ever. With "owned" channels—such as database marketing, social media, and content marketing—they have more control than ever. But businesses need help in tapping into these multidimensional opportunities.

The new mission of the newspaper sales staff isn't simply to sell more advertising (though that can be part of the solution), but to aid clients in overcoming digital fragmentation and capturing new customers. Perhaps this means building them a better website, helping them with social media engagement, or enabling their e-mail and text marketing efforts.

Q. How should newspapers incorporate mobile into multiplatform sales?

The growth of mobile platforms is staggering. Well over 50 percent of U.S. consumers have smartphones. They check them more than 100 times each day. And increasingly, they use them to make buying decisions. Mobile users want information that is up-to-date and personalized. Often, they're searching for local content—whether a recommendation for an auto mechanic, a restaurant review, a nearby event, or a real-time local news story. Newspapers can utilize mobile experiences to regalvanize the identity and value that they've fostered for their geographic communities. News isn't the only vehicle to do this. The *Dallas Morning News* uses mobile media to update high school sports contests. For the *Chicago Tribune*, it's about daily commutes and nearby hotspots via its RedEye app.

Mobile advertising hasn't kept up with rapid consumer adoption, but there is optimism that locally targeted advertising carrying personalized experiences that help users choose businesses is a strong path forward. We encourage sales teams to sell mobile—whether targeted display, local search, text campaigns, or websites—as part of a multiplatform offering that parallels the multiplatform experiences being emphasized on the content side.

Q. Where are the revenue opportunities in new channels?

Whereas mobile platforms present opportunities to reinforce geographic community, interactive channels such as social media, shopping marketplaces, and vertical content expand the definition of community beyond strict geographic lines to include audience affinities, passions, and causes.

These new communities built around affinities also present new revenue possibilities. Local businesses can sponsor topical contests (such as most-creative pet photo, football picks, or honor-student nominations) that live on a variety of platforms—website, Facebook page, e-mail newsletters, mobile—and create greater "stickiness" with readers. Robust online and mobile shopping applications—with updated listings, reviews, products, photos, menus, and social feeds—help residents make buying decisions. Merchants highly value these conversions. New content verticals open up sponsorship opportunities.

Q. Newspapers have assets that extend deep into their communities. How can sales teams leverage these assets to create online-to-offline connections and value for marketers?

One of newspapers' tried and true assets is their physical presence in the community, covering local events and influencing the public agenda in that market. Even in a digital age, there remain significant offline opportunities to engage the community in ways that create incremental revenue. In fact, digital platforms can strengthen offline opportunities by creating greater reach, awareness, and engagement.

Events present the most obvious and robust offline opportunity. They can take many flavors: town hall discussions, community roundtables and debates, business expos, bridal events, career fairs, home shows, music festivals, and many more. There are just as many opportunities to monetize: sponsorship, booths, premium seating, VIP packages, merchandising. Newspapers are uniquely positioned in their communities to create and execute these events and use their print and digital assets to drive their success.

If the newspaper also offers a mobile option as well as the opportunity to "sponsor" certain editorial content, the advertiser has the ability to connect and interact with readers in all four of the "spheres"—public, social, tribal, and psychological—mentioned above. And that increases the value of the advertisement even further.

This suggests that, instead of selling print and online advertising separately, most community newspapers should play to their strengths and competitive advantage by aggressively seeking to convert top print advertisers to a dual print and online schedule, priced at an appropriate premium that begins to capture the true value to the advertiser. In addition, they should consider ramping up their mobile offerings and creating niche products that advertisers can sponsor.

There are numerous advantages to this for the newspaper. When both editions are combined, the print edition is no longer the "mature" one while the digital edition is the "nascent" one. Sold together, the print and online editions are a dual-platform medium that offers the advertiser one-stop shopping. It is a much stronger competitor to traditional local mediums, such as radio, television, and billboards, or newer digital ones—all which are essentially offering only a single platform for delivery.

In addition, by selling the two editions as a package, the local newspaper can reset pricing expectations—especially for the digital component. From the beginning, digital advertising pricing has been dictated by the large online giants who stress "eyeballs" (their strength) over engagement (a community newspaper's strength). Most local merchants are not interested in reaching more eyeballs, but only in making sure their advertisements are seen by residents in the community and prompt them to act. "I want my ad to bring feet through the door," as one merchant put it.

Aware of the value that a cross-platform medium actually delivers to advertisers—and with a rate card that conveys that value—community newspapers are well positioned to begin *profitably* pursuing new revenue opportunities. Next, the sales staff needs to learn how to hit the street selling differently—and strategically.

Strategic Management of the Sales Force

With advertising revenues plummeting, the sales effort in many community newspapers has become more and more unfocused, even frantic, in recent years. As one salesman describes his typical week: "It seems like we're constantly chasing smaller and smaller dollars. We're doing more special sections, hoping to pick up small advertisers to make up for the loss of big advertisers. If you are breathing, I'll try to sell you an advertisement." This unfocused, scattershot approach—which chases low-margin, low-return accounts in an effort to replace lost print revenue—also comes with a huge opportunity cost. It prevents a community newspaper from repositioning itself as a true cross-platform advertising medium for the digital age.

"In any sales organization, laser-like focus is the best way to turn around the numbers," says Nancy Adler, who has more than two decades of experience leading sales and marketing management at media companies, ranging in size from the *Wall Street Journal* to *Crain's New York Business*. In consulting with community newspapers in recent years, she has found that "sales reps on small papers are often chasing smaller and smaller sums—especially as the dollars spent on print advertising are shrinking. If you are the ad director of a small paper, it's very easy to re-flexively add another special print advertising section without evaluating whether it is worth the time and effort—or whether it is really serving the advertiser or reader well."

In contrast, a strategic approach is a top-down exercise. The vision and the pace are set by the publisher and advertising director. There are three elements in the strategic management of a sales force:

- First, publishers and ad directors need to identify high-priority accounts—those current and potential advertisers with the most upside potential.

- Next, they need to focus staff time and attention on developing services and content packages for these high-priority advertisers, using a consultative sales approach that stresses the integrated print/online solutions.
- And finally, they need to track the sales effort on a routine basis, recognizing successes and adjusting strategy as needed.

"In the beginning, when our very survival was at stake, I made two mistakes," says Palmer of the *Daily Herald*. "I didn't prioritize and threw too many products at the sales force. They felt loaded down. And I didn't stress digital enough. I wish I'd been as big a supporter two years ago as I am now. I've come to understand it has to be in everything we sell."

Publishers and ad directors undertaking a strategic approach should first do a simple benchmarking exercise to identify high-volume, high-margin advertisers, as well as potential new customers with upside potential and former high-volume merchants who have recently moved their marketing dollars to a competitor. At most community newspapers, more than half of the yearly advertising revenue comes from 80 to 100 advertisers. In many community newspapers, very few of the high-volume advertisers are purchasing the online edition, which suggests there is significant return on "upselling" these accounts and convincing them to purchase both print and digital.

Having prioritized these accounts, publishers and ad directors then need to do an inventory of current offerings. They should look for existing and potential cross-platform franchises that might offer an attractive "sponsorship" opportunity, such as certain types of content (a sports calendar, for example) or a community page built around a special interest like parenting or quality-of-life issues. Emphasizing "sponsorships" has several advantages for a community newspaper. Financially, sponsorship packages move the newspaper away from its heavy print advertising reliance and begin to establish a higher "value" for advertisements that run in the digital edition, especially when purchased in tandem with the print. Also, sponsorship packages are usually sold on a schedule ranging from six months to a year, which allows sales representatives to focus on retention of high-priority advertisers instead of continually chasing "new" advertisers.

After completing the inventory of current and potential content packages, publishers and ad directors should then establish revenue targets for each of the high-priority advertisers, tying these targets to the sales of integrated print/online packages and sponsorships of content. Outside of regular sales calls, the publisher or advertising director also need to meet with high-priority advertisers to solicit feedback. An annual "check-up" visit is useful for two reasons. First, it provides the newspaper with useful information, such as how the local television station is selling against the newspaper. But just as important, it begins to position the newspaper as a "collaborator" with local merchants, especially when the publisher or advertising director shares proprietary data about the local community or the paper's readers. (For an example of an annual advertiser survey, see businessofnews.unc.edu.)

After conducting a round of high-priority advertiser interviews and setting sales targets for each of these accounts, publishers next need to focus on incorporating "consultative selling" into the newspaper's sales culture.

When publisher Dave Neill reorganized the advertising department at the *Naples Daily News*, he was seeking to move the sales approach "away from generalist to specialist." Specifically, he wanted to get away from the routine in which an account executive has a 9:00 A.M. "appointment with the liquor store . . . at ten, they got an appointment with the nail salon, at eleven they got an appointment with an ambulance-chasing attorney." With the Naples sales staff assigned to specific industries—such as health and wellness, real estate, or food—"they're able to share national industry trends, they're able to share regional economic trends," Neill says.

For a newspaper sales representative in the predigital world, success usually depended on maintaining a good relationship with local advertisers and being known as a reliable "order-taker and processor"—someone who could make sure that an advertisement got into the newspaper on the right day and in the correct form. In this new era, relationships are still important in the sales process. Since most newspaper representatives live locally, advertisers say they tend to "trust" newspaper salespeople more than those with television stations or digital outlets who live out of town.

Nevertheless, local merchants want more. During a time of immense confusion in the marketplace, they are looking for advice. So while they still "trust" the newspaper representatives to handle their advertising efficiently, they often perceive the salespeople with other mediums as more "credible." In contrast to newspaper representatives, these salespeople come armed with data that speak to the reach and efficiency of the audience they deliver. "In order to close the credibility gap with local advertisers—and build on the trust that still exists in the marketplace— newspaper publishers need to change the mindset of their advertising staff," says Adler. "Sales representatives need to become 'marketing consultants' for their advertisers."

As the Naples example illustrates, true consultative selling involves more than just providing "numbers" and data to counter a competitive claim. It begins with sales representatives doing advance homework—being up-to-date on business conditions in the community and understanding the impact they might have on particular merchants. Then they need to sit down with local advertisers periodically, asking pertinent questions and listening for clues as to how they want to grow their business or respond to local economic challenges. Finally, sales representatives need to come up with a "marketing plan" that achieves the advertisers' goals, matching it to the mediums and the audience that the newspaper delivers.

Such a change in behavior—from selling space to selling solutions—does not come easily in most newspapers. In a recent Pew report, several newspaper executives admitted that, in the advertising department especially, "implementing cultural change was among their most daunting tasks." Therefore, consultative selling needs to be both mandated and modeled from the top down by the publisher and the advertising director, and it needs to be constantly reinforced through training and rewarded through compensation. That is why publishers will need to significantly revamp their sales compensation plans to reward both consultative and cross-platform sales, which will be discussed in the next section.

A consultative, integrated sales approach requires an integrated sales team in which all representatives are responsible for selling both print and online advertising, with the emphasis on selling combination packages. Progress toward the established revenue targets needs to be monitored on a routine basis—monthly, quarterly, and yearly. Ad directors need to track and publicize on a monthly basis the number of integrated print/online presentations made to existing and potential clients. Staff meetings should be used to discuss successes as well as lessons learned so the sales approach can be refined to reflect feedback from the market.

When Neill began reorganizing the *Naples Daily News* sales effort in 2009, his goal was "to have each individual salesperson be a resident expert in an industry. I first laid out the vision to the mangers, telling them why I thought we needed to blow up the current system and roll the dice. But I didn't push down an agenda. I involved everyone in the planning, and as a result, I had maybe 80 percent buy-in from the sales staff from the beginning. We started with real estate, which was our lowest risk, biggest category. Seeing is believing, and relatively quickly, the holdouts—who initially freaked out because they had to give up accounts they'd had for years—came on board when they saw the early successes we had."

Consultative selling, says Neill, is about "reengaging with the community and the market you serve. Now our customers are dealing with smarter account executives who know how to put together an effective program across multiple platforms. All our account executives sell both print and digital, and—in contrast to many newspaper advertising representatives—all have the knowledge and authority to make decisions on the spot when talking with clients. We're not selling ads anymore; we're selling campaigns."

Day-to-day strategic management of the sales effort is the final and critical step in transitioning advertising staff from the print era to a cross-platform mindset. It involves developing cross-platform solutions, prioritizing the sales effort, and "selling campaigns," not advertising, so that advertising departments "reengage" with the markets they serve. Publishers and ad directors will need to lead by example, modeling behavior along the way. They will need to align goals and performance standards with the new strategy. And they will need to manage the effort on a day-to-day, month-to-month, and year-to-year basis as the newspaper sales staff navigates exciting, but uncertain, times.

Setting Up the Sales Force for Success

As Harvard's Ron Heifetz points out, adaptive change is never easy. Without leadership, most people—and organizations—will opt to continue doing what they know best. The role of strategic leaders—publishers and ad directors—is to nurture a "new DNA" in the sales organization. "Salespeople are very motivated by money," says Palmer. "So if you want to change a salesperson's behavior, you have to set them up for success, so they can make their bonus and commission."

Currently, says strategy consultant Jed Williams, newspaper advertising staffs are simply "following the money" since the overwhelming majority of their bonuses and commissions are tied to print advertising. They are "falling back on the only thing they know how to do": selling space in the print edition. In order to change behavior and break this "path dependence," as the economists label it, newspapers need to simultaneously and sequentially follow three protocols. They need to revise the rate card, revamp the compensation system, and create a structured training program that teaches everyone in the advertising department how to sell the newspaper in the digital era.

Revising the rate card is the first step, says *Rutland Herald* general manager Catherine Nelson, who discovered more than 172 listed rates when she joined the 12,000-circulation paper in 2006. Based on her twenty years of experience consulting with community newspapers ranging in size from 5,000 to 150,000 circulation, she says, "No community newspaper ever routinely uses more than nine—maybe ten—rates. So you start with understanding and identifying which rates are used most frequently and then simplifying the rate card around these rates." Once the rate card is simplified, "then you calculate combination rates for each of the platforms you are offering—based on the different levels and types of audiences you are delivering on each platform."

With the *Herald*'s simplified and revised rate card, "it is practically impossible for a merchant to buy print only," says Nelson, "and that is by design, since if you hand a merchant a rate card, he will automatically gravitate toward the lowest rate—without regard for whether it is accomplishing what he wants to accomplish. So this rate card sets up the salesperson to do what's in the merchant's best interest, and get his message out across multiple platforms, instead of just print."

As Bruce Kyse of the *Santa Rosa Press Democrat* points out, in order to move the needle and increase multiplatform revenue, "you need to change the point of reference for *both* the salesperson and the local businessman, who may be falling back on historical patterns and seeing you as a print-only vehicle." That is why, two years ago, he temporarily revised the combination rate at the Santa Rosa paper, giving a discount on print advertising to merchants who purchased the digital edition as well. "While the average rate went down, digital advertising went through the roof," he says. "Overnight, we had repositioned ourselves in the market. We got a group of businesses to start thinking about us as digitally savvy instead of print-only—which made selling cross-platform much easier the next time the salesperson walked through the door."

Having revised the rate card, publishers next need to revamp the compensation system to reinforce and reward cross-platform sales. At Santa Rosa, Kyse created a new system based on three types of sales: transactional, which were handled by a call center that sold special sections and digital-only accounts; relationship-based, which stressed upselling of mid-sized accounts; and strategic sales, which focused on multiplatform sales to major accounts. The amount of compensation potential for a sales rep increased with the difficulty of the sale. "If there is no activity with an account for six months, we reassign it to another salesperson," he says.

"When we introduced the new sales compensation plan, we did away with everyone's account base. We moved from a system of the salesperson owning the account to the newspaper owning the account."

At the *Columbia Daily Herald*, Palmer has also revamped the compensation system to stress prospecting. "In the past, the older sales guys could maintain their income by just being good order-takers," he says. "I don't need order-takers. I need people who can sell." He has raised the commissions on digital sales and often encourages competition among teams "to see who can sell the most of a certain product. I'll split the sales staff in half, and the winning team that month gets a bonus."

When Neill reorganized the Naples advertising staff, placing every sales representative on an industry-specific team, he decided to continue to compensate on individual effort, not team performance. "Nevertheless," he says, "members of the industry teams quickly realized they could all make more money if they shared information and worked together. It didn't have to be a case of win-lose. All boats could rise."

Regardless of whether a newspaper utilizes a team- or individual-based compensation system, it needs to stress and reward prospecting for major new accounts and multiple-platform sales, including upselling existing accounts, Neill says. "With prospecting, especially major accounts, you have to be patient with the sales cycle and take the long-term view. It took two years to land NetJets, our first major national advertiser. Our compensation system now rewards the patience and professionalism of the account executives who prospect and land big accounts." In other words, it rewards consultative selling—and a whole new type of behavior.

The final step in the process of nurturing new sales DNA is to provide a structured training program that "gives the advertising staff the tools they need to be viewed by the market as true consultants," says Kyse, who instituted a four-tier training program at Santa Rosa. Before a sales rep can advance to the next tier, "you have to pass a test, which involves going out and selling the type of product you just learned to sell in the classroom." Sales reps basically have one year to advance through all four tiers and become certified, says Kyse, "or, you are out."

Palmer takes a similar carrot-and-stick approach to training: "I tell the order-takers, 'I'm glad you were a great order-taker, but you can't make a living now just being an order-taker. I'm going to invest in you, and give you training and teach you to sell. But if you can't learn how to sell advertising, then you need to find some other place to be an order-taker. I need you to be hungry.' This is about the paper's survival." Training, says Neill,

From Selling "Space" to Selling "Solutions"

Nancy Adler has more than two decades of advertising and marketing experience, managing sales efforts at the *Wall Street Journal*, CNBC, and *Crain's New York Business*, where she is currently marketing and sales director. Since 2010 she has been advising publishers and advertising directors involved in the Community Newspaper Project on revamping and reinventing their sales efforts.

Q. How does "consultative sales" differ from traditional sales?

Many media advertising representatives say they are already doing "consultative selling," but in fact they are doing more selling than consulting. And usually they are merely selling the publication or media outlet they represent.

A recent study by the Pew Research Center identified internal tensions between the "legacy" and digital sales cultures as the biggest challenge to their business success. That's why the best route for most community newspapers is to reposition themselves as a cross-platform medium—and make everyone on the staff responsible for selling both print and digital. In order for the sales staff to sell a cross-platform concept, they need to first educate themselves about how to match the medium with the message. Certain platforms are better for achieving certain marketing goals. For example, digital works really well in aiding a transaction. Print often works well in introducing awareness of a product. They work even better together because the advertiser is increasing his reach and repeat exposure to the message.

Next, sales representatives need to understand the unique audience that the newspaper is delivering across its various platforms and how engaged people are with the content. Then, they need to understand what goal or goals the advertiser is trying to achieve. In other words, consultative selling requires knowledge of the medium, the audience, and the advertiser's goals. This means newspaper sales representatives need to move from simply "selling space" in the print edition to, instead, "selling solutions" and marketing options.

Q. What is the best way to move from selling space to selling solutions?

Both publishers and sales representatives need to learn a totally new way of doing business. Though it seems obvious, one of the most effective ways to train advertising representatives is to incorporate a simple "case study" into a routine sales meeting. Each week, for example, a sales representative discusses a current or potential account. The other sales representatives then help one another prep for a "consultative" visit with this account—anticipating questions and concerns that a particular merchant may have, identifying viable competitors, and sharing information about the local market and solutions that have worked for other advertisers. Such a "case study" approach creates organizational knowledge and support for behavioral change.

Q. Why might a sales force resist such a move?

The primary reason for resistance from the sales staff is that, at least initially, it is much more time-consuming to prepare for and conduct consultative sales calls than it is to simply "sell space." Prior to the consultative sales call, newspaper sales representatives need to spend time boning up on the local market and on the marketing options available to advertisers so they can anticipate and counter a competitor's argument. In addition, they need to be knowledgeable about the audience that a newspaper is delivering—the demographics, the interests and passions of the readers, and their engagement with the news and information that the paper produces.

Instead of merely flashing the latest circulation figures, sales representatives conducting a "consultative" meeting will spend a significant amount of time asking questions and then listening to the advertisers' responses so they can suggest thoughtful marketing solutions. Sales representatives often view this as an "opportunity cost" since such time spent preparing for and conducting these meetings prevents them from selling more space in the print edition, and that, ultimately, affects their commissions. Therefore, publishers will want to revamp the sales compensation system to encourage consultative selling.

Q. Does consultative selling take more time than the traditional newspaper sales alternative?

In reality, after an initial ramp-up period, consultative selling is actually much more time efficient—for both the newspaper and its sales representatives—than continuing business as usual. It also has much more impact on the bottom line, especially when consultative selling is paired with strategic management of the sales force—one that prioritizes efforts around high-value advertisers and rewards representatives that sell cross-platform solutions. During a time of immense confusion in the local marketplace, consultative selling acknowledges the new realities, in which community newspapers face many competitors, old and new, for the advertising dollar. It builds on the trust that newspapers still enjoy in the local market and allows the sales staff to reassert some control over their destinies.

is "essential to getting ad staffs away from the assembly-line, manufacturing approach to sales that we practiced in recent years. You can revamp the compensation system and reorganize the advertising department, but unless you teach salespeople a new way to do it, they'll attempt to do it the way they've always done it."

Therefore, publishers and ad directors trying to change sales behavior should employ all the tools they have at their disposable—revising the rate card, revamping compensation, and investing in training. In this new world order, newspaper advertising staffs need to anticipate and meet the rapidly shifting demands in the local market. In order to pursue new revenue *profitably*, advertising sales staffs need to be reeducated about how to match the medium with the message and how to convey the real value that a community newspaper—repositioned as a cross-platform medium—delivers. And then they need to reeducate local advertisers on how to get a better return for their marketing dollars by fully utilizing all the platforms that the newspaper offers.

If publishers and advertising directors commit to revamping their newspapers' business models and changing the focus and sales effort, community newspapers should be able to sustain cross-platform revenue growth at an average annual rate of 6 percent or more, so that a decade from now, more than half of the revenue that sustains good journalism is coming from platforms other than the advertisements sold into the print newspaper. By embracing digital and positioning community newspapers as cross-platform mediums—instead of print-only ones—advertising departments have a unique moment in time to carve out a competitive advantage for their papers in the local market. Sales representatives who understand the unique audience that community newspapers are delivering, as well as the marketing needs of local merchants, can craft a compelling story as to why newspapers are a very viable twenty-first-century advertising medium. And in doing so, they will deliver the money to support good journalism in the digital age.

The Whiteville Experience Pursuing New Revenue

The *News Reporter* has faced the same advertising challenges as most other community newspapers: significant declines in both classified and display advertising and insignificant digital revenues which, until recently, amounted to less than 10 percent of total ad dollars. In 2008 and 2009, when display began to fall dramatically, ad director Mickey Greer moved quickly to protect the print advertising business. He stayed in constant contact with his clients, the 100 or so high-volume advertisers who contributed more than half of total sales revenue.

The other three members of the sales staff focused on the smaller clients, but only Dean Lewis—considered "a quick learner" by his peers at the *News Reporter*—became a "digital expert." An enthusiastic and energetic salesman, Lewis learned most of what he knew about selling digital "space" from a team of outside sales specialists associated with the vendor who handled the newspaper's content management system. These representatives spent several weeks in the Whiteville area in 2008 selling banner and business-directory ads on whiteville.com to local merchants, resulting in $90,000 in revenue. But less than half of these digital advertisers renewed when their contracts were up because "they didn't think the digital ads had been seen by anyone," remembers Greer. Although Lewis remained a very big proponent of the digital edition, that experience left Greer very worried that whiteville.com, with its very low digital rates—and apparently low response rate—could undermine the print edition.

So in the fall of 2010, when editor Les High and his sister, Stuart, in charge of special projects, first became intrigued with the prospect of creating complementary print and online "community pages," Greer cautioned them that "doing a combined sale of the two editions may not be a good idea." In the spring of 2011, Stuart and Greer sat down with sales consultant Nancy Adler—who had sold advertising across multiple platforms, including print, online, mobile, and broadcast—and began analyzing five years of advertising data, looking to identify trends among top-priority accounts and categories of business. "Whiteville is like most newspapers. A majority of the revenue comes from a small percentage of the clients," Adler says. "Mickey naturally was worried about losing existing print advertisers. But every client I've had recently is on multiple platforms."

So Adler tried to focus the discussion on "whether we could grow the business by enticing high-volume display print advertisers to purchase both print and online." But Greer wanted to focus the sales effort on adding "new" advertisers. At something of a strategic impasse, Adler decided to focus her efforts on redoing the rate card.

"Regardless of which way we went, I knew we needed a new rate card that captured the real value of an integrated buy," says Adler. "The digital rate was so low [roughly 5 percent of the print rate] that it just didn't make financial sense for the paper to simply sum the print and online rates together. There would be a lot of money left on the table in that scenario." But before she could begin revising the rate card, she immediately discovered two additional issues with the digital edition: the type of advertising and the number of visitors. "First there was the issue that the banner and directory-type ads weren't very engaging. So I wanted to think about moving away from these types of advertisements," she says. "And then there was the issue with traffic on the site. Whiteville.com has 1,000 unique visitors a day—which is quite something for a paper of its size. But it wasn't a good buy for most local merchants to purchase it alone—it wasn't going to bring feet through the door. However, if you paired the strong engagement and loyalty of those visitors with the loyal subscribers of the print edition, you could have a valuable proposition to offer local merchants. You could think about all sorts of ways to make the two advertisements work together and really use the digital ad to interact with readers."

Given the extended reach and exposure that the dual platforms offered, Adler calculated that the *News Reporter* could justify a new integrated rate priced at a 50 percent premium to print only—"and that was before I figured in the tremendous engagement readers had with the content. The loyalty of the customers for both the print and online editions was *very* strong, which meant they were *very* engaged with the editorial content and more likely to notice an advertisement that was adjacent to the content. You get increased 'share of mind' if your ad is associated with content that readers are truly engaged with."

In the end, Adler recommended several pricing options, with premiums ranging from 20 percent to 30 percent above the print-only rate. And instead of selling "advertisements," she recommended selling "sponsorship of specific content—such as the sports calendar—and 'entitlement sponsorships' of an entire community page." (For an example of the proposed rate card and the sales sheets, see businessofnews.unc.edu.)

With a new rate structure in place by the spring of 2012, the *News Reporter* editorial and advertising staff committed to a fall launch of the

"Sports of All Sorts" page timed to coincide with the beginning of high school football season. But before the sales staff had a chance to begin identifying potential sponsors, Greer died unexpectedly of a heart attack. The entire community was shaken. "Mickey knew the history of every advertiser. So when he died, we [the *News Reporter*] lost all that history," says Stuart. "And in the community, he was *the* face of the *News Reporter* for many merchants who saw him around town all the time. People who didn't speak regularly to Dad or Les talked to Mickey all the time."

Without a succession plan in place, the three Highs looked internally for a new advertising director and quickly settled on Lewis, the "digital expert." In this new role, Lewis felt it was very important to get the Sports of All Sorts page launched on time. Without the extensive client "history" that Greer possessed, he decided to approach three advertisers from his own client list and convince them to buy into the new community-page concept. McDonald's signed on as sponsor of the "Athletes of the Week" feature, and a local realtor sponsored the athletic calendar. A local health supply store was enlisted as "entitlement sponsor" of the Sports of All Sorts page.

Two of the three sponsorships were sold below the recommended amount. Nevertheless, it was higher than the previous rate for a combination print and online schedule, and it established the precedent that sponsorships would be sold on an extended timeline (preferably six months or longer). In addition, because the sponsorship had print, digital, and mobile components, the *News Reporter* could now be viewed by advertisers as a cross-platform advertising medium.

Sports of All Sorts was an immediate hit in the community. Unique visitors to whiteville.com averaged more than three times what they had during previous football seasons. And the three sponsors liked both their placement on the page and the reaction of their customers. So Stuart turned her attention to the next two community pages. Working with Adler and a group of UNC students, she began crafting sponsorship packages for "Plugged-In Parents" (aimed at the approximately 20,000 parents in the community) and "My Community" (designed to keep citizens of Columbus County up-to-date on such quality of life issues as education, safety, health, and the economy). The initial goal was to launch these two pages sequentially in the spring and summer of 2013.

As with Sports of All Sorts, there would be an "entitlement sponsor" who would receive a banner ad at the top of both the print and online community pages (saying "sponsored by"), plus a smaller ad at the bottom of the printed page and a second interactive ad for the online version. In addition, the *News Reporter* hope that the entitlement sponsor of My Community would cosponsor (with the paper) a series of quarterly breakfast meetings to discuss quality-of-life issues in the community (such as the state of education, health care, and the local economy). The entitlement sponsor of the Plugged-In Parents page would cosponsor a family-related event or show. With these online and offline "opportunities," the entitlement sponsors would reach current and potential customers across multiple venues, where they would be most receptive. In other words, by sponsoring content on the community pages and using multiple platforms, advertisers would substantially increase the effectiveness of their message.

In addition, there would be four sponsors of specific content in both My Community and Plugged-In Parents. These sponsors would be entitled to "space" adjacent to both the print and online editorial material—for example, the "High-Five" calendar or the "Recipe-of-the-Week" for Plugged-In Parents. The online space could be designed as an interactive ad that would link directly to the sponsor's own website.

But in the late fall of 2012, as the *News Reporter* editorial team worked to finalize the content for Plugged-In Parents, Lewis began to express doubts about the recommended rates for sponsors, which he felt were "too high" for local merchants. Only six months into his new role, he also expressed concerns about identifying likely sponsors since he could not think of any top candidates from his own client list, largely developed during the time when he handled digital advertising sales.

After consulting with Les, Stuart decided to delay the launch of both pages until the spring and summer of 2014 so the advertising staff could be retrained to sell cross-platform sponsorships. Almost immediately, she and the sales representatives were presented with another unexpected opportunity and challenge. In only two months, they had to learn how to position and sell advertising for 954, the paper's new quarterly lifestyle magazine. Les, who had been mulling the idea of a magazine for some time, decided to "fast-forward it" when his father learned that someone from "outside" the county was launching a publication. "We need to own Columbus County," he said.

The magazine debuted in April 2013. Both Les and Stuart considered the magazine to be a success from both an editorial and advertising standpoint—and another example of how the *News Reporter* was rapidly becoming a cross-platform medium that offered its advertisers many ways to reach its various audiences. In his inaugural column to readers, Les touted 954's "unique tie-in to the Web and social media. Each page of 954 can be viewed through a link on whiteville.com or at the magazine's website, 954mag.com. Advertisers are not only able to advertise on the print pages, their products and services are shared on Facebook, Instagram, and Twitter, allowing media-savvy advertisers several platforms with which to reach customers."

As Stuart sees it, "The magazine was something of a turning point for us. We started experimenting with producing some of the new editorial content we would be producing for the 'Parenting' community page—such as the do-it-yourself column. And it allowed us to approach many of our longtime advertisers with something new: color display advertising that automatically linked to the Web. So it was a combination print and on-line sale. Many of the advertisers in the magazine increased their spending with us" by opting to add the magazine to their newspaper schedule.

Based on the success in selling the magazine, Stuart began to "dream big with the community pages." She revived Adler's original idea of growing advertising revenue by enticing high-volume print newspaper advertisers to sponsor the community pages. She and Les identified four regional and national retailers, headquartered in North Carolina, as potential entitlement sponsors for the two pages. One (a regional bank) did not advertise in the *News Reporter* even though it was one of the county's largest employers. But the other three did. Two (a department store and a home-improvement chain) mostly purchased preprinted inserts. The other one (a regional health-care facility that was also a major employer) advertised only in the print edition.

Stuart felt the regional bank and the health-care facility were potential candidates to sponsor My Community (given their strong community presence), and that the department store and home-improvement chain might be convinced to sponsor Plugged-In Parents (since they both targeted parents, especially mothers). She turned over her ideas to the UNC student group. Taking a cue from the "consultative sales" approach of the advertising department at the *Naples Daily News*, the students began by researching potential sponsors—noting, among other things, their target customers (and how this related to the subject matter on the community pages), their business challenges and opportunities, their advertising history (and how they allocated their marketing dollars), recent news stories and trends that might affect their business in Columbus County, and their long-standing relationship with the *News Reporter*.

Next, they put together an initial marketing plan for all four companies and a sales presentation kit that included both a print and online digital mock-up of the community page. After several revisions and additions, they turned the materials over to Stuart and staged a mock sales presentation for the *News Reporter* advertising staff. (Examples of the sales kits are available on businessofnews.unc.edu.)

Lewis was an active, good-natured participant in the role-playing exercise and made several strategic suggestions on how to price the sponsorships. Noting the "tight" budgets of local merchants, he suggested that the sponsorship costs be listed on a monthly basis instead of a six-month or yearly basis—"because it seems less." But he was also insistent that "we ask for a one-year commitment for the sponsorships, and not give them a six-month option, unless they push back. That way we can focus on retention and not have to sell this sponsorship every month."

Simultaneously, Stuart, Les, and Lewis approached local store managers and asked for an introduction to the appropriate person in either the company or ad agency who could make the decision to purchase the entitlement sponsorship. "We realize that we cannot delegate selling entitlement sponsorships of these community pages to the advertising sales representatives. Les and I need to be involved in the actual sales call, as well as Dean," says Stuart. "We're asking for a lot of money—and a schedule—so potential sponsors need to know that we are committed to this."

As Stuart reflects on her decision to revive Adler's idea of using sponsorships of community pages as a way to entice print-only advertisers to use both print and mobile, she acknowledges that "the past two years has truly been about learning as we go. There is so much to learn and you have to move quickly. But with each success, you get more and more confident. You know you are not going to hit a home run every time, but you learn and move on."

Indeed, the advertising department had come a long way in only a year's time. While Greer's sudden death had shaken the staff and been a significant emotional setback, both Stuart and Lewis had stepped forward and interjected a new sense of purpose and enthusiasm in the advertising department—and a special appreciation for the various platforms that the *News Reporter* was beginning to offer its advertisers. As a result of the magazine launch, the sales staff was beginning to understand how to match an advertiser's message with a digital medium, how to position the newspaper (and its sister publication, *954*) as a cross-platform medium, and how to sell strategically by focusing on high-priority clients.

For Les, the success of both Sports of All Sorts and *954* meant that "everyone at the paper had begun to think beyond just the print edition." He and Stuart still hope to improve on a number of editorial and advertising features for both publications, including the rollout of new video and mobile delivery as well as tie-ins to Facebook. But for the first time since whiteville.com was established in 1998, he was beginning to see a strategic path.

Nothing in life goes as you plan it, Les reflects. Stuart's decision to return to the *News Reporter* had been very timely—and a key reason for the success of the changes at the newspaper so far. "She could just see things that Dad and I were too close to see," he says. Or as Harvard's Heifetz would say, Stuart was the "confidant" that Les could rely on to help him "get up on the balcony" so he could see the big picture. She also brought a fresh pair of eyes to the marketing and sales approach.

As the paper had moved from creating a new strategy to implementing it, Les had come to terms with the fact that he would, at some point, have to reduce costs associated with the print edition of the newspaper. But he feels like the *News Reporter* has made a significant step toward becoming a cross-platform medium with the introduction of the community pages and *954*. And he feels like the advertising department is poised to aggressively, but strategically, begin to hit the street selling differently and pursuing new revenue opportunities.

"It involved a change in mindset—for all of us," says Les. "For me, it was about moving from 'protecting' the print edition to understanding that our future is directly linked to the digital edition—and mobile and whatever comes next. It's about being future oriented, not living in the present. It's about believing that we have a future and being excited about it."

PART III The New World Order

Most of the time, if you are honest with yourself, you know that your vision of the future is just your best estimate at the moment. Plans are no more than today's best guess. . . . [Therefore] the practice of leadership requires the capacity to keep asking basic questions of yourself and of the people in your organization and community.

—Ronald A. Heifetz and Marty Linsky, *Leadership on the Line: Staying Alive through the Dangers of Leading* (Harvard Business School Press, 2002)

For more than three decades, I had the privilege of working as both a journalist and a business executive on some of the nation's smallest and largest newspapers. As I advanced from my first job as cub reporter on a twice-weekly paper in my hometown to business-side masthead positions on both the *New York Times* and the *Wall Street Journal*, I came to appreciate how very fragile our newspaper ecosystem is. Most "outsiders"—including today's consumers of news, business strategists, and investors—do not appreciate or even comprehend the complexity of the interrelationships among and within newspaper organizations.

I chose to focus this book on community papers since they form the base of the newspaper ecosystem. A crack in the foundation compromises the integrity of the entire structure. However, I would be remiss if I did not also helicopter up and consider the implications of this new world order for other organizations that are part of this fragile system, including the big-city cousins of community newspapers, the metros—which are also involved in a life-and-death struggle—as well as the hundreds of institutions that support the country's 11,000 papers, such as press organizations, nonprofit foundations, and universities.

Each of these interrelationships is worthy of exploring in a book. Indeed, several of my esteemed colleagues in the profession and academy have recently tackled one or more of these issues in much more depth than I can in this section of the book. Rather, my intent in the final two chapters is to come full circle, and, from my perspective as a journalist, business executive, and educator, provide a top-level survey of the changed landscape and begin to consider the implications for the missions and strategies of all newspapers—and the institutions that support them—as they attempt to accommodate the new world order.

CHAPTER EIGHT
The Far-Reaching Implications

Economists often use the imagery of a hurricane to describe the process of creative destruction. In a storm's immediate aftermath, when we observe the altered shoreline, our attention is most often focused on the wreckage—not on the scattered seeds of renewal inconspicuously left behind as the waves receded.

Two decades after the Internet made landfall, the newspaper industry is still adapting. But it is much easier to determine the broad strokes of what papers must do to survive in this new environment. Based on the experiences of other industries, we know that *all* newspapers—the community, metro, and national papers—must pursue a three-pronged strategy that streamlines costs associated with the legacy print product while they simultaneously transition their readers and advertisers to multiplatform delivery of content. But the specific challenges newspapers will face will vary by market and community. Therefore, the key question for owners, publishers, and editors becomes: by pursuing this three-pronged strategy, can our newspaper make enough money to continue to supply the sort of "accountability journalism" that "feeds" our democratic and capitalist systems?

"Going forward, what is an achievable and sustainable profit margin? That is the real question all of us are dealing with," says John Mitchell, publisher of the independently owned *Rutland Herald.* "Could we put out a good paper with a 5 percent margin? Maybe so. But then, my family has never been in it for the money. We see newspapers as a public trust."

Warren Buffett, who now owns more than sixty community newspapers in Nebraska, New York, and North Carolina, has told investors in his company that he believes 10 percent margins are achievable, especially with publications in small and midsized markets. But what about the country's ninety or so largest papers—the national and metro papers that sit atop the newspaper pyramid? They face very different market and journalistic challenges than those that community newspapers must over-come. Can they achieve a 10 percent margin—or even a 5 percent margin? And is either level sufficient to fund the quality accountability journalism they produced in the latter half of the twentieth century?

What makes the calculation of a future margin so difficult is that news-papers are "not one business, but two," as Poynter analyst Rick Edmonds points out. Good newspapers serve both readers and advertisers well. Suc-cess with one group does not guarantee success with the other. According to a story in the *New York Times*, in his first meeting with reporters after purchasing the *Washington Post*, new owner Jeff Bezos "told reporters that the paper should focus on delivering important, compelling stories to its readers. If they do that, advertisers will come."

"In any commodity situation [as newspapers now face], the business strategy advice is to seek a differentiation," says economist Eli Noam. This means that successful newspapers will first differentiate themselves from competitors, as Bezos suggests, by offering unique content that readers want—in other words, by being the "most credible and comprehensive sources of news and information readers care about."

But they also have to assemble the *right* size and the *right* type of audience to attract advertisers, which have historically provided the lion's share of rev-enue that supports the news operations of most newspapers. The audience of readers has to be large enough to attract major advertisers in a particular market and to be divided into smaller segments that allow smaller or spe-cialized advertisers to target a specific group of engaged readers. This means that a newspaper needs to provide a broad menu of news and information—content that is of interest to people living in a specific region as well as that which is of interest to people with certain affiliations and passions.

"Realistically, no single news organization" can now produce all the news and information—both the geographic and special-interest information—that their readers and advertisers want and expect in the digital age "and do it well, through its own economic and editorial resources," says Noam. Therefore, newspapers that survive and thrive—and achieve sustainable profit margins—will understand how to take advantage of the new eco-nomics of networking, he says. In an era of reduced margins, individual newspapers must learn to "rely substantially on others" to help them both produce and deliver this content and grow their audience so they remain attractive to advertisers.

Noam's vision of "networks" is very different from the chain-ownership model of the twentieth century, in which companies acquired newspapers in different geographic markets and allowed them to operate relatively independently of one another. In the twenty-first century, by belonging to a network—either a formal or informal one—a newspaper can more efficiently control costs, but more important, it can tap into resources that allow it to build community among readers across multiple platforms and grow new advertising revenue.

For a community newspaper, such a network might extend across a region and include formal working relationships with other small papers in the region, the metro paper in the state capital, and local and regional nonprofit news organizations, press associations, and area colleges and universities. The mission and service that each of the networked members provides will most likely be very different from what they delivered previously, but their contributions will be essential to sustaining "good" journalism at all levels.

This chapter considers some of the implications of the evolving newspaper ecosystem of the twenty-first century, which looks to be much more complex and interdependent than it has been in the past. It begins by focusing first on the special challenges and opportunities confronting the metro papers, which serve as vital "middlemen" between community papers and national news outlets. It then considers the changing role of other organizations that support this fragile ecosystem: the nonprofit news organizations attempting to provide "accountability journalism," foundations funding research on new digital tools and applications, and the press associations that have historically assisted newspapers with legal and business concerns. Finally, it considers how universities training tomorrow's newspaper employees must respond. In a networked world, strategic decisions made by individual members ripple through the system and ultimately determine the financial fortunes of all who are connected.

The Challenges Facing Metro Papers

Creative destruction typically moves across an industry in waves. Invariably, the segments that suffer first and longest are those that are the last to achieve a strong financial footing. Such is the case with the country's eighty-five or so metro and regional newspapers.

In the latter two decades of the twentieth century—prior to the explosion of the Internet—the *Wall Street Journal* and the *New York Times* took advantage of satellite printing, piggybacked on the delivery systems of other metro newspapers, and broke away from their heavy reliance on the New York market where they were based. (*USA Today*, a national newspaper established in 1982, was never a metro paper.) Repositioned as "national newspapers" with an audience across the continent, the *Times* and the *Journal* today enjoy strong loyalty from their digitally savvy, affluent subscribers who are willing to pay a premium price to get the unique content these papers provide—and, in turn, attract national advertisers willing to pay a premium to reach them.

The key strategic question facing these two national brands today is not one of survival. Rather it is this: with reduced margins, do these two papers have the financial resources to continue to grow their audiences *and* develop the storytelling expertise across multiple platforms—video and digital as well as print—that both readers and advertisers expect? Can the *Times* survive as an independent company, or will it follow the path of the *Journal*, acquired by the News Corporation in 2008, and be subsumed by a larger company? Either way, given their strong brand credibility, few media analysts doubt that these two national "newspapers" will survive in some form.

The prognosis for many metro papers is less certain. During the same years that the *Wall Street Journal* and The *New York Times* were retooling their business strategies, reporters at metro papers such as the *Los Angeles Times*, the *Philadelphia Inquirer*, and the *Washington Post* were roaming the globe, producing world-class journalism on a par with these two national newspapers and earning numerous Pulitzer Prizes for their efforts.

But the business models of these metro papers remained tethered to the geographic regions they served. The majority of their subscribers were located in the suburbs, and fewer and fewer of them came into the central city to work or shop. Yet the vast majority of their advertising revenue came from local businesses hoping to reach these consumers in the greater metro area. Unlike papers in smaller markets, they faced competition for advertising dollars from a variety of sources, including regional television stations with signals that could reach these far-flung customers. And many of the metros had high fixed costs, driven by union contracts and a distribution system that could extend more than 100 miles out from the city's center.

Conventional business wisdom holds that you never want to be caught "in the middle," where you can be attacked by competitors on both sides. But in many ways, that is where the country's eighty-five or so metro newspapers find themselves—betwixt and between—as two distinct business models begin to emerge, one for community papers and the other for the national giants.

For national papers, it's all about "scale"—spreading the net as wide as possible and attracting a sizeable audience, one engaged with the content and willing to pay a premium to get it. This upscale audience then attracts national and global advertisers who want to reach them, giving the national papers two potentially significant streams of revenues—one from their audience and the other from their advertisers. For community newspapers, the key to success is to stay close to home; know the market well; and create content that engages readers, connects people to their community, and attracts local advertisers in the much smaller geographic area they cover.

Metros face significant challenges with pursuing either strategy. In order to "go national," as the *Wall Street Journal* and the *New York Times* did, a metro newspaper must offer content that resonates with readers in cities across the country. Then it must determine whether it can accumulate an audience that is sizeable *and* affluent enough to pay a premium to receive the specialized content, or if these readers will attract advertisers willing pay a premium to reach them. Could the *Washington Post*, for example, create a financially successful national newspaper for political junkies, or for those whose fortunes are tied to decisions made in the nation's capital, such as government contractors, lobbyists, and bureaucrats? Similarly, could the *Los Angeles Times* create a successful national publication for those who follow the entertainment business? How much would either paper have to spend to create and aggregate the sort of content that would differentiate it from existing competitors in the broadcast, magazine, and online worlds that already produce and distribute similar content? Could they charge either advertisers or readers enough to justify the increased costs? And could such a venture ever be more than a sideline business?

For most metros, therefore, following in the footsteps of the *Wall Street Journal* and the *New York Times* is not a feasible option, forcing them to consider the alternative and stay closer to home. But compared to papers in small and midsized markets, many metros today serve areas without the well-defined and cohesive sense of political, economic, or social identity that is typical of small communities. Editorially, how do metros and regional papers create unique content that "builds community on many platforms," attracting and engaging residents of a diverse, sprawling geographic area? And how do they successfully pursue new advertising revenue when they face a much more competitive environment—one that includes regional television stations, for example, that can deliver a larger audience to area merchants, or specialty magazines and digital sites that can deliver a more engaged and targeted one?

Considering the unique challenges that metros face, it is understandable why investors and strategists tend to underestimate what it will take to turn around these newspapers—as illustrated by the succession of owners in recent years at the *Philadelphia Inquirer*, the *Chicago Tribune*, and the *Minneapolis Star Tribune*, for example. Many new owners focus initially on efficiencies—shedding legacy costs by vacating buildings, reducing pension obligations through a variety of means, and laying off staff. Without barriers to entry, newspapers have to drastically reduce costs to remain competitive, but that is at best "a short-term remedy," says economist Noam, since it fails to address the underlying problems with readership and advertising.

Boston Red Sox owner John W. Henry acknowledged this when he purchased the *Boston Globe* in 2013 from the New York Times Company for $70 million—considerably less than the $1.1 billion the *Times* paid in 1993. "I'm not sure that anyone has successfully put forward a sustainable financial model for metros given the magnitude and consistency of revenue declines," he said, and quickly added: "But if I were going to bet on one, it would be the *Boston Globe*."

Like Buffett, Poynter's Rick Edmonds is optimistic that when the dust settles, most "well-managed" newspapers—including metros—can achieve a 10 percent profit margin. But they must focus on addressing the reader and advertising issues. Successful metros, he says, "will establish some method of getting readers to value and pay for content. Second, they will keep an eye out for doing more experiments faster. And third, they will get the pacing right, as they exchange high-margin print advertising dollars for other streams of lower-margin revenue."

This suggests that metros will need to create a third path to profitability, one that draws on tactics employed by national and small newspapers but is modified to address the specific market challenges and opportunities they face. In order to profitably pursue new revenue, successful metro papers, like the national papers, will need to develop a "sophisticated" understanding of their advertisers' needs, says former BBDO executive JoAnn Sciarrino. Faced with robust competition for advertising—competition that includes regional television and national search and e-commerce firms—metro papers, she says, can only stand above the fray if they develop the internal sales skills that will help their advertisers tell their stories on multiple platforms. Metros, therefore, need to truly embrace consultative selling and create an in-house digital agency to aid clients in extending their reach and efficiency. "Your mid-sized businesses that populate most metro areas have the same marketing needs—social media, search optimization—as the large, national brands," she says. "But they do not have the budget that would justify hiring a regional or national ad agency to provide the guidance. Metro papers can provide that service for a fee with an in-house agency and simultaneously enhance the loyalty of the advertiser."

In order to get readers to "value and pay for content," metro papers— like the smaller community papers—need to understand what drives connection to the larger geographic region, as well as to the many diverse subgroups that inhabit the region. A strong sense of "community" in a metro area is often associated with the professional sports teams located there, points out Edmonds, or with local collegiate teams. Therefore, creating and nurturing cross-platform communities for sports fans of all sorts, for example, becomes a way for metro papers to connect and engage with a certain segment of readers, and, potentially, it creates an opportunity for newspapers to charge readers for proprietary content delivered through mobile applications.

But unlike smaller newspapers, metros need to provide many—not just several—points of entry for the diverse population that inhabits the region. This suggests that the successful metro papers will feature a rich tapestry of multiplatform communities built around the special passions, affiliations, and ethnic identities of the residents in the region.

The question then becomes: can these sites and pages for multiple "communities" of special interests produce enough revenue to *also* fund the sort of regional "accountability journalism" that metros have provided in the past? If not, then in order to continue to "set the agenda" for debate of public-policy issues that affect the state and region, metro editors will need to learn how to take advantage of "the economics of networking," as Noam calls it.

In the de facto monopolistic world of yesterday, metro papers tended to treat all other media outlets as "competitors," including small community and ethnic publications in the suburbs and outlying regions and local broadcast and cable television stations. Each vied for "the scoop." Is that the best way to do business in the networked world of today, when every news organization is dealing with limited resources?

Orage Quarles, publisher of the *News and Observer* of Raleigh, which is owned by McClatchy Newspapers, has been a strong advocate for relaxing the regulations on cross-ownership of television and newspaper stations serving the same metropolitan area, which the Federal Communications Commission (FCC) has so far resisted. "When we [McClatchy] bought the *Charlotte Observer*, it allowed us to make strategic decisions on what our future would look like. And we decided that investigative journalism, hard news, and sports would be what we'd focus on," he told an audience of readers attending an FCC symposium in 2013.

In 1996 the Raleigh-based paper won the Pulitzer Gold Medal for Public Service for its investigative reporting on the impact of large-scale commercial hog farming on the economy and environment of eastern North Carolina. By 2013, as a result of three rounds of layoffs, newsroom staffing levels were approximately half of what they had been when the prize was awarded.

As Quarles points out, with severely depressed margins and diminished staffing, metro papers must decide what they will *not* do. The choices about what not to cover means that there will be "holes" in coverage—unless such newspapers figure out how to take advantage of networking to provide differentiated and compelling content.

As metros contemplate their future, there are many new avenues to explore, and as Edmonds cautions, they need to do "more experiments faster." For example, is it possible for metro newsrooms to become a hub at the center of a formal network that collates and synthesizes the work of the smaller community and ethnic newsrooms, in the process providing context for issues of regional concern? What are the roles and expectations of the individual community and ethnic newspapers in this network?

Similarly, is it possible for metro papers to form a partnership with local television stations, using available technology to film and transcribe legislative committee meetings so that they can be made available to the public and later accessed and used by media outlets in joint investigative pieces on environmental issues? Is collaboration in some matters, rather than competition, a better model for all community-based news organizations, especially as it concerns coverage of public-policy issues?

Henry said that his first action after purchasing the *Boston Globe* would be to build "a community commitment and effort" since "being a part of the leadership of the *Globe* provides an opportunity to play a significant role with others in this community's present and future." But with significant revenue declines, how do metros like the *Globe* cover not just communities of special interest but also the larger geographic region that they serve—especially if they go it alone?

In the latter half of the twentieth century, the *Globe*'s influence spread far beyond the confines of the Boston area to include much of New England. Time will tell how expansive Henry's view of "community" is. Metros that continue to take an expansive view will need to create a new journalistic model for covering a large geographic region, one that taps into the existing network of for-profit news organizations as well as the emerging nonprofit groups. For as Noam points out, with limited resources, "no single news organization" can realistically produce all the important news and information that adequately informs citizens and public officials in a diverse, sprawling metropolitan area. Simultaneously, metros will need to think expansively about ways to pursue new sources of profitable revenue from both readers and advertisers so that they can continue to be the vital journalistic "middle man" in the news ecosystem, spotting and linking together the grassroots concerns that various community news organizations in the region uncover.

All successful strategies allocate scarce resources to areas that add the most value. For metros, the challenge is figuring out how to reconnect and engage with readers and advertisers as they establish a third business model that draws on the strategic lessons learned and tactics employed by the community newspapers and the national giants.

Reimagining the News Ecosystem

Just as newspapers of all sizes need to figure out how to better collaborate and partner with each other, they also need to take full advantage of the thousands of new nonprofit flowers that are blooming. These nonprofit organizations provide news that can fill the journalistic "holes" created by the cutback in staffing of newsrooms, giving reporters or advertising salespeople tools they can use to either build community or pursue new revenue opportunities. Some nonprofits also provide training to help those on the editorial and business sides better utilize scarce resources.

When I transitioned from industry to the academy in 2008, it was becoming apparent to many people who cared about newspapers—nonjournalists as well as journalists—that the economic ecosystem that supported the premier national, metro, and community papers in the latter half of the twentieth century was disintegrating. Quite often, in public forums, I would be asked if I believed a "nonprofit business model" would save newspapers. I responded that I thought nonprofit news organizations could play an important role during this time of transition. However, I cautioned that since economics limited the scale and scope of what non-profit organizations could contribute, it was imperative that they be integrated into the new ecosystem that was emerging so that all news organizations could receive maximum benefit.

From the beginning, the amount of funds available to support nonprofit journalistic enterprises has been a fraction of the advertising revenues that newspapers have traditionally relied upon to pay the bills for the news operation. Indeed, when revenues plummeted in 2008, many owners and publishers of existing newspapers quickly did the calculations and realized it would be best if they could remain for-profit despite substantially diminished advertising and profit margins. Even the large nonprofit news organizations—such as ProPublica, the national investigative news organization that was founded with an initial three-year, $30 million grant from the Sandler Foundation—cannot begin to match the resources of the *New York Times*, with a reported annual news budget of approximately $200 million and advertising revenues of more than three times that amount. Indeed, those initial grants made by foundations and wealthy individuals to start nonprofit organizations are most often intended to fund only the first couple of years of operation. Without significant advertising or reader support, the founding editors have had to obtain additional funding from the small circle of foundations supporting journalistic endeavors, even as more and more "competing" start-ups petition for a share of the limited supply of money.

As a result, most of the surviving nonprofits today are small, stand-alone operations scattered in towns and cities across the country, not clustered in one location the way that technology companies are around Silicon Valley, where they can draw economic benefit from their proximity to one other. There are, however, clusters of nonprofits within various regions and states throughout the country. Some of the country's larger newspapers—notably the *Times*, which published an investigative piece by ProPublica that won a Pulitzer in 2010—have actively partnered with the nonprofit sector. But many editors are unaware of nonprofits in their own backyard, and if they are aware, they may well see them as competitors and not potential partners.

Similarly, many editors and publishers are unaware of the new digital tools and applications that have been developed by nonprofit "incubators." The Knight Foundation, for example, has distributed several million dollars in small grants ranging from $50,000 upward, modeled on the "incubator" approach used by many venture capital firms. An individual or group is given a small initial grant intended to fund the development of both a prototype for a digital enterprise and a business model. Even though some organizations, such as the nonprofit Investigative Reporters and Editors, Inc., provide training in how to use these journalistic tools for a nominal fee, a relatively small percentage of reporters and editors have taken advantage of the training.

So although nonprofit journalism entities are limited in size and scope, they have the potential to fill a significant gap in the news ecosystem during this period of transition and disruption—provided that owners, publishers, and editors fully incorporate them into their own strategic plans and provide reporters with the training to use them. The same is true of other existing organizations in the newspaper support network—especially the state press associations, which have traditionally provided three services to members: they lobby legislatures on behalf of the industry; they provide legal counsel, especially on journalistic issues; and they offer training and retooling sessions for newspaper employees. In recent years, with their lobbying efforts, many state associations have been focused on retaining longstanding revenue streams, such as requiring that municipalities continue to post legal notices in their local papers, and *not* on helping newspapers aggressively grow new revenue streams. Their legal service, a godsend to small papers, is often adversarial—aimed at gaining access to public records from recalcitrant officials, for example, and not on thinking expansively about the opportunity to make government more transparent in the digital era. And while most state associations provide training sessions for both journalists and salespeople, they often feature a hodgepodge assortment of vendors pushing specific tactics that may create short-term results but do little to reposition the newspaper for the long term.

Newspapers pay to play in these organizations. Publishers and editors who sit as officers need to be reassessing the mission of state and regional press associations and determining how member news organizations can better utilize them to help with the transition. Would it be more economically beneficial, for example, if newspapers paid more and, in return for the increased dues, expected the state press associations to provide in-depth, structured training programs that help journalists take advantage of the new digital tools or sales representatives learn how they can hit the street selling differently and significantly increase the amount of multiplatform advertising revenue?

In addition to fighting to obtain specific public records, should press associations be pressing government agencies for easy digital access to all of their documents and reports? "At a time we're supposed to have more transparency than ever, it often feels like openness in government is going backwards," observes John Mitchell of the *Rutland Herald*. Presenting before the Federal Trade Commission in June 2010, economist James Hamilton pointed out: "Lowering the cost of discovering stories is a content-neutral, platform-agnostic way to support accountability in journalism. . . . Government already funds the development of software tools that are related to public goods in fields such as national security and education. And the same logic of supporting public goods [with] positive externalities should lead agencies to support efforts to lower the cost of reporters who are covering public affairs."

Reimagining a profitable digital future for newspapers necessarily involves reenvisioning a bigger role for nonprofits in the news-gathering process and a much different role for the traditional supporting industry organizations, such as press associations. Newspaper publishers and editors need to understand that it is in their long-term economic interest to tap into these resources. They need to actively seek out ways to collaborate, pooling resources with the nonprofit news organizations to bring transparency to government or asking that the industry groups (such as press associations, to which they pay fees), provide structured training for reporters and advertising sales representatives. And they need to support these efforts by giving their staff members the day—or the week—off to receive training so they can more effectively report or sell.

As Harvard's Ron Heifetz puts it, owners, publishers, and editors need to "get up on the balcony" and understand that it is in their long-term best interest to be fully invested in the success of this nonprofit support network. Individually or grouped together, these nonprofit organizations—some of which are start-ups and others that have been around for decades—cannot fill the gap created by the chaos that has swept the industry. But, integrated into the newspaper ecosystem, they have the potential to stem the loss of news and revenue and allow owners, publishers, and editors to better allocate scare resources to endeavors that add value for their readers and advertisers.

Training Tomorrow's Newspaper Leaders

At a January 2008 summit titled "Journalism in the Service of Democracy," sponsored by the Carnegie Corporation, Bill Keller—then executive editor of the *New York Times*—confessed that he was a recent "convert to the cause of journalism schools." An English major at Pomona College, he

The Role of Nonprofits in Filling the Gap

Paul Steiger served as managing editor of the Wall Street Journal from 1991 to 2007 and was founding editor and CEO of ProPublica, an independent non-profit news organization that in 2010 won the first Pulitzer Prize for online investigative journalism. ProPublica was founded with an initial grant from Herbert and Marion Sandler, who pledged $10 million a year to support the effort. This is excerpted from the question-and-answer session that followed Steiger's presentation "From Mainstream Media to a Non-Profit News Startup" at UNC–Chapel Hill in February 2012.

Q. What do you see as the role of nonprofit news organizations in the digital era? How replicable is the model that ProPublica has?

Four billion dollars in newsroom payrolls have vaporized in the last five years. So what is a little tiny pipsqueak operation like ProPublica with its little 10 million dollar [annual] budget doing thinking it can make up that gap?

The answer is we cannot make up that entire gap. Anytime there is a major restructuring of an industry, there is a loss of skin, fat, muscle, and bone. And trying to figure out "what is what" is a challenge. Without question, there was some waste. When you have huge profits, like the industry had, there is some excess expenditure—but most of that has been squeezed out of the system. There is also a substantial loss of muscle and bone.

Some of this [filling the gap] will have to come from the nonprofit sector. Part of my mission, starting in 2010, when I became much more of a fund-raiser, was not only to raise money for ProPublica but also to try and make the point to the world of philanthropy that, while there was no need for them to direct their resources to newspapers five or ten years ago, it is now an appropriate designation for you to send some of your money. Just as it is appropriate to send some of your money to museums and ballet companies and orchestras.

Not everybody is buying into that logic, but more and more people are. The FCC recently did an exhaustive study on the state of news for a democracy. They did some calculations that if there was just a modest shift in the focus of existing philanthropy in the United States, there would be enough to support a substantial increase [in non-profit news gathering]—nothing like getting us to the same levels as the BBC, but it would support [more news gathering] on public television and public radio in the United States, plus about 100 ProPublicas.

It's not an enormous shift, but will it happen overnight? No. Will the vast majority of our news come from a nonprofit source? No. I'm arguing that [so far] the only place that has demonstrated a need for philanthropic support is investigative reporting and possibly foreign reporting.

There are other would-be ProPublicas, and they're getting support. The Center for Investigative Reporting at Berkeley has been around for twenty years. The Center for Public Integrity in Washington has had some hiccups, but they've been around for quite some time. Plus, there are more and more small hyperlocal investigative organizations. Like restaurants, many will fail; but many succeed.

told a group of deans, professors, and students that he had previously believed the best training for young reporters was an apprenticeship under a "grizzled editor" at a small newspaper. But because of recent reductions in newsroom ranks, he continued, very few grizzled editors remained—and those that were still around did not have time to train a young reporter. As a result, he said, "I've come to think of journalism schools as maybe the last resort."

Journalism schools—like business schools in this country—are a twentieth-century invention. Unlike schools of medicine and law, which require aspiring members of those professions to obtain a diploma from an accredited institution and pass a licensing exam, a formal journalism or business education is still optional today. You can become a celebrated journalist or a skillful business strategist without attending professional school. And most likely, whether you attend a professional school or not, you will climb up the ladder by serving in multiple "apprenticeships," often in several companies.

But industry turmoil over the last two decades has rendered obsolete the apprenticeship model of the twentieth century in which inexperienced journalists moved progressively from smaller papers to larger ones until they "arrived" at a large paper such as the *Philadelphia Inquirer* or the *New York Times*. With newsroom staffing down by more than one-third over the last decade, there are fewer reporting positions at the larger papers.

This raises provocative questions about the role of the country's 500 journalism schools, many of which are not only training future journalists but also advertising, marketing, and strategic communication specialists. Should the primary focus of "journalism schools" be on teaching the basics—practical, how-to instruction on using the new technology to communicate or sell across multiple platforms? Or should they focus on training high-functioning leaders who know how to ask the right questions and put issues, research, and events in a larger context when framing either a story or a business strategy? How much deep knowledge of a specific area should graduates have? How much hands-on experience working with clients should they be given? What sort of research should the faculty be pursuing—classic theoretical communication inquiries or problem-solving endeavors with immediate benefits for the industry?

From 2005 to 2011, the Carnegie-Knight Initiative on the Future of Journalism Education attempted to both pose and answer these questions. In announcing the inquiry, which involved eleven of the nation's top journalism schools, Vartan Gregorian, president of the Carnegie Corporation, argued that the digital revolution had moved "journalists to the forefront of diffusing knowledge to the next generation." The Knight Foundation set forth the premise that "in today's changed world of news consumption, journalism schools should be exploring the technological, intellectual, artistic, and literary possibilities of journalism to the fullest extent, and should be leading a constant expansion of improvement in the ability of the press to inform the public as fully, deeply, and interestingly as it can."

As Harvard University professor of government and the press Thomas Patterson notes in his book *Informing the News: The Need for Knowledge-Based Journalism* (2013), there is a clear imperative for journalism schools to break out of their twentieth-century paradigm—that of serving as "industry-oriented trade schools" and a "feeder system" to the news industry. "For the first time in their history, journalism schools are positioned to play a major part in setting the standards for quality journalism," he says. "News outlets have traditionally set the standards, which journalism schools have then used as the benchmark for their training programs. . . . Today, the news industry is facing the challenge of declining audiences and shrinking revenues, which has centered its attention more on its financial health than on the quality of its journalism."

Business schools faced a similar identity crisis in the latter three decades of the twentieth century, when creative destruction was sweeping across the technology, manufacturing, retail, and services industries. This meant that business-school graduates needed in-depth knowledge of subject matter, as well as an analytical framework for processing and reacting to information and understanding the implications. The best business schools realized that they needed to teach not only the basics of finance, accounting, and marketing but also strategy and organizational behavior. In addition to teaching management skills, business schools began to teach leadership in all its dimensions.

That is the opportunity for journalism schools today. They must move away from merely training students for their first job on a "small paper," where they will perfect the basics before moving up to larger newspapers. Instead, journalism schools should be training students "to lead" in a news organization of any size, from a small community weekly to a metro daily. And the faculty should provide timely, practical industry research, even as it contemplates possibilities and outcomes that are not yet on the radar of today's practitioners.

What is the role of newspaper publishers and editors in helping to shape the curriculum and research agenda of journalism schools during this time of immense disruption? Too often, when asked for their input, publishers and editors have responded by citing a specific, basic skill set—not a strategic one. "I need a reporter who can use social media," they say, or "I need an advertising sales rep who can sell digital." As, I hope, the previous chapters in this book have pointed out, the skills needed by the smallest community newspapers are not that different from those that the metro and national newspapers require. *All* papers, regardless of size, should be seeking journalists and advertising/marketing specialists who can think strategically—that is, see the challenges as well as the opportunities. And *all* papers should be thinking strategically about how they pay and deploy these new graduates.

Many of the students I have taught—and who have worked on this project—have developed a passion for community newspaper journalism. But they worry that they will become low-paid "content gerbils," reporters assigned to write five or so daily "hyperlocal" stories, blog, tweet, and manage a Facebook page—with no time during the typical workweek to use the more-advanced analytical skills they developed in journalism school. "And how can you put down roots in a community and raise a family on the salary I would be paid?" asked one student, summarizing the other prevailing fear of his colleagues.

Re-creating journalism schools requires that the newspaper industry and the academy seek a "both/and" approach instead of the "either/or" dichotomy of choices that existed in the twentieth century. Or as Patterson observes, in the twenty-first century, journalism schools should be imparting *both* "content knowledge" *and* "process knowledge."

"I've been doing this since college," says Tennessee publisher Mark Palmer. "This is my fifth newspaper. We certainly live in interesting times, as they say. But I'm having fun in a different way than I have before. For those who are curious, it's a great time to be in the business." That is the challenge for the academy: producing graduates who are curious *and* trained to apply critical analytical judgment to new situations and opportunities. The newspaper industry should be insisting that journalism schools train tomorrow's newspaper owners, publishers, and editors to seize the possibilities that are emerging. In return, they should be rethinking how they create and sell newspapers, and how they reward and compensate graduates who want to put down roots in a community and support the mission of the local paper.

Speaking to a group of media executives and analysts at the Paley Center for Media's 2007 International Council meeting in Silicon Valley, Verizon's chairman and CEO Ivan Seidenberg reflected on his own attempts over the previous two decades to manage his company's transition from the ubiquitous telephone wires that dotted the landscape in the twentieth century to the wireless era of the twenty-first century. "The minute you think you know how to define the future," he observed, "you stop being able to see it."

While the outlines of a new ecosystem are becoming apparent, it is still too early to predict the winners and losers. There are a number of key questions that need to be answered. Chief among them is: what sort of return on investment and profit margins are the owners of newspapers—the private-equity groups, investment firms, chains, and independent businessmen—expecting? Will they take the long-term or short-term view? Will the profit margins these papers produce support good journalism in our metro newspapers as well as in our community publications?

Ownership by a chain or investment firm does not necessarily preclude good journalism. In the 1980s, the thirty-two newspapers in the Knight Ridder chain, the second largest in the country, received roughly a quarter of the 136 Pulitzer Prizes awarded, a figure equal to the total prizes awarded to the nation's five largest news organizations: the *New York Times*, the *Wall Street Journal*, the Associated Press, the *Los Angeles Times*, and the *Washington Post*.

But we are also entering an era of reduced margins. In order to achieve margins that support good journalism, owners need to allow publishers and editors the latitude to experiment and craft strategies that respond to the specific challenges in a market, whether at the community, metro, or national level. And publishers and editors must learn a new paradigm—one that takes advantage of the economics of networking. They need to figure out when to collaborate and when to compete, how to more fully incorporate nonprofit organizations into the network, and what to expect of universities that are training tomorrow's publishers and editors.

Leadership, says Ron Heifetz, "is the capacity to keep asking basic questions of yourself and of the people in your organization and community." We are only beginning to articulate those questions as the seeds of renewal, scattered throughout the ecosystem, begin to emerge.

CHAPTER NINE
Crafting a New Beginning for Newspapers

Our journeys are often punctuated by insights or "epiphanies" that prompt us to change course and explore a route not previously envisioned. Sometimes, the terrain becomes so difficult that we are forced to detour. Other times, we gradually realize that the path we set out on is not the one that will get us to the destination we'd hoped.

All of the owners, publishers, and editors of community newspapers profiled in this book have experienced that insightful moment when they realized that the world as they knew it had changed irrevocably—and that they must set out on a different course. The paths they have chosen reflect the specific challenges and opportunities of the communities they serve.

The Chicago Spanish-language weekly *La Raza* is aggressively pursuing multiplatform delivery of its journalism and advertising. Small-town editor Sallie See in West Virginia is using her strong presence on Facebook to enhance both the news coverage and the marketing capabilities of the weekly *Hampshire Review*. Others, such as *The Pilot* in an upscale North Carolina resort and retirement community and the *Columbia Daily Herald* in an economically depressed area of Tennessee, are seeking to diversify, launching a broad range of print and digital publications and business extensions, including in-house ad agencies and the purchase of a local bookstore. All have acknowledged that they must aggressively change their business models to reflect the new realities—simultaneously reducing costs associated with the legacy print edition, building vibrant community across multiple platforms, and strategically pursuing the new revenue opportunities this affords them.

As the experiences of the *Whiteville News Reporter* illustrate, the path we envision at the beginning of a journey is never straightforward. Four years into the journey, it is still too early to know exactly where the new path will lead for Whiteville—and for the other newspapers who have committed to it. Some may evolve from print-only to pure digital delivery. For the foreseeable future, most papers will likely commit to multiplatform delivery, with print as a diminished, but key, element. As Whiteville's Stuart High, special projects director for the *News Reporter*, puts it: "We are learning as we go."

Most community newspapers have moved out of the denial stage that framed many responses during the first decade of dealing with the Internet. In learning a new way of operating, all the newspapers are opening themselves up to the possibility of crafting a new beginning for themselves in the twenty-first century.

A Story Based on Three Epiphanies

In *The Art of Possibility: Transforming Professional and Personal Life* (2002), conductor Benjamin Zander points out that "our senses bring us selective information about what is out there" and then we construct—or invent— our own story about what it means. In my own professional journey— from newspaper journalist to publishing executive to professor—there have been three "aha" moments, which occurred roughly a decade apart and build chronologically and logically on one another. Two occurred before the dawn of the Internet age. But if anything, they are even more relevant in the digital age. These insights are the story behind this book, and they form, I hope, a call to action for owners, publishers, and editors and will inspire a recommitment to the important and historic mission of community newspapers everywhere.

EPIPHANY 1: Healthy community newspapers support both
our democratic and capitalist way of life at the most basic level—
in our villages, towns, city blocks, and counties where we work,
play, spend our incomes, and elect our public officials.

The seed for this book was planted in the summer of 1969, when, as a freshly minted high school graduate whose sole journalistic experience consisted of editing the school newspaper, I was hired as a reporting intern on my hometown paper. Every weekday at about 10:30 A.M., John Henry Moore, the second-generation owner and editor of the twice-weekly, independent *Laurinburg (N.C.) Exchange* (circulation 10,000), would rise from his desk and amble two blocks downtown to the café on Main Street for a cup of coffee with town merchants and leaders.

Moore would return an hour later with a couple of "tips" for the advertising director, a handful of story ideas for all three of the full-time reporters, plus enough two- and three-paragraph short items to fill his "Odds and Ends" column, which ran down the left side of the front page. His typical column covered everything from contentious zoning issues to store openings and a Little Leaguer's pitching achievements. A snapshot of the community, Moore's column quickly became addictive reading, even for someone like me, who had aspirations of leaving my hometown in the rearview mirror as soon as possible. And his editorials often picked up on issues bubbling just below the surface that had only been hinted at in his front-page column.

Today, the *Laurinburg Exchange*, now published five days a week, is owned by an investment firm based in Ohio. This private company, which owns ninety-eight other newspapers in small towns spread throughout the country, is highly leveraged and runs its papers so as to maximize cash flow to pay down the debt. It has consolidated printing and editing functions for all its various properties, leaving only a small staff at each of its newspapers responsible for reporting and selling advertisements to local merchants.

The "Odds and Ends" column is long gone—along with the "stalwarts," the reporters who had been there for decades and knew everyone in town. Today, there are two general-news reporters whose bylines appear several times in most editions of the paper. They try hard to cover the breaking news in Scotland County, which has the state's highest unemployment rate. But they do not have the time—nor the experience and perspective— to do the sort of analytical stories that residents so desperately need as they try to overcome the significant challenges they face.

The editorial page seldom addresses these issues, and without the sorts of "observations and tips" that were part of the "Odds and Ends" column, there is no journalistic mechanism for providing context and building community among the disparate factions in the county, or for detailing the "facts" behind issues that could affect the region for years. As an example, in 2006 a New York firm hoped to build a huge "megadump" in the northern part of the county, adjacent to the environmentally sensitive state game lands. That effort was halted—not by the paper, which often ran almost-verbatim press releases put out by the company, but by a group of vigilant local citizens and state officials who fought hard to break through the noise and misinformation put out by the strong lobbying effort of the dump's proponents. According to one state report, such a "megadump" in the state's poorest county could have had environmental and economic consequences two centuries or more into the future.

The community journalism that "Mr. Moore" practiced did not rise to the level of the courage required of Leslie Thompson and Willard Cole at the *Whiteville News Reporter* when they took on the Ku Klux Klan in the 1950s; but his "Odds and Ends" column and his pointed editorials informed and educated citizens of Scotland County about issues—large and small—that could affect the quality of life in that community. That is why economists call such journalism "an economic good," and why it is critical that strong community newspapers—even those that do not aggressively pursue investigative journalism but merely provide context—survive in the digital era.

EPIPHANY 2: Good journalism alone is not sufficient to save newspapers. In a competitive situation, a newspaper must also have a flexible and "forward-looking" business plan that addresses the needs of both its readers and advertisers.

In many ways, the 1970s were a golden age for newspaper journalism. Watergate reporting inspired enterprising, investigative journalists to be aggressive in covering all sorts of public issues. Society pages were breaking free of their shackles and venturing into consumer-affairs reporting. And the front page of many newspapers sported not just the standard "inverted pyramid," wire-service style of reporting (the Five Ws—who, what, when, where, and why) but also cleverly and creatively written "feature leads" that attempted to pull readers into the story.

However, this was also the decade in which many afternoon papers ceased to exist. By the dawn of the 1980s, there were only a handful of "two-newspaper" towns. Betting against the trend—and confident good journalism would prevail—the Times Mirror Company purchased the afternoon *Dallas Times-Herald* in 1969 and took on the then-stodgy *Dallas Morning News*. Throughout the 1970s and early 1980s, Dallas became a magnet for journalists hoping to participate in "one of the last great newspaper wars" of the twentieth century.

Like most reporters and editors in the predigital era, I was blissfully ignorant of the "business" of journalism. I realized that newspapers were supported by two streams of revenue: readers and advertisers. But I did not realize that the vast majority came from advertisers who wanted to reach certain readers and entice them to buy their goods and services.

In 1982 a fire on board a commercial airline flight out of the Dallas–Fort Worth airport—a major news story that occurred on my watch as a *Times-Herald* assignment editor—provided a quick lesson in the economics of newspaper journalism. Arriving at work the morning after—proud that the *Times-Herald* had "beaten" the competition with a couple of "exclusives" on the air disaster—I spied the large delivery trucks bound for the upscale northern suburbs still in the press bay. In that moment, I realized that business decisions—much more than good journalism—would ultimately determine the fate of the *Times-Herald*.

Acknowledging that the trend was against afternoon newspapers, Times Mirror had decided to convert the *Times-Herald* from afternoon to morning publication in 1977. No doubt "the folks in corporate"—with the best of intentions—didn't want to ruffle the feathers of loyal afternoon newspaper readers by forcing them to change their daily routines. So they elected to gradually "phase in" the conversion over several years, starting with the inner-city routes, which were easier to reach but less affluent, and whose residents were not as desirable for advertisers as those in the northern suburbs. Even with only a rudimentary knowledge of the newspaper business, I instinctively grasped that morning in 1982 that this gradual phase-in not only had left many *Times-Herald* readers in the dark on a major news story but also had left the newspaper vulnerable with its retail advertisers, who hoped to convince those same coveted suburbanites to shop at the upscale malls and department stores that day.

Indeed, over the next couple of years, the dynamic in the Dallas newspaper war shifted quickly. Circulation, which reached a peak in the mid-1970s, declined throughout the 1980s, and retail advertisers—whose revenue, in essence, "funded" the news operation—deserted the *Times-Herald* and moved to the *Morning News*. The last edition of the *Times-Herald* was published in 1991.

Today, there is a parking garage where the *Times-Herald* newsroom and pressroom were once located. Most of the journalists moved on quickly in the 1980s to larger news organizations—including the *Los Angeles Times*, *Newsday*, and the *New York Times*, where Bill Keller, an alumnus of the *Times-Herald* during that era, became executive editor in 2003. And Dallas joined the legions of other cities—large and small—with only one newspaper.

The experience in Dallas brought home a painful lesson about the economics of good journalism: in a highly competitive situation (such as the Internet presents), you cannot depend on your journalistic reputation to keep you safe. You also have to take into account the needs of the advertisers, who have historically provided the vast majority of revenue and profits.

Time is not on your side. Things can change quickly, and you are suddenly facing a tipping point. Therefore, community newspapers today need to commit to a goal of aggressively revamping their cost and revenue structures and reinventing their business models. They need a business strategy that anticipates all outcomes and a roadmap for responding quickly to changing preferences of readers *and* advertisers.

EPIPHANY 3: The expectations of both readers and
advertisers have changed dramatically in recent years.
This requires that newspaper editors and publishers adopt
a new way of thinking about community—and nurturing it.

In 1994 I first started contemplating the ramifications of a "borderless" society—one defined not by geography but rather by our interests and affinities. As senior vice president of strategic planning at the *New York Times*, I was responsible for overseeing development of strategies for two ventures: the launch of a national edition of the *Times* that would be delivered in markets across the country and the simultaneous introduction of a digital version, nytimes.com, that could be accessed around the globe. Both endeavors had the potential to ensure the *Times*'s editorial and financial success in the twenty-first century.

The challenge was one of "repositioning" a New York–based publishing enterprise as a "national newspaper" in both the print and the online worlds. The rollout of the national print edition in the mid-1990s was so successful financially (significantly boosting circulation and advertising revenues and overall profitability) that it may come as a surprise to learn that there were a number of valid objections raised to the proposed strategy. Many on the business side (especially in the advertising and circulation departments) worried that the *Times* was "too New York" to be accepted by readers and advertisers outside the metropolitan area.

To allay those concerns, the *Times* conducted extensive research over several years on current and potential readers of both its print and digital editions. What the *Times* discovered was that there was a certain type of person who had a natural affinity for the type of content that the *Times* published—whether he or she resided in Dallas or New York. These were people who tended to actively engage in all that the world had to offer and viewed New York City as a cultural and commercial center. They wanted to be "in the know" about what was happening in that trend-setting city and viewed the *Times* as the "most credible and comprehensive source" of all the news and information they cared about—including national and world affairs, politics, cultural events, and significant trends in business and society.

Because readers valued the *Times*'s credibility, they were more engaged in the content of the paper—both the news and the advertising. This active engagement made them an attractive audience for advertisers and enabled the *Times* to charge both readers and advertisers of its print and online editions a significant premium over its competitors.

Like all newspapers, the *New York Times* has been challenged over the last decade as it has sought to adjust to the digital age. It has encountered many of the same issues as community newspapers: Should it charge readers to access the content online? If so, how much? Should it protect the high-margin print advertising or aggressively pursue the lower-margin digital ads? Should it migrate into video production? What is the role of the long-form, contextual journalism for which the *Times* is known, in contrast to Twitter?

However, the insight gained from research at the dawn of the Internet age enabled the *Times* to reposition itself as a national newspaper from a New York–centric one, even as it strengthened the loyalty of its current readers during a time of tremendous disruption and competition from multiple media outlets. The ubiquitous Internet has made it possible to connect readers of all newspapers—not just the large national ones like the *Times*—with other "people just like us" who share the same affinities, affiliations, and affections (or passions). Advertisers are keen to reach these people. By nurturing many communities across multiple platforms, newspapers build loyalty among readers first, who then attract advertisers who want to reach them. That is why it is critical that community newspapers take an expansive view of community so they can follow their customers and the money.

The Internet provides newspaper editors and publishers with both a challenge—of cutting through the noise and clutter—and an opportunity. The strong newspapers will focus on using the new digital tools that the Internet has unleashed, the various applications and mobile access, to nurture an expansive notion of community. Both readers and advertisers are expecting it.

Absorb and Trust

As these three epiphanies illustrate, good journalism alone is not sufficient to guarantee financial success for newspapers. But without good journalism, newspapers are merely commodity products that can easily be supplanted by competitors in a digital era.

When I was appointed Knight Chair of Journalism and Digital Media Economics in 2008, I welcomed the opportunity to return to my journalistic roots and focus on the country's community newspapers. With the entire newspaper ecosystem under assault, I realized that their long-term survival was also in jeopardy. While their economic concerns were not yet as critical as those of the metro newspapers, I had come to realize and appreciate that the country's 11,000 community publications formed the base of an immense news pyramid that supported the larger national and regional news organizations where I had worked for the previous three decades.

By covering the issues and events in communities overlooked by the regional and national organizations, these newspapers had the ability to improve the quality of life of residents in those towns and regions they served. On a day-to-day basis, the best of these papers produced the majority of the "news that feeds democracy," as author Alex Jones puts it, staying in touch with grassroots issues and trends that might grow to be a regional or national concern. If the foundation of the news pyramid was damaged, the country's entire news ecosystem it supported would be in jeopardy. Therefore, their role—though often overlooked—was as important and critical as ever.

At roughly the same time, a Knight Foundation report, *Informing Communities*, worried about an emerging "digital divide" in this country between affluent urban areas, which were heavily wired, and isolated communities, which were not. So I sought out three prize-winning papers known for their public-service journalism in rural, economically depressed North Carolina counties. Especially in the latter half of the twentieth century, the state's newspapers—large and small—developed a reputation for aggressively pursuing the sort of investigative, enterprise journalism that a recent FCC report notes is in jeopardy today. Since 1950, six of the state's newspapers have won the coveted Pulitzer Gold Medal for Public Service, one winning it twice. Three of those awards have gone to some of the smallest papers ever to win: Whiteville's *News Reporter*, the *Washington Daily News*, and the *Tabor City Tribune*.

I quickly enlisted the Whiteville and Washington papers—and added the *Wilkes Journal-Patriot*—in an endeavor to test new strategies and tactics. But while the editors at Whiteville and Washington eagerly embraced the opportunity to receive assistance in navigating the digital divide,

Journal-Patriot editor Jule Hubbard held back. He attended every meeting, but he displayed a polite reserve about committing to the project. Hoping to discover why, I began a phone conversation by saying: "I know there is a lot to absorb." After a long pause, he replied, with what I imagined to be a sly smile: "Oh, we've absorbed what you've said. We're just trying to decide whether we trust it."

"Absorb and trust." I immediately jotted those words on a sheet of paper that I have kept on the top of my desk pad as a constant reminder of what is at stake for newspapers as well as the communities they serve. There is a lot for editors and publishers to absorb and learn—a whole new way of thinking about the news business. In committing to new business models, publishers and editors are constantly weighing the implications those changes will have on the long-standing trust they have earned from the communities they serve.

Of the three original newspapers, the *Whiteville News Reporter* has made the most progress, with the *Journal-Patriot* following in its footsteps about two years behind. The Wilkes County paper now has a redesigned, interactive website and is starting to use its digital edition to enhance its sports coverage. The Washington paper, sold in 2010 to a chain in Alabama, has opted out. But from that original group of three, the project has expanded to include more than two dozen papers from the West Coast to the urban heartland of the country and remote rural areas of Appalachia.

Economists use the term "creative destruction" to describe what's been happening to newspapers. Those two words, placed together, embody both the threat and the opportunity. There are no guarantees. Based on what we have witnessed in other industries faced with similar disruptions, those who batten down the hatches and try to wait out the storm most likely will not survive. Those who understand that there is a "new normal" and risk embracing the creativity unleashed by the Internet have the potential to not only survive but also thrive.

So much is at stake, because the best newspapers are more than just businesses. They serve a vital role in informing, educating, and improving the quality of life for all residents—immigrants who need to learn the systems and the "ways" of living in a new country as well as longtime citizens who live and work in remote, economically depressed communities and struggle to find solutions to their everyday problems. What if there were no *La Raza*? How would Chicago's Latino immigrants learn about the consequences of funding cutbacks in mental-health care and how that affects Spanish-speaking residents? Who—or what organization—would provide context linking the drug wars in Mexico to gang violence on Chicago streets?

And what if, sixty years ago, Leslie Thompson and Willard Cole had not stood up to the Ku Klux Klan? At the height of the violence and intimidation, the Whiteville mayor pleaded with the governor of North Carolina to stop the paper's coverage because "it was bad for business."

Indeed. Thompson's stand cost the *News Reporter* almost a decade of profits. But in the end, it allowed Columbus County to enter the latter half of the twentieth century unencumbered by the stigma of a KKK stranglehold. Today, the county faces many of the same problems afflicting other rural areas of the country bypassed by the digital highway, including high unemployment and low household income. What additional economic, political, and social problems would Columbus County be confronting today *if* the *News Reporter* had looked the other way?

The best community newspapers have been described as "vitamin supplements for their communities," the "soul that people turn to in order to find out the truth," "an anchor," and the "tie that binds together" people in a community by providing the sort of news and information "that feeds democracy." That is why it is so important that owners, publishers, and editors demonstrate the courage and leadership of their forebears and begin the journey of re-creating their business models and crafting a new chapter—a new beginning—for community newspapers in the twenty-first century and the digital age.

Acknowledgments

His obituary in 2008 noted that John Henry Moore, who was the long-time editor and publisher of the *Laurinburg (N.C.) Exchange* and my first boss, would be remembered for "challenging his community through his writing, believing that a strong community needs a strong newspaper to prosper."

A book such as this is always a collaborative effort that reflects the insights and influences of colleagues and associates who have trained, mentored, supported, challenged, or inspired us. Often, they have done all of the above. My training as a journalist began in the summer of 1969, when I walked through the doors of my hometown paper and met John Henry Moore. In the years since, I have been fortunate to work with and learn from some of the world's legendary editors, those who are well known, including Max Frankel of the *New York Times* and Paul Steiger of the *Wall Street Journal*, as well as those who are lesser known, such as the late Roy Parker Jr., editor of the prize-winning and spunky *Fayetteville (N.C.) Times*, founded in 1973 when many newspapers were already disappearing. From these mentors, I came to appreciate the vitally important role of newspapers in informing our democracy and building strong communities.

The late James K. Batten, CEO of Knight Ridder Inc., was the first to impress upon me the power of technology to both transform newspaper journalism and destroy the business model that underpins it. "If you care about good journalism, then you need to learn the business," he told me in the early 1980s, as I lamented the economic struggles of the *Dallas Times-Herald*. His advice prompted me to pursue a master's in business administration at Columbia University. Over the next two decades, a host of colleagues and mentors at the *New York Times*, the *Harvard Business Review*, and the *Wall Street Journal* gave me numerous opportunities to apply the business concepts I learned at Columbia, creating and implementing strategies that enabled those venerable journalistic institutions to grow revenues and profits by embracing technological change.

My colleagues in the academy have also contributed directly and indirectly to the insights in this book. Several faculty members here at the UNC School of Journalism and Mass Communication collaborated with me on research and encouraged me to build on the groundbreaking journalistic research on newspapers done by retired UNC professors Donald Shaw and Philip Meyer. I am especially indebted to Ferrel Guillory, director of the Program on Public Life; Ryan Thornburg, director of the Rural Open Block project; and JoAnn Sciarrino, Knight Chair in Digital Advertising and Marketing. Faculty members at other institutions have graciously provided insights from their own research and helped me apply these to community newspapers, most especially Ron Heifetz, senior lecturer at Harvard University's John F. Kennedy School of Government; Richard Foster, senior fellow at Yale University's School of Management; and James Hamilton, professor and director of the journalism program at Stanford University.

Financial support has come from the McCormick and Knight Foundations, which provided grants to underwrite the research and test strategies. Two longtime media executives—Nancy Adler and Margarita Lam—gave extensively of their time and expertise, providing consulting advice to both the students and the papers participating in the project. Susan King, dean of the School of Journalism and Mass Communication, has encouraged me to make this research endeavor a priority. My research associate, the indefatigable and ever-resourceful Christine Shia, has cheerfully and proficiently guided work behind the scenes as this book evolved over the last four years from instructional website to its current form. My husband, Harrison Abernathy, an Episcopal minister and former newspaper journalist, was the first to encourage me to write this book and since has invested considerable time and thought in reading each of the rough drafts, making sure the insights can be understood by anyone who cares about good journalism. Finally, but not least, I am very grateful for the enthusiastic support and insightful contributions of UNC Press, including editor Jay Mazzocchi and editorial director Mark Simpson-Vos, who gave me excellent feedback on the original proposal and suggested the book's dramatic arc, focusing on the individual stories of innovative community newspapers that are striving to stay relevant and profitable in the twenty-first century.

The bibliography lists more than three dozen publishers and editors who have either worked directly with the UNC team on this project or graciously shared their stories. This book would not have been possible without the unselfish cooperation of the *Whiteville News Reporter* (Jim, Les, and Stuart High), the *Washington Daily News* (Ray McKeithan), the *Wilkes Journal-Patriot* (Jule Hubbard), *La Raza* (Fabiola Pomareda and Jimena Catarivas), the *Rutland Herald* (John and Rob Mitchell and Catherine Nelson), the *Hampshire Review* (Sallie See), the *Fayetteville Observer* (Charles Broadwell), *The Pilot* (David Woronoff), the *Deseret News* (Clark Gilbert), the *Santa Rosa Press Democrat* (Bruce Kyse), the *Naples Daily News* (David Neill), and the *Columbia Daily Herald* (Mark Palmer).

Over the last five years, almost 200 students have worked on this project. Many have continued to contribute even after they have graduated. All are acknowledged on the website; the contributions of these students stand out: Anika Anand, Jin Ah Bae, Kaitlyn Barnes, David Bockino, Stewart Boss, Kate Caison, Fitch Carrere, Jeanne-Marie DeStefano, David Enarson, Sarah Frier, Clayton Gladieux, Christopher Helton, Eliza Kern, Kevin Kiley, Alex Kowalski, Tariq Luthun, Claire McNeill, Jeff Mittelstadt, Evan Noll, Steven Norton, Jeanine O'Brien, Lucia Parker, Alexandra Perez, Carolina Peterson, Chase Pickering, Rebecca Putterman, Mary Alice Rose, Hanna Samad, Gloria Schoeberle, Paula Seligson, Savona Smith, Nick Shchetko, Victoria Stillwell, Marshele Waddell, Sam Wardle, Nick Weidenmiller, Gillian Wheat, Eric White, Jed Williams, Tianyue Ye, and Michelle Zayed.

For all this help and the privilege of working on many newspapers that served their communities well, I will always be most grateful.

How to Use the Complementary Instructional Website

The act of writing and producing a book such as this involves extrapolation of main points gleaned from numerous interviews and years of research. It is what business strategists refer to as "zooming out" so that you can address the changing environment, acknowledge main events and trends transforming the landscape, and then point out pathways to a new destination. Therefore, much of what informs this book has ended up on the cutting-room floor.

So, taking advantage of the interactivity and interconnectedness of the digital age, I have designed the complementary website http://businessofnews.unc.edu to provide additional depth and understanding for owners, publishers, and editors of news organizations who wish to "zoom in." While the book focuses primarily on the issues facing legacy community newspapers, the website focuses more broadly on the business of news and can be used by members of start-up nonprofit organizations as well as established news operations of any size looking to reconnect with their audiences and advertisers.

The site is divided into four areas, which can be accessed sequentially or referred to individually as needed. It acknowledges that many news organizations share similar characteristics, but each community and "market" is unique.

"Getting Started" provides instruction on nurturing an effective strategic process within your own news organization. This section consists of three short (ten-to-fifteen-minute) videotaped lessons that guide you through the process of gathering information, establishing priorities, and creating a strategy that plays to the unique strengths and challenges of your community and news organization. The lessons address the mechanics of how to define a mission and a vision, set strategic goals, and measure success against those goals. Each lesson has downloadable worksheets with exercises that can be completed individually or in a group setting.

"Digging Deeper: Strategy Implementation" focuses on how the various newspapers spotlighted in this book are shedding legacy costs, building vibrant community on many platforms, and pursuing new revenue opportunities. There are numerous examples of how newspapers have implemented these three strategies, as well as interviews with publishers and editors elaborating on how their thinking evolved to accommodate marketplace realities. There is also a summary of key ideas from each of the nine chapters in the book.

"Learning More: Additional Resources" recommends books, newsletters, blogs, and other sources you can consult for more information on specific topics. For example, if you want to learn more about strategy implementation, this section offers brief summaries of several seminal texts cited in this book, focusing on key concepts. (You can download the excerpts from these books for a copyright fee or click through a link to purchase a book.)

"Staying Up-To-Date" offers you the opportunity to engage in discussion with others in the profession, as well as with the students and professors at the University of North Carolina who have contributed to this book. We are living in fast-paced times. As we learn more, we will update our site and our book with relevant research and findings. So consider this website an iterative work in progress—not unlike the planning process on which you are about to embark.

The biggest lesson we took away from our efforts over the last five years is this: if community news organizations are to survive and thrive in the digital era, owners and managers—publishers, editors, and advertising directors— will need to not only think differently but also act differently. We hope this book and the website get you started on the journey.

Bibliography

Books and Research Reports

Adner, Ron. *Wide Lens: A New Strategy for Innovation*. London: Portfolio Penguin, 2012.

Beath, John, and Yannis Katsoulacos. *The Economic Theory of Product Differentiation*. Cambridge: Cambridge University Press, 1991.

Boston Consulting Group. *The Experience Curve Reviewed: IV. The Growth Share Market or the Product Portfolio*. 1973. Report recaps the ideas the company created in 1968.

Buffett, Warren E. "Annual Letter to Berkshire Hathaway, Inc." February 2013.

Carnegie Corporation of New York. *Improving the Education of Tomorrow's Journalists*. New York: Carnegie Corporation, 2005. Online at http://carnegie. org/publications/.

Carter, W. Horace. *Virus of Fear*. Tabor City, N.C.: W. H. Carter, 1991.

Christensen, Clayton M. *The Innovator's Dilemma: When New Technologies Cause Great Firms to Fail*. Boston: Harvard Business Review Press, 1997.

Christensen, Clayton M., and Michael E. Raynor. *The Innovator's Solution: Creating and Sustaining Successful Growth*. Boston: Harvard Business School Press, 2003.

Collins, James C. *Good to Great: Why Some Companies Make the Leap—And Others Don't*. New York: Harper Business, 2001.

Deloitte. *State of the Media Democracy Survey, 2012*. Online at http://www.deloitte. com.

Donatello, Michael C. "Assessing Audiences' Willingness to Pay and Price Response for News Online." Ph.D. diss., University of North Carolina at Chapel Hill, 2013.

Foster, Richard, and Sarah Kaplan. *Creative Destruction: Why Companies That Are Built to Last Underperform the Market—And How to Successfully Transform Them*. New York: Doubleday, 2001.

Gaerig, Andrew. "New Economics of Advertising: The Principle of Relative Constancy Reconsidered." Student thesis, University of North Carolina at Chapel Hill, 2010.

Hamilton, James T. *All the News That's Fit to Sell: How the Market Transforms Information into News*. Princeton, N.J.: Princeton University Press, 2004.

Heifetz, Ronald A., and Marty Linsky. *Leadership on the Line: Staying Alive through the Dangers of Leading*. Boston: Harvard Business School Press, 2002.

Hussman, Eliza. "Valuing Newspaper Website Content: What People Are Willing to Pay for and Why." Student thesis, University of North Carolina at Chapel Hill, 2012.

Jones, Alex. *Losing the News: The Future of the News That Feeds Democracy*. Oxford and New York: Oxford University Press, 2009.

―――, ed. *A Report on the Carnegie-Knight Initiative on the Future of Journalism Education*. Boston: Joan Shornstein Center on the Press, Politics, and Public Policy, Harvard University, 2011.

Jones, Michele Kathleen. "Accurate as of the Time Stamp: Newspaper Journalism Ethics in a Time of Economic and Technological Change." Ph.D. diss., University of North Carolina at Chapel Hill, 2010.

Jurkowitz, Mark, and Amy Mitchell. "Newspapers Turning Ideas into Dollars: Four Revenue Success Stories." Pew Research Center's Project for Excellence in Journalism, February 11, 2013. Online at http://www.journalism.org/ analysis_report/newspapers_turning_ideas_dollars.

Kaplan, Robert S., and David P. Norton. *The Strategy-Focused Organization: How Balanced Scorecard Companies Thrive in the New Business Environment*. Boston: Harvard Business School Press, 2001.

Katzenbach, Jon R., and Douglas K. Smith. *The Wisdom of Teams: Creating the High-Performance Organization*. Boston: Harvard Business School Press, 1993.

Kiley, Kevin R. "No News at Breakfast—I'll Take It to Go: College Students' Habits and What They Indicate about Future News Use." Honors thesis, University of North Carolina at Chapel Hill, 2010.

Knee, Jonathan A., Bruce C. Greenwald, and Ava Seave. *The Curse of the Mogul: What's Wrong with the World's Leading Media Companies?* New York: Penguin Group, 2009.

Knight Foundation. *Informing Communities: Sustaining Democracy in the Digital Age: The Report of the Knight Foundation on the Information Needs of Communities in a Democracy*. Washington, D.C.: Aspen Institute, 2010.

Kotter, John. *Leading Change*. Boston: Harvard Business School Press, 1996.

Manpower Development Corporation. *The Building Blocks of Community Development*. Durham, N.C.: MDC, Inc., 2002. Online at http://www.mdcinc. org/sites/default/files/resources/The%20Building%20Blocks%20of%20 Community%20Development.pdf.

―――. *Building Communities of Conscience and Conviction*. Durham, N.C. MDC, Inc., 1998. Online at http://www.mdcinc.org/sites/default/files/resources/ Building%20Communities%20of%20Conscience%20and%20Conviction.pdf.

Mathews, Forrest David. *Community Effectiveness: What Makes the Difference?* Kettering Foundation, 1987.

Merritt, Davis. *Knightfall: Knight Ridder and How the Erosion of Newspaper Journalism Is Putting Democracy at Risk*. New York: AMACOM, 2005.

Mersey, Rachel Davis. *Can Journalism Be Saved? Rediscovering America's Appetite for News*. Santa Barbara, Calif.: Praeger, 2010.

Meyer, Philip. *The Vanishing Newspaper: Saving Journalism in the Information Age.* Columbia: University of Missouri Press. 2009.

Nagle, Thomas T. *The Strategy and Tactics of Pricing: A Guide to Growing More Profitably.* Upper Saddle River, N.J.; Pearson/Prentice Hall, 2006.

Noam, Eli. *Media Ownership and Concentration in America.* Oxford and New York: Oxford University Press, 2009.

Parker, Lucia. "Coming Back for More: The Importance of Reader Loyalty for FayObserver.com." Student thesis, University of North Carolina at Chapel Hill, 2009.

Patterson, Thomas E. *Informing the News: The Need for Knowledge-Based Journalism.* New York: Vintage Books, 2013.

Peach, Sara. News on the Go: Field Notes on Storytelling for Mobile Devices. Online at http://reesenewslab.org/projects/news-on-the-go/.

Pew Research Center. *Pew Internet and American Life Project.* "Technology and Media: Mobile." Online at http://www.perwinternet.org/topics/Mobile.aspx?typeFilter=5.

———. *The Pew Research Center's Project for Excellence in Journalism: The State of the News Media, an Annual Report on American Journalism,* 2013. Online at http://stateofthemedia.org/.

Picard, R. G. *Economics and Financing of Media Companies.* 2nd ed. New York: Fordham University Press, 2011.

Porter, Michael. *Competitive Strategy: Techniques for Analyzing Industries and Competitors.* With a new introduction. New York: Free Press, 1998.

Reichheld, Frederick. *The Ultimate Question: Driving Good Profits and True Growth.* Boston: Harvard Business School Press, 2006.

Reichheld, Frederick F., and Thomas Teal. *The Loyalty Effect: The Hidden Force behind Growth, Profits, and Lasting Value.* Boston: Harvard Business School Press, 1996.

Schumpeter, Joseph A. *Capitalism, Socialism, and Democracy.* New York: Harper & Row, 1950. Contains Schumpeter's first use of the term "creative destruction," also known as "Schumpeter's gale," which was influenced and adapted from the work of Karl Marx.

Shaw, Donald. *The Rise and Fall of American Mass Media: Roles of Technology and Leadership.* Bloomington: Indiana University, 1991.

Simons, Robert L. *Seven Strategy Questions: A Simple Approach for Better Execution.* Harvard Business Review Publishing, 2010.

Paley Center for Media International Council. *International Council 2007 Briefing Summary. Convergence: What's Next?* New York: The Paley Center for Media, June 13–15, 2007.

Waldman, Steven, and others. *The Information Needs of Communities: The Changing Media Landscape in a Broadband Age.* Federal Communications Commission, July 2011.

Wardle, Sam. "Hangings to Hurricanes: What Readers Want from Their Community Newspaper's Website." Student thesis, University of North Carolina at Chapel Hill, 2010.

White, Eric Lee. "New Media in the Newsroom: A Survey of Local Journalists and Their Managers on the Use of Social Media as Reporting Tools." Student thesis, University of North Carolina at Chapel Hill, 2012.

Williams, Joseph Edgar (Jed). "Wired for the Future? Creative Destruction and the Continual Renewal of the Associated Press." Student thesis, University of North Carolina at Chapel Hill, 2010.

Zander, Rosamund Stone, and Benjamin Zander. *The Art of Possibility: Transforming Professional and Personal Life*. Penguin Books: New York, 2002.

Articles and Presentations

Abernathy, Penelope Muse. "A Nonprofit Model for the New York Times?" Paper presented at the Duke Conference on Nonprofit Media, May 4–5, 2009.

———. "Opening Remarks to the Federal Trade Commission." Paper presented at the Third Workshop for the Future of Journalism, National Press Club, June 15, 2010.

Abernathy, Penelope Muse, and Richard Foster. "The News Landscape in 2014: Transformed or Diminished? (Formulating a Game Plan for Survival in the Digital Era)." Paper presented at the Yale University Conference on Information, the Law and Society, November 12, 2009.

Arthur, W. Brian. "Competing Technologies, Increasing Returns and Lock-In by Historical Events." *Economic Journal* 99 (March 1989): 116–31.

Beaujon, Andrew. "Warren Buffett Expects His Paper to Deliver 10 Percent Returns." Poynter online, May 6, 2013, http://www.poynter.org/latest-news/mediawire/212599/buffett-expects-10-percent-return-from-newspapers/.

Broadwell, Charles. "Business Is Business; 'Mistakes' Happen." *Fayetteville Observer*, August 25, 2013.

Burton, Joe. *A Marketer's Guide to Understanding the Economics of Digital Compared to Traditional Advertising and Media Services*. New York: American Association of Advertising, McCann Worldgroup, 2009.

Carr, David. "Newspaper Monopoly That Lost Its Grip." *New York Times*, May 12, 2013.

Carroll, Rory. "California Newspaper Defies Industry Wisdom to Stay Alive." *The Guardian* (UK), July 23, 2013. Online at http://www.theguardian.com/world/2013/jul/23/california-newspaper-industry-wisdom.

Connell, Christopher. "News 21: Are Next-Generation Journalists the Future of a Profession in Transition?" *Carnegie Reporter* 5, no. 3 (2009). Online at http://carnegie.org/publications/carnegie-reporter/single/view/article/item/229/.

David, Paul A. "Clio and the Economics of Qwerty." *American Economic Review* 75, no. 2 (May 1985): 332–37.

Ellis, Justin. "Monday Q & A: Raju Narisetti on Designing for Mobile, the Paywall Fallacy, and Reinventing Ads." *Neiman Journalism Lab Email Newsletter*, March 4, 2013.

Erdem, T., M. P. Kean, and B. Sun. "The Impact of Advertising on Consumer Price Sensitivity in Experience Goods Markets." *Quantitative Marketing and Economics* 6 (June 2008): 139–76.

Gary, Loren. "The Work of a Modern Leader: An Interview with Ron Heifetz." Harvard Management Update Series. Boston: Harvard Business School Publishing, 1997.

George, Lisa M., and Joel Waldfogel. "The *New York Times* and the Market for Local Newspapers." *American Economic Review* 96, no. 1 (March 2006): 435–47.

Haughney, Christine, and Michael D. Shear. "Bezos Is a Hit in a *Washington Post* Newsroom Visit." *New York Times*, September 5, 2013.

Healy, Beth. "John Henry Adding *Globe* to his Boston Constellation: Red Sox Owner Had Two Advantages to His Bid: A Local Profile and a Cash Offer." *Boston Globe*, August 4, 2013.

King, Susan. "The Carnegie-Knight Initiative on the Future of Journalism Education: Improving How Journalists Are Educated and How Their Audiences Are Informed." *Daedalus* 139, no. 2 (Spring 2010): 126–37.

Lamberg, Juha-Antti, Kalle Pajunen, Petri Parvinen, and Grant T. Savage. "Stakeholder Management and Path Dependence in Organizational Transactions." *Management Decision* 46, no. 6 (2008): 846–63. Bingley, UK: Emerald Group Publishing.

McCombs, M. E., and D. L. Shaw. "The Evolution of Agenda-Setting Research: Twenty-Five Years in the Marketplace of Ideas." *Journal of Communication* 43 (Spring 1993): 58–67.

McCombs, Maxwell E., and Donald Shaw. "The Agenda-Setting Function of Mass Media." *Public Opinion Quarterly* 36, no. 2 (Summer 1972): 176–87.

McCombs, Maxwell, Jack Nolan, and Jesse H. Jones. "The Relative Constancy Approach to Consumer Spending for Media." *Journal of Media Economics* 5, no. 2 (Summer 1992): 43–52.

Miles, Raymond E., Charles C. Snow, Alan D. Meyer, and Henry J. Coleman Jr. "Organizational Strategy, Structure, and Process." *Academy of Management Review* 3, no. 3 (July 1978): 546–62.

Murdoch, Rupert. Speech to the American Society of Newspaper Editors, April 13, 2005.

Paterno, Susan. "Is McClatchy Different?" *American Journalism Review* (August/September 2003): 17–28.

Perry, Mark. "Free Fall: Adjusted for Inflation, Print Newspaper Advertising Will Be Lower This Year Than in 1950." Carpe Diem Blog, posted September 6, 2012, http://mjperry.blogspot.com/2012/09/freefall-adjusted-for-inflation-print.html.

Rayport, Jeffrey F. "Advertising's New Medium: Human Experience." *Harvard Business Review* 91, no. 3 (March 2013): 76–85.

Robinson, Scott E., and Kenneth J. Meier. "Path Dependence and Organizational Behavior: Bureaucracy and Social Promotion." *American Review of Public Administration* 36, no. 3 (September 2006): 241–60.

Stecklow, Stephen. "Despite Woes, McClatchy Banks on Newspapers." *Wall Street Journal*, December 26, 2007.

Stiller, Burkhard, Kevin Almeroth, Jorn Altmann, and others. "Content Pricing in the Internet." *Computer Communications* 27, no. 6 (2004): 522–28.

Sydow, Jorg, Georg Schreyogg, and Jochen Koch. "Organizational Path Dependence: Opening the Black Box." *Academy of Management Review* 34, no. 4 (2009): 689–709.

Thornburg, Ryan. "For OpenBlock, Big Improvements from Small Newsrooms." PBS.org Idea Lab article, July 21, 2013, http://www.pbs.org/idealab/2013/07/for-openblock-big-improvements-from-small-newsrooms.

Waldfogel, Joel. "The Four P's of Digital Distribution in the Internet Era: Piracy, Pricing, Pie-Splitting, and Pipe Control." *Student's Guides to the U.S. Government Series* 7, no. 2 (2010): 3–20.

Wanta, W. "The Messenger and the Message: Differences across News Media." In *Communication and Democracy: Exploring the Intellectual Frontiers in Agenda-Setting Theory*, edited by Maxwell E. McCombs, Donald L. Shaw, and David H. Weaver, 137–51. New Jersey: Lawrence Erlbaum Associates, 1997.

Wanta, W., and S. Ghanem. "Effects of Agenda Setting." In *Mass Media Effects Research: Advances through Meta-Analysis*, edited by R. W. Preiss and others, 37–51. New Jersey: Lawrence Erlbaum Associates, 2007.

Williams, Peter J., and Richard E. Caves. "What Is Product Differentiation, Really?" *Journal of Industrial Economics* 34, no. 2 (December 1985): 113–32.

Interviews

Adler, Nancy. Sales, marketing, and strategy executive, New York, in discussion with the author during collaborative work with the author, 2009–13.

Broadwell, Charles. Publisher, *Fayetteville (N.C.) Observer*, in discussion with the author during collaborative work with the author, 2009–13.

Carter, Hodding, III. Journalist and politician, former assistant secretary of state for public affairs in the Jimmy Carter administration, in discussion with the author, May 2013.

Catarivas, Jimena. Publisher, *La Raza*, Chicago, in discussion with the author, May–August 2013.

Clark, John. Executive producer, Reese Felts Digital News Project, University of North Carolina at Chapel Hill School of Journalism and Mass Communication, in discussion with the author, June 2013.

Cross, Al. Director, the Institute of Rural Journalism and Community Issues, University of Kentucky, in discussion with the author, May 2013.

Edmonds, Rick. Media business analyst and leader of News Transformation, Poynter Institute for Media Studies, in discussion with the author, September 2013.

Franklin, Stephen. Award-winning journalist and former labor writer and foreign correspondent for the *Chicago Tribune*, in discussion with the author, 2012–13.

Gilbert, Clark. President and CEO, Deseret Digital Media and *Deseret News* (Utah), in discussion with the author, August 2013.

Greer, Mickey. Advertising manager, *Whiteville (N.C.) News Reporter*, in discussion with the author, 2010–11.

Guillory, Ferrel. Director, Program on Public Life, University of North Carolina at Chapel Hill, in discussion with the author during collaborative work, 2009–13.

Hamilton, James. Professor of communication at Stanford University and digital strategist, comments made during a panel meeting at the Federal Trade Commission, "How Will Journalism Survive the Internet Age?," June 15, 2010; and in discussion with the author, 2001–13.

Heifetz, Ronald A. Senior lecturer in public leadership, John F. Kennedy School of Government, Harvard University, in discussion with the author, June–August 2013.

High, Jim. Publisher, *Whiteville (N.C.) News Reporter*, in discussion with the author, June 2013.

High, Les. Editor, *Whiteville (N.C.) News Reporter*, in collaborative work with the author, 2009–13.

High, Stuart. Special-projects director, *Whiteville (N.C.) News Reporter*, in collaborative work with the author, 2011–13.

Hubbard, Jule. Editor, *Wilkes Journal-Patriot* (North Wilkesboro, North Carolina), in collaborative work with the author, 2005–13.

Kyse, Bruce. Publisher, *Santa Rosa (Calif.) Press Democrat*, in discussion with the author, July–August 2013.

Lewis, Dean. Advertising director, *Whiteville (N.C.) News Reporter*, in discussion with the author, 2010–13.

McFarland, Mary Kay. Lecturer, West Virginia University, and project coordinator, West Virginia Uncovered, in discussion with the author, July 2013.

McKeithan, Ray. Former president and publisher, *Washington (N.C.) Daily News*, in collaborative work with the author, 2009–13.

Mitchell, John. Publisher, *Rutland (Vt.) Herald*, in discussion with the author over a period of weeks in 2013.

Mitchell, Rob. Editor, *Rutland (Vt.) Herald*, in discussion with the author over a period of weeks in 2013.

Neill, David. President and publisher, *Naples (Fla.) Daily News* 2010–13, in discussion with the author, July 2013.

Nelson, Catherine. Vice president and general manager, *Rutland (Vt.) Herald* and *Times Argus* (Vermont), in discussion with the author, August 2013.

Palmer, Mark. Publisher, *Columbia (Tenn.) Daily Herald*, in discussion with the author, August 2013.

Pantelis, Magdalena. General manager, *Dziennik Zwiaskowy, Polish Daily News*, and informancjeusa.com, in discussion with the author, July 2013.

Pomareda, Fabiola. Managing editor, *La Raza* (Chicago), in discussion with the author, May–June 2013.

Quarles, Orage. Publisher, *News and Observer* (Raleigh, N.C.), at an FCC symposium at the University of Chapel Hill School of Journalism and Mass Communication, February 20, 2013.

Sciarrino, JoAnn. Former BBDO executive and Knight Chair in Digital Advertising and Marketing, University of North Carolina at Chapel Hill, in discussion with the author, 2011–13.

See, Sallie. Editor, *Hampshire Review* (West Virginia), in discussion with the author, May–June 2013.

Shaw, Don. Professor emeritus at the University of North Carolina at Chapel Hill School of Journalism and Mass Communication, in discussion with the author, April 2013.

Steiger, Paul E. "From Mainstream Media to a Non-Profit News Startup," talk at University of North Carolina at Chapel Hill School of Journalism and Mass Communication, February 20, 2012.

Thornburg, Ryan. Associate professor, University of North Carolina at Chapel Hill School of Journalism and Mass Communication, in collaborative work with the author, 2009–13. For OpenBlock information, see https://github.com/openplans/openblock.

Waldman, Steven. Senior advisor to the chairman of the Federal Communications Commission and visiting senior media policy scholar, Columbia University, New York, in discussion with the interviewer Stewart Boss, January 2013.

Williams, Jed. Vice president, consulting and senior analyst, BIA/Kelsey, in discussion with the author, March–July 2013.

Woronoff, David. President, North Carolina Press Association, and publisher, *The Pilot* (North Carolina), in discussion with the author, May 2013.

Index

insightful moment and, 215; Internet-enhanced content of, 42; Internet two-pronged attack on, 40–48; legacy costs and, 5, 41, 47–48, 98–100, 101–2, 115–18; local accountability of, 26–27, 126, 147; magazines created by, 100, 135–36, 148, 156, 191, 192, 193–94; mission of, 4, 17–22, 32, 81, 119; most-read features of, 105; network economics and, 199; new beginning for, 224; new definition of, 2, 3; number of publication days of, 47; numbers of, 21; online editions of, 49–50; period of transition for, 63; political activism of, 12, 17–18; pre-Internet profit margins of, 34; Pulitzer Prizes awarded to, 12, 13, 20, 23, 33, 54, 94, 117, 222; rate card revision and, 183; reader loyalty to, 5, 123, 147; reasons for change and, 33–53; reasons for survival of, 26–27; revenue decline of, 17; special-interest communities and, 80, 85, 120, 125–26; three-pronged strategy and, 19, 62–63, 84–85, 96–97, 197; traditional definition of, 20; unique audience delivered by, 187; unique content of, 46, 102

Community pages or sections, 188–94

Company psychology, 80–81

Compensation (sales rep), 183–84, 187

Competition: competitive advantage, 4, 6–7, 38, 63, 85, 177; competitive disadvantage, 47, 53; competitive environment, 4, 48–53, 69, 201–5, 218, 219; vs. collaboration, 214

Competitive Strategy (Porter), 51

Computer-assisted reporting, 131–32

Computers: ownership numbers, 49. *See also* Digital *headings*; Internet; Websites

Confidants, importance of, 89–90, 97

Confirmation bias, 57

Congressional Quarterly, 112, 130

Consultative selling, 181–82, 185–86, 192, 203

Consumption habits, 49, 64, 88, 133, 164

Content creation, 41, 42–47, 65, 102; ad sponsorship of, 189; context and, 121; costs of, 46–47; reader interests and, 121, 124–26

Core business. *See* Cash cow

Cost per thousand (CPM), 45, 68, 173

Costs, 4–5; fixed, 41, 46, 47, 53; reduction of, 61, 72, 75, 85, 116, 215; segregation of, 46–48; streamlining of, 197; traditional, 40, 41; transformative change and, 71. *See also* Legacy costs

Cost structure, 55; lethal destruction and, 63; revamping of, 98–99

CPM. *See* Cost per thousand

Creative destruction, 1–2, 4, 41, 56, 63, 223; creative survival possibilities and, 7, 8, 41–42, 70–75, 84–85, 199; hurricane imagery and, 197; legacy costs and, 41; tipping point and, 36–37

Creative Destruction (Foster), 41, 64–65, 70–71, 73

Cross, Al, 24, 26, 28–29, 49–50, 129, 147

Cross-ownership (newspaper/TV station), 110, 111, 204

Cross-platform delivery, 4, 63–75, 100, 119–54; advertising messages and, 6–7, 17, 69, 85, 156–69, 172, 175–78, 185, 188–94; advertising rates and, 173–74, 177, 182, 183; change prospectors and, 82, 85–86; competitive advantage of, 6–7, 83, 85; employees' new skills and, 111, 112, 117–18; lack of cohesive vision for, 62; revenue and, 187; sales and, 175–77; sales force compensation and, 183–84; shedding legacy costs and, 101; special-interest community and, 134, 203; transformation to, 101, 114; vibrant community and, 65–68. *See also* Digital edition; Multiple platforms; Print edition

Cultural lock-in, 73, 81

Customer base, 63, 82; digital edition and, 72; implementing new strategy and, 85; loyalty of, 65–68, 85, 87–88,

122, 143; tipping point in, 74. *See also* Readers

Daily Herald. See Columbia (Tenn.) Daily Herald

Daily newspapers, 21, 107; U.S. numbers of, 2. *See also* Metro and regional dailies; National newspapers

Daily News. See Polish Daily News; Washington (N.C.) Daily News

Dallas Morning News, 218–19; SportsDay app, 139, 143, 176

Dallas Times-Herald, 218–19

Daniels, Jonathan, 12

Data analysis, 86; digital mapping application, 128–29, 131–32

De facto monopoly, 35–40, 41, 51 Defenders against change, 82, 84, 96

Delivery routes. *See* Printing and distribution

Deloitte survey, *State of the Media Democracy Survey*, 48, 49, 133

Delta Democrat-Times (Greenville, Miss.), 18

Demographics: advertising audience, 164–65; aging print-edition readers, 102, 116, 135; choice of medium, 49, 50, 53, 62, 63, 66, 102, 115–16, 133, 135, 140, 149; digital vs. print edition, 164; Facebook users, 140, 167; special-interest communities, 149

Denver Post, 134

Deseret News (Salt Lake City), 72, 79, 100, 113; Deseret Digital Media, 80, 110; Deseret Management Corporation, 79, 109, 110–11; Deseret Media, 72, 114, 175; newsroom staff layoffs and, 109–10; readers' special interests and, 134; transformation of, 80, 86, 110

Design and printing business, 156

Detroit Free Press, 107

Detroit News, 107

Digital advertising, 43, 56, 95–96, 155–94; complexity of, 166–67; cross-platform sales and, 175–78, 185;

display ads and, 69; in-house agency and, 61, 155, 158, 166; local merchants and, 159, 177–78; pricing of (*see* Rates); print revenue vs., 68

Digital age, 13, 18, 26, 40–53, 69, 86, 222–23; community definition and, 4, 67, 125–26; community newspaper disadvantage and, 41–48; ease of information retrieval and, 86, 128–33; extent and pace of change and, 33–34; four arguments for change and, 53; free information and, 43; interactivity and timeliness of, 163; investigative journalism and, 209; journalism schools and, 211; local news and, 119; marketing and, 162, 167; mission of community newspaper and, 32; multiple advertising outlets and, 162; negative effects of, 18; news sources and, 20; nonprofit news organizations and, 209–10; public records and, 129. *See also* Internet; Mobile devices

Digital edition, 2, 4, 16, 99, 121, 200; charging for, 142–47; communities and, 96, 120–21, 124; employee responses to, 111, 117–18; following customers to, 72; high-traffic articles of, 86, 145; interactive features of, 105–6; as key to future profitability, 56, 88; loyalty to, 66; moving print readers to, 104–5; new opportunities for, 112; pay wall and, 43–44; popularity of, 48–50, 95; readers of, 50, 59–60, 66, 87, 115–16, 124, 140; revenue from, 45; selling to advertisers of (*see* Digital advertising); strategic planning for, 220, 221. *See also* Websites

Digital mapping, 128–29, 131–32

Digital tools, 149, 150, 151, 154, 206–7; public-affairs reporting and, 128–33

Disaggregation of content (unbundling), 42, 43, 45, 46

Distribution. *See* Printing and distribution

Diversification, 100, 155–56, 215